Churchill's Socialism

Churchill's Socialism:
Political Resistance
in the Plays of Caryl Churchill

By

Siân Adiseshiah

CAMBRIDGE
SCHOLARS
P U B L I S H I N G

Churchill's Socialism: Political Resistance in the Plays of Caryl Churchill, by Siân Adiseshiah

This book first published 2009

Cambridge Scholars Publishing

12 Back Chapman Street, Newcastle upon Tyne, NE6 2XX, UK

British Library Cataloguing in Publication Data
A catalogue record for this book is available from the British Library

ISBN (10): 1-4438-1318-4, ISBN (13): 978-1-4438-1318-1

For Charlie and Xanthe

TABLE OF CONTENTS

ACKNOWLEDGEMENTS

This book is based partly on PhD research carried out at the University of Birmingham, research that could not have been undertaken without the financial support of an Arts and Humanities Research Board studentship. My PhD supervisor, Professor Tony Davies, provided me with just the right balance of intellectual guidance and the freedom to pursue my interests, as well as showing much kindness and support. I must also thank Professor Lizbeth Goodman, who strongly encouraged me to pursue the book's publication and offered useful advice on changes. I am very grateful, too, to Professor Una Chaudhuri for reading a draft of the manuscript and offering encouragement and support as well as a positive appraisal. Dr Robert Wilcher also contributed a generous endorsement of the book. Professor Stephen Regan has been tremendously supportive over the years and has given me particular encouragement over the publication of this book.

I am very thankful to colleagues from the School of Humanities and Performing Arts at the University of Lincoln for covering my teaching whilst I was on research leave, leave that enabled me to finish writing this book. Dr Erin Bell, Chris Golby, Dr Rupert Hildyard, Dr Chris Marlow, Dr Charlie McGuire, and Dr Alan Shadforth must all be thanked for providing very helpful commentary on drafts of chapters. I am grateful, too, to Dr Graeme Chesters, who helped me to negotiate dimensions of Left opposition with which I was less familiar.

I am also very appreciative of the support offered by my post-natal friends, and particularly Jose, support that helped me to cope with sleep deprivation and dirty nappies whilst finishing the book. I am also indebted to political discussions and long-term friendships with ex-Ruskin students, Callum, Chris, Gav, Paul,–and Shad in particular. I have also valued the warmth and generosity shown by my sister, Kam, her partner, Gary, and my wonderful niece, Havana. I should also acknowledge my lovely baby daughter, Xanthe's contribution, without which the book certainly would have been finished earlier, but life would have been much duller. And lastly, I would like to thank Charlie for conveying absolute faith in the book from beginning to end, and for his friendship, support, and love.

INTRODUCTION

Caryl Churchill's highly respected position in the canon of contemporary dramatists is secure and well-earned. Part of her acceptance into the mainstream is due to her distinctive approach to playwrighting, distinctive because of her peculiar ability to connect with concerns of the contemporary moment and her particularly innovative manipulation of dramatic form and style. It appears too, though, that Churchill's success is less connected with her desire for a socialist society ("decentralised, non-authoritarian, communist, non-sexist–a society in which people can be in touch with their feelings, and in control of their lives"[1]), and more a result of the appropriation of her work by critical approaches that prioritise gendered and postmodernist themes. This latter approach is particularly well illustrated in Sheila Rabillard's edited collection, *Caryl Churchill: Contemporary Re-presentations*.[2] Although there has been brief attention paid in the past to Churchill's socialist politics, the positioning of her work within the framework of socialist concerns has become a distant memory.[3] This is partly due to the flourishing of feminist theory and gender studies in the 1970s and 1980s, a body of theory informing many of the theoretical approaches to her work, and also due to the dominance of poststructuralism and postmodernism in critical theory during this same period, a dominance that prioritised a focus on language, signification, and modes of representation. As part of this trajectory, Marxist, socialist, and class-based frameworks were considered increasingly to be outdated and were relegated to marginal positions within the academy.

---

[1] Caryl Churchill, Interview by Judith Thurman, *Ms* (May 1982): 54.
[2] Sheila Rabillard, ed., *Caryl Churchill: Contemporary Re-presentations* (Winnipeg: Blizzard Press, 1997).
[3] See Ruby Cohn, "Modest Proposals of Modern Socialists," *Modern Drama* 25 (1982): 457-68; Christian W. Thomsen, "Three Socialist Playwrights," in *Contemporary British Drama*, eds. Malcolm Bradbury and David Palmer (London: Edward Arnold, 1981), 156-75; Linda Fitzsimmons, "'I won't turn back for you or anyone': Caryl Churchill's Socialist-Feminist Theatre," *Essays in Theatre* 6.1 (November 1987): 19-29; Janelle Reinelt, *After Brecht: British Epic Theater* (Ann Arbor: University of Michigan Press, 1994).

Rabillard's collection includes a range of perspectives on a variety of plays from *Light Shining in Buckinghamshire* to *The Skriker*.[4] In the Introduction, Rabillard describes the essays as responding to the "temporal pressure to re-examine socialist-feminist readings of Churchill's works," and as "introducing the possibility of departures (whether subtle or overt) from the prevailing emphasis upon Brechtian feminist paradigms."[5] However, while feminist appropriations of Churchill's work have been exciting and persuasive, socialist approaches have tended to focus on ways in which Brechtian methods have been used for feminist ends. The Brechtian paradigm has often become shorthand for an engagement with a socialist framework, an engagement that does not necessarily consider notions of class, anti-capitalism, and social revolution very much at all. Rabillard's postmodern characterisation of Churchill's later work, such as *Icecream*[6] and *The Skriker*, is offered, in part, as (a teleological) justification for a move away from "Brechtian feminist paradigms" and "socialist-feminist readings" of her earlier work.

Although Churchill's work clearly lends itself to postmodernist readings, the domination of such approaches has resulted in serious neglect of the socialist impulses that inform her work. The later plays in particular are often characterised as postmodern–as reflecting the dissolve of the totality, and depicting the incoherence of the political. But these readings overlook another narrative, a narrative that often questions, opposes, and challenges the implications of a postmodern abandonment of grand narratives and political agency. Churchill also seems to have fallen victim to the tendency to read women writers differently, to prioritise the feminism of their work, and view them apart from the supposedly more masculine politics of socialism, Marxism, and class struggle. It is therefore time for a new book on Churchill's work, one that reframes some of her most significant plays within a socialist context.

I situate Churchill's work in relation to socialist and Marxist theoretical and political thinking and activism from the late 1960s to the early 2000s. The eight plays selected are representative of an incisive intervention into anti-capitalist politics, but they also constitute a trajectory that reflects the move away from the revolutionary optimism of the late

[4] Churchill, *Light Shining in Buckinghamshire*, in *Caryl Churchill Plays: 1* (London: Methuen, 1985), 181-241 (hereafter cited in text as *LS*); *The Skriker*, in *Caryl Churchill Plays: 3* (London: Nick Hern, 1998), 239-91 (hereafter cited in text as *Skriker*).
[5] Rabillard, Introduction to *Caryl Churchill*, ed. Rabillard, 7-13; 8.
[6] Churchill, *Icecream*, in *Caryl Churchill Plays: 3* (London: Nick Hern, 1998), 55-102.

1960s and early 1970s towards a growing pessimism arising from the seemingly relentless endurance of Thatcherism in the 1980s and early 1990s, the break-up of Eastern Europe, and the continued retreat and fragmentation of the British Left. This political and cultural context is discussed in Chapter 1 at length and in some detail, and provides a new contextual framework within which to locate Churchill's work. Much of Churchill's drama resonates with the language of the British Left, a Left that incorporates many forms, including: trade unionism, Labourism, anti-imperialist struggle, revolutionary socialism, communism, anarchism, radical environmentalism, and anti-capitalism. Writing this particular political context for Churchill inspires readings of her plays with a political inflection that is often overlooked, an inflection that provokes a more complex depiction of politics in her drama.

Chapter 2 introduces all eight plays through a consideration of the politics of utopianism. The wish for an alternative society and the desire for what is not (yet) tangible connect the diverse forms of Left opposition and reflect a reverberation thematically across Churchill's drama. The complex, but dynamic field of utopian studies facilitates exploration of the implications of the stimulating conjuncture of utopia and theatre. The suggestiveness of the theatrical space, a space of potentiality, makes it peculiarly apt for thinking through utopian dramatic possibility. The politics of utopia cuts across the chapter topics of Marxist and feminist historiography, the intersection of class and gender, the end-of-history thesis, and radical environmental politics. All of Churchill's plays seem to be expressive of the utopian, or on some occasions, the dystopian. The politics of utopia responds to a signification in Churchill's plays that is unaccounted for in other political fields. The traces of desire, the sense of yearning for an altogether different social context; or conversely, a critique of, or satire on, spaces that are starved of the utopian, can be found in much of her drama.

Plays that engage explicitly with Left concerns have been selected, starting with *Light Shining* and *Vinegar Tom*, which were both performed and published in 1976.[7] They are discussed together as history plays in Chapter 3, in which the plays' dialogue with Marxist and Marxist-feminist historiography is the primary focus. The English revolution is a deeply potent, historical event for Marxists and socialists, in terms of its recuperation as class conflict: as the first national victory of the bourgeoisie and the radicalisation and mobilisation of large sections of the

---

[7] Churchill, *Vinegar Tom*, in *Caryl Churchill Plays: 1* (London: Methuen, 1985), 129-79 (hereafter cited in text as *VT*).

peasantry, artisans, and day-labourers. Alongside *Light Shining*, which is a play that draws on classical Marxist material, *Vinegar Tom* poses uncomfortable questions regarding the silences in historical enquiry, both liberal and Marxist alike, over the mass slaughter of (predominantly female) "witches."

Top Girls (written 1980-2 and performed in 1982) and *Fen* (written in 1982 and performed in 1983) are discussed in relation to the interaction of class and gender identities in Chapter 4.[8] Anxiety over retreat from socialist, collectivist, and community-based politics that characterised the late 1970s and 1980s permeates the dramatic narrative of *Top Girls*. The play is a critical response to the outward world of privatisation and individualism, but at the same time is an inward-looking analysis of the current opposition to late capitalist society. Its particular concern is the preoccupation of contemporaneous feminism with individual success within capitalist economics, which automatically excludes large numbers of working-class women. In an interview with Laurie Stone, Churchill explained that *Top Girls* was prompted by the experience of having a right-wing woman prime minister, the idea expanding after visiting America where she "met several women who were talking about how great it was that women were getting on so well now in American corporations, that there were equal opportunities." She accepts "that's certainly part of feminism," but says, "it's not what I think is enough. I'm saying there's no such thing as right-wing feminism."[9] *Fen* conveys the other side of the privatisation equation with its depiction of rural, female labour working relentlessly to increase the profits of the farmer, multinational capitalists, and city speculators. The play accentuates the feminist neglect of an anti-capitalist agenda and simultaneously exposes the dearth of anti-sexist and feminist activism within socialist and Marxist circles.

Chapter 5 considers *Serious Money* (written and performed in 1987) and *Mad Forest* (written and performed in 1990) with respect to the political moment at the end of the 1980s that connected the demise of the Soviet bloc, the celebration of monetarism, and the hegemony of the age of "post-isms" and "end-isms."[10] *Serious Money* uses the old-form of City

---

[8] Churchill, *Top Girls*, in *Caryl Churchill Plays: 2* (London: Methuen, 1990), 51-141 (hereafter cited in text as *TG*); Churchill, *Fen*, in *Caryl Churchill Plays: 2* (London: Methuen, 1990), 143-92 (hereafter cited in text as *Fen*).

[9] Churchill, Interview by Laurie Stone, reprinted in *File on Churchill*, ed. Linda Fitzsimmons (London: Methuen, 1989), 61.

[10] Churchill, *Serious Money*, in *Caryl Churchill Plays: 2* (London: Methuen, 1990), 193-309 (hereafter cited in text as *SM*); Churchill, *Mad Forest*, in *Caryl*

Comedy to satirise the world of the stock exchange in the City of London with its fast, brash depiction of a ruthless, predatory, and exploitative "community," whose drive to accumulate profits determines the lives of billions of workers worldwide. The celebration of moneymaking prefigures the death of communism–the only perceived threat to capitalism–and thus the disintegration of any serious challenge to free-market liberal democracies, as famously heralded by Francis Fukuyama.[11] With its dramatisation of the Romanian revolution, *Mad Forest* is a polytonal narrative of the mass uprising and the overthrow of Nicolae Ceauşescu. The dialogue that took place between the production company and students in Bucharest informs its intense sensitivity to the variety of voices included. The desire to embrace a diversity of Romanian perspectives, in conjunction with the confusion of socialists and Marxists over how to respond to these tumultuous events is echoed in the play's political hesitation. However, although everything is up for grabs, commitment to human agency, empowerment, and solidarity is consistently played out as moments of hope and inspiration.

The sixth and final chapter analyses two plays, *The Skriker* (1994) and *Far Away* (2000), through a consideration of the predominance of war and an escalating deterioration of the relationship between the human and non-human natural worlds.[12] Within this decade, unremitting warfare involving Britain and Western allies as central protagonists is a dominating feature, the brutality of which is reflected in the apocalyptic sensibility of both plays. This chapter raises the question of whether the same sense of socialist commitment can be traced in plays that have been frequently labelled as postmodern articulations of political confusion. In a period where Left opposition has retreated yet further, or mutated into a less recognisable and less united force, a force exemplified by its smallness and fragmented structure, the difficulty of political theatre to maintain a commitment to socialist concerns provides the challenge this chapter addresses. *The Skriker* to some extent foregrounds incoherence as a defining feature of the contemporary moment; however, this sense of incoherence is not celebrated as a liberating postmodern development in the play but is rather lamented as stultifying, and satirised as narcissistic and politically reckless. *Far Away*, too, does more than dramatise a politically unintelligible world. Its apocalyptic vision of terror–of all-out

---

Churchill Plays:3 (London: Nick Hern, 1998), 103-81 (hereafter cited in text as *MF*).

[11] See Francis Fukuyama, "The End of History," *The National Interest* 16 (Summer 1989): 3-18.

[12] Churchill, *Far Away* (London, Nick Hern, 2000) (hereafter cited in text as *FA*).

global warfare within which animals, plants, trees, and every other constituent of the natural world participates–is a frightening admonition of the implications of globalisation and environmental destruction. Again, like *The Skriker*, *Far Way*, whilst utilising a postmodern aesthetic, simultaneously problematises aspects of postmodernist thinking, particularly the fetishisation of language and representation at the expense of ethical commitment and political action.

CHAPTER ONE

SOCIALIST CONTEXTS

> There's been a lot of talk ... about 'the times' as if they were a force of nature–we are part of them just as much as the government, the city and business interests, and our opposition can be part of them.[1]

As stated in the Introduction, Churchill has expressed her desire for a non-authoritarian, communist society.[2] She has also famously, although hesitantly, accepted the labels of socialist and feminist playwright.[3] Many of Churchill's plays engage with such subjects as struggle, oppression, power, revolution, human subjectivity and agency, and display a dynamic relationship with Left thinking, as well as an especially sensitive understanding of the nuances of dominant ideologies. Contextualising her plays' treatment of political subject matter within Left debate produces a range of political perspectives that, at times, compete against other, more postmodern, readings of Churchill's drama.

Dominant discourses in the academy on the evaluation of post-1960s historical and cultural change are remarkably hegemonic in their consensus. This consensus proposes a move away from a society characterised by Fordist mass and standardised production techniques, capital and labour conflict, and strong collective identities, towards post-Fordist, flexible specialisation production techniques, and a postmodern

---

[1] Churchill, Letter to the Chairman of the English Stage Company (3 November 1989), reprinted in *About Churchill: The Playwright and the Work,* by Philip Roberts (London: Faber, 2008), 115-17, 116.

[2] See Introduction, note 1.

[3] I use the term "hesitantly" because Churchill states, "I've constantly said that I am both a socialist and a feminist. Constantly said it. If someone says 'a socialist playwright' or 'a feminist playwright' that can suggest to some people something rather narrow which doesn't cover as many things as you might be thinking about. I get asked if I mind being called a woman playwright or a feminist playwright, and again it depends entirely on what's going on in the mind of the person who says it." Unpublished interview by Linda Fitzsimmons, in *File on Churchill* (London: Methuen, 1989), 89.

culture identifiable precisely for its lack of stable identification. This view assumes a breakdown of traditional categories resulting in, what cultural theorist, Stuart Hall, and former editor of *Marxism Today*, Martin Jacques, describe as "diversity, differentiation and fragmentation, rather than homogeneity, standardisation and the economies and organisations of scale which characterised modern mass society."[4] Churchill's later work may well be more conducive to postmodern readings. However, deferral to a postmodernist paradigm as a self-explanatory framework for thinking about Churchill's drama, or referencing postmodernity as a *given* historical and cultural realty, often eclipse alternative perspectives, perspectives that facilitate the expression of more of the plays' political potential. The language of postmodernism becomes, ironically, limiting and deterministic in its assumption of a *de facto* postmodern landscape. A historical narrative that relies upon a move away from Fordism to post-Fordism, from modernism to postmodernism–like any other historical narrative–is one that privileges a particular perspective and reflects the interests of the authors of the history. Hence, an important aspect of producing a political context for Churchill's work is to examine ways in which this historical narrative came to dominate perspectives on this period, and to explore the implications of this move for the British Left.

The Left in Retreat (1980-2000)

I do not want to suggest there was a shift of the whole of the British Left away from class politics, or that this direction coincided precisely with the re-election of the Conservative Party led by Margaret Thatcher in 1979. The discourses of the New Left were framed around the notion of disillusionment with Labour's reformism or gradualist approach to socialism, its experience of Stalinism in the Communist Party, and its attempt to discover alternative revolutionary routes.[5] This meant, to varying degrees, a decentring of the working class as the predominant agent of social transformation and a growing preoccupation with the ideologies of consumption and cultural practices. However, in contrast, the revolutionary Left led a "return to the class," and considered labour and trade union politics a crucial forum within which working-class struggle

---

[4] Stuart Hall and Martin Jacques, Introduction to *New Times: The Changing Face of Politics in the 1990s*, eds. Stuart Hall and Martin Jacques (London: Lawrence and Wishart in association with *Marxism Today*, 1989), 11-20, 11.

[5] The New Left is discussed in more detail on pages 17-23.

could be mobilised.[6] A campaign to democratise and re-claim the Labour Party, initiated in the late 1970s by the Bennite Left, Tribune, and others continued with gusto into the 1980s, gaining some successes such as the 1981 Wembley conference agreeing to set up an electoral school that required mandatory reselection of MPs amongst other democratic measures. This trajectory peaked with Tony Benn losing the deputy leadership election of the Labour Party by a whisker in 1981. Notwithstanding this Left activity, this chapter's subtitle does respond, nevertheless, to an acceleration and consolidation of a move by the New Left tradition, the Communist Party, sections of the Labour Left, feminist, and Campaign for Nuclear Disarmament (CND) activists away from traditional socialist forms of organising towards more of a concentration on electoral and coalitionist approaches.

The early 1980s witnessed battles within the Communist Party between "modernisers," who tended towards Eurocommunism and used Gramscian theories of hegemony and "war of position"[7] to validate this direction, and the "traditionalists," who wished to remain involved in more conventional forms of socialist organisation. Frequent debate took place over whether socialists should join the Labour Left, or build socialist unity outside of the Labour Party. Nevertheless, there was a realignment of sorts of the Left after Labour lost the 1983 election. This involved Tony Benn, Arthur Scargill, Militant, Socialist Workers Party and other Trotskyist organisations, as well as (to some degree) those in the Communist Party, who considered the main problem to be Labour's lack of a principled socialist backbone. In contrast, there were the contributors to the later New Times project, such as Hall and Jacques, and the Eurocommunists, who believed that part of the problem was aspects of socialist theory itself, which Thatcherism, to some extent, had exposed.

Monetarism is a dominating characteristic of Thatcherism; however, a move away from Keynesian economics was clearly pursued by Labour in the mid- to late 1970s; significantly, this occurred just after Labour was re-elected for the second time in October 1974 on one of its most Left-wing programmes. Memories of a perfidious Labour government and the Winter of Discontent of 1978/79 caused disillusionment and distrust of Labour amongst working-class voters, imbuing the seeming newness and radicalism

---

[6] For example, Militant Tendency, who insisted on the centrality of Labour and trade union politics, had 1000 members by the end of 1975, 4,700 members in 1983, and over 8,000 by 1986. See John Callaghan, *The Far Left in British Politics* (Oxford: Blackwell, 1987), 204-5.

[7] Hegemony and "war of position" are discussed in more detail on pages 22-23.

of Thatcherism with a certain attraction.[8] Debates within the Left over the nature of Thatcherism, particularly in terms of the inter-relationships of economic, political, and social forms, dominated the period. The Left playwright, David Edgar comments on the shifting of political meanings such as that of the welfare state. Once viewed as benign paternalism, the welfare state was now "magically transformed into the promoter of irresponsibility, indiscipline and disorder."[9] Trade unions too, changed from being integral elements in the political economy to promoters of recklessness, disharmony, and anarchy. Transformation of the political idiom was a key element to the success of the political and economic vision of Thatcherism.

This transformation of the political idiom involved the rejection of the permissiveness of the 1960s, a return to Victorian virtues of discipline, and a transformation of a section of the working class into the "undeserving poor," a section of the community characterised by dependence on the welfare state, a large proportion of which were single mothers. But this conservative social attitude was combined with a radical liberation of capital and the free market. The public shift towards an acceptance of the necessity for economic liberalism accompanied by social and political conservatism has been a significant dimension of the way the 1980s has been constructed. Raymond Williams attempted to equate negative forms of cultural expression, such as the seeming submission of large sections of the public to the diminution of communities, with "factors which arise from the dislocation, rather than the alternative reading, as the evidence of some essence of the people which Thatcher has in some way managed to distil."[10] But this environmental explanation offered by Williams for the rightwards shift of the British public seems not to be given particular attention or significance by many commentating on this period.

Nevertheless, there remained a sharp polarisation in the 1980s between the ideologies of Thatcherism and a socialist politics based upon an amalgamation of Left forces such as the industrial militancy of Scargill and the National Union of Mineworkers (NUM), the Greenham Common

---

[8] For an account of the Labour government's role in identifying the working class and trade unions as the constituency that must pay for the economic downturn, which in turn neatly facilitated the Tories' designation of the trade unions as the source of the nation's problems, see Michael Rustin, "The New Left and the Present Crisis," *New Left Review* 121 (May-June 1980): 63-89, 64.

[9] David Edgar, *The Second Time as Farce* (London: Lawrence and Wishart, 1988), 13.

[10] Raymond Williams, "Problems of the Coming Period," *New Left Review* 140 (July-August 1983): 7-18, 11.

women, the Bennite faction of the Labour Party, Liverpool and Lambeth
Councils, and Ken Livingstone and the Greater London Council (GLC).
However, the Thatcher regime mounted an effective challenge to Left
opposition, by, for example, breaking the 1984-85 Miners Strike, de-
unionising the major media outlets at Wapping, and abolishing the GLC.
This, in conjunction with the lack of, or move away from, class-based
politics within certain influential sections of the Left seems to have
inadvertently aided, as Edgar says, "the highly successful Thatcherite
endeavour to Americanise people's conception of the working-class." This
new conception involved the separation of "the full-time employed
proletariat from the part-time or unemployed section" and the importation
of "a new vocabulary–'the inner cities,' 'the underclass'–to define the
latter."[11] An attempt, too, to re-categorise a significant section of the
working class–who were increasingly finding employment outside of the
industrial sector–as middle class, was to some extent successful.

The representation of a fragmented working class, aided by the end of
full employment, deterioration of manufacturing, selling off of huge stocks
of council housing, retracting the welfare state, and encouraging the
pursuit of private property seemed to bolster sections of the Left
(particularly the New Times project) in their relegation of the working
class to that of a constituency status–just one constituency amongst many–
as opposed to a primary oppositional force. While there was recognition
by the Left that it was in the interests of Thatcherism to vehemently pursue
the claim that the working class no longer existed, or was heterogeneous
beyond identification, much was conceded to this way of thinking. Eric
Hobsbawm claimed, "it was a crisis not of the class, but of its
consciousness."[12] Whatever it was–and certainly part of the problem with
class politics was the (mis)conception that the working-class subject was a
white, male, manual labourer–class as a category was no longer an
automatically agreed upon, and shared, locus of analysis of change
amongst some of the Left, and particularly the Left intelligentsia.
Publications such as André Gorz's *Farewell to the Working Class* were
indicative of this retreat from social class towards new historical
subjects.[13]

The break-up of Eastern Europe and the introduction of Glasnost in the
USSR were also significant events in this post-Fordist narrative.[14] The

---

[11] Edgar, *The Second Time as Farce*, 124.
[12] Eric Hobsbawm, *Age of Extremes* (London: Michael Joseph, 1994), 305.
[13] André Gorz, *Farewell to the Working Class* (London: Pluto Press, 1982).
[14] This book is primarily concerned with placing Churchill's plays in the context of
British Left debate; hence, the idiom of this debate is retained in order to explore

Left responded to these calamitous events with excitement, hope, fear, and despair simultaneously. While the "Manifesto for New Times" praised Mikhail Gorbachev's "honesty to admit that socialism has suffered from the arrogance of omniscience and the stagnation of bureaucracy,"[15] and congratulated the creativity of Perestroika, political scientist, Fred Halliday alluded to the rise of nationalist conflict and warned of the increase in xenophobia, racism, religious conservatism, and the engendering of new right-wing organisations across most of the new states.[16] Halliday lamented the capitalist restructuring of Eastern Europe and expressed regret over what he saw as the soon to be forgotten revolutionary achievements of 1917. Nonetheless, a politics seeking to work within the economic framework of capitalism and one that saw the defeat of communism as bringing with it the necessity of denouncing the revolutionary narrative initiated in 1917 became a dominating position within influential sections of the Left. Many influential Left commentators viewed the break-up of Eastern Europe as cause for reappraisal of Marxism and socialism. Mary Kaldor went as far as to question the usefulness of the word "socialism," and asked, "is social justice an adequate substitute for the term 'socialist'?"[17] Hence, the idiom of the Left became progressively abandoned by prominent and influential Left commentators.

The fragmentation of Eastern Europe from a coherent bloc, and the reappraisal, once again, of socialism, made an important contribution to the discourse of post-Fordism. The idea that we moved into a post-Fordist era of capitalism, a period characterised by the break-up of the manufacturing industry, sudden increase of growth in the information

---

the extent to which Churchill's work is illuminated through this context. However, I acknowledge Ludmilla Kostova's discussion of the simplification and homogenisation of identities that takes place when the term "Eastern Europe" is employed, and therefore I use the term with hesitation. "Inventing Post-Wall Europe," in *Beyond Boundaries: Textual Representations of European Identity*, ed. Andy Hollis (Amsterdam: Rodopi, 2000), 83-84.

[15] "The Manifesto for New Times," in *New Times*, eds. Hall and Jacques, 448-53, 453. The contributors to "The Manifesto" were Beatrix Campbell, Marian Darke, Tricia Davis, David Green, Joanna de Groot, Ron Halverson, Steve Hart, Martin Jacques, Charlie Leadbeater, Bert Pearce, Jeff Rodrigues, Mhairi Stewart and Nina Temple, and the Manifesto was amended by the Communist Party Executive Committee.

[16] Fred Halliday, "The Ends of Cold War," *New Left Review* 180 (March/April 1990): 5-23, 11; 22.

[17] Mary Kaldor, "After the Cold War," *New Left Review* 180 (March/April 1990): 25-37, 37.

technology sector, globalisation, the increased freedom of capital, and a cultural change towards anti-authoritarianism (including in relation to trade unions and the labour movement), underpinned this embrace of a multiplicity of oppositional constituencies. Sociologist, John Urry claimed the changed economic structure did not produce homogeneity in terms of social class and pointed instead to the diversity of identities organised around "issues of gender, the environment, nuclear weapons, urban inequalities, racial discrimination, social amenities, level of rates, and so on." [18] He emphasised the fluid and decentralised nature of many of these groups and their tendency towards suspicion of centralised, hierarchical modes of organisation, including the Labour movement. There was some dissent from this position by Left cultural theorists, such as Dick Hebdige, who explained "postmodern pessimism" of the Jean Baudrillard kind as "symptomatic of the crisis of a particular intellectual formation (male, white, European) shaped in the crucible of student politics of 1968." [19] Disappointed by the failure of the revolutionary upheavals of 1968 to result in permanent change, many Leftist intellectuals, Hebdige argues, turned their talents to a more sceptical and cynical political philosophy. Nevertheless, Hebdige's perspective is similarly framed by an emphasis on the proliferation of identities and subcultures, which, perhaps, in turn leans incautiously towards a depoliticising, postmodern relativism.

Hall responded astutely to the political nuances and ambiguities of what he considered to be "new times." He described the contradictory nature of modernity, emphasising the simultaneous production of wealth and poverty. A newly acquired abundance of choice existed within the confines of a seemingly boundless range of consumption preferences but this emphasis on choice was symptomatic of an existence characterised increasingly by division and isolation. Globalisation was a neo-imperialist project based upon enriching the West at the expense of the poverty-stricken South. Hall described "the city–privileged scenario of the modern experience for Baudelaire or Walter Benjamin" as "–transformed into the anonymous city, the sprawling city, the inner city, the abandoned city." [20] However, while tracing the increasing destructiveness of the capitalist system, Hall and the New Times project (particularly in comparison with the New Left of the 1960s) simultaneously no longer appeared to consider

---

[18] John Urry, "The End of Organised Capitalism," in *New Times*, eds. Hall and Jacques, 94-102, 99-100.
[19] Dick Hebdige, "After the Masses," in *New Times*, eds. Hall and Jacques, 76-93, 87.
[20] Hall, "The Meaning of New Times," in *New Times*, eds. Hall and Jacques, 116-34, 124.

revolutionary solutions. Politics became preoccupied with margins and individual subjectivities, and was susceptible to Terry Eagleton's terse appraisal of deconstruction, a practice that "like much cultural theory … can allow one to speak darkly of subversion while leaving one's actual politics only slightly to the left of Edward Kennedy's." According to Eagleton, deconstructionists think that "the current system of power can be ceaselessly 'interrupted,' deferred or 'pushed away,' but to try to get beyond it altogether is the most credulous form of utopianism."[21]

Eagleton's comments highlight the political limitations of poststructuralist and postmodernist discourses. Cultural theorist, Fred Inglis claims, "there is something repellent in the mischievousness with which the deconstructionists toy with the loss of hope in the face of the ugliness of the times."[22] At the same time, philosopher, Kate Soper saw advantages in this very recognition, a recognition that should lead to the re-alignment with principled political positions, which in turn brings with it the engagement with "more than theory."[23] Hence, from within cultural theory, there is certainly a discernible Left critique of the politically limiting implications of postmodernism;[24] however, on balance, it is clear that a great deal of theoretical and political ground was ceded simultaneously. Furthermore, whilst Marxist theory has been in the doghouse for the last three or four decades for grand narrativising and subsuming (and thus effectively occluding) other oppressions, such as those based upon gender and race under the category of social class, class itself has been virtually eclipsed as a category in critical theory.

The move away from class in political practice as well as in theory was coterminous with a change in political expectation, but this retreat from the aim of "changing the world" also seemed to be informed by a compromise with aspects of Thatcherite ideology. Sociologist, Michael Rustin, in his persuasive critique of the New Times project, pointed to the "unfortunate concessions to values that are probably better simply

---

[21] Terry Eagleton, "In the Gaudy Supermarket," Review of *A Critique of Post-Colonial Reason: Toward a History of the Vanishing Present* by Gayatri Chakravorty Spivak *London Review of Books* (13 May 1999): 3-6, 6.

[22] Fred Inglis, "The Figures of Dissent," *New Left Review* 215 (January/February 1996): 83-92, 91.

[23] Kate Soper, "Postmodernism, Subjectivity, Value," *New Left Review* 186 (March/April 1991) 120-28, 123.

[24] See also Frederic Jameson, "Postmodernism, or The Cultural Logic of Late Capitalism," *New Left Review* 146 (July/August 1984): 53-92; Terry Eagleton, *The Illusions of Postmodernism* (Oxford: Blackwell, 1996); Alex Callinicos, *Against Postmodernism* (Oxford: Blackwell, 1989).

regarded as those of the other side." Appropriating key Thatcherite principles (individualism, consumption, efficiency, and modernisation) so as to mount a more effective challenge to those very principles is what Rustin saw the New Times project as mistakenly undertaking. Rustin argues,

> the idea of a 'progressive restructuring of society,' or 'socialist modernisation,' gives centrality to vapid notions of 'modernity' which in this form should have no place in socialist programme-making. It should be a question of modernisation or restructuring for what or whom.[25]

As Rustin argues, the move of emphasis away from production towards consumption in analyses of post-Fordism masks the fundamental basis of consumption, namely that the ability to consume depends upon the earning of wages (production); therefore, the supposedly old-fashioned foci of Marxist cultural analysis (production relations, ownership of property, class relations) remain the foundations of cultural life.

Another significant section of the Left, which developed in the early 1990s, and whose departure was of a non-traditional socialist orientation was the radical environmental movement. Marxists and environmentalists have had an uneasy relationship historically, with the former viewing the primary contradiction in society as that between labour and capital, the latter identifying the contradiction as one between productive growth and the sustainability of the planet.[26] However, the ecologically oriented, non-violent direct action strategies used by environmental groups such as Reclaim The Streets, Earth First!, and Critical Mass, displayed, according to Graeme Chesters, "an 'antagonistic' or 'intemperate' orientation towards the normative system of production, distribution, exchange and consumption."[27] In other words, unlike mainstream environmentalists such as Greenpeace, the Green Party and Friends of the Earth, the radical environmental movement was interested in the way that environmental concerns intertwine with production, distribution, exchange, and consumption. Their antagonistic approach also meant a decreased negotiability of goals. Alberto Melucci explains that "antagonist movements embody goals and forms of action that are not negotiable with the existing

---

[25] Michael Rustin, "The Trouble with 'New Times,'" in *New Times*, eds. Hall and Jacques, 303-20, 313.

[26] For a helpful discussion of the compatibility between Marxism and ecological approaches, see Reiner Grunmann, "The Ecological Challenge to Marxism," *New Left Review* 187 (May/June 1991): 103-20.

[27] Graeme Chesters, "Resist to Exist?" *ECOS* 20.2 (1999): 19-25, 20.

arrangement of social power and with the forms of political hegemony exercised by dominant interests."[28] Unlike the New Times project, which appropriated or negotiated with Thatcherite principles, radical environmentalists sought to practice a politics fundamentally different to these.

Drawing on a variety of resources such as the radical art practices of Dada and the surrealists, the revolutionary tradition of Situationism and theorists such as French neo-Marxist Henri Lefebvre and philosopher Gilles Deleuze, the diverse groups and activists that made up the radical environmental movement aimed to subvert, disturb, and reclaim, rather than lobby, negotiate, and influence the political process. Chesters explains,

> reclaiming streets is not instrumental, goal oriented action aimed at convincing or cajoling public opinion to influence those in power, such as is the model for many other types of highly symbolic action, Greenpeace and the Brent Spar for example. Rather, it is a celebration of the possibility of participation in the public sphere, unmediated by institutions, it is as much about returning pleasure to politics and politics to the streets, as it is about car free space.[29]

This amalgamation of aesthetics, celebration, and radical politics is often manifested in non-traditional forms of action, such as carnival. It is argued that the politics of street parties is traceable in the activists' production of communal and social space, one that resists capitalist spatial hegemony. It is a form of activity that is not so much representative as productive in its creation of utopian moments in the immediate present.

Marxists responded to the eco-anarchism of the radical environmental movement with caution. The latter's absence of a cohesive organisational structure, the lack of an overarching theory connecting struggles, the preoccupation with culture and aesthetics, and the move away from workplace activity, were some of the problems that thwarted effective collaboration between revolutionary socialists and radical environmentalists. The seemingly directionless character of the radical environmental movement and its lack of an engaged relationship with class struggle were among some of the issues that troubled Marxists. Additionally Marxists tended to suspect the utopian pre-figuration (the notion that the future can

---

[28] Alberto Melucci, *Challenging Codes: Collective Action in the Information Age* (Cambridge: Cambridge UP, 1996), 39.
[29] Chesters, "Resist to Exist?" 23.

be lived out now) of the environmentalists as a form of idealism.[30] Not surprisingly this non-traditional method of struggle–the absence of a restrictive organisational structure, the emphasis on creativity, and the notion of "living the revolution"–is precisely what attracted environmentalists. Traditional, revolutionary socialist forms of organising, whether Leninist or not, were seen as stifling and as having the potential to reconstitute oppressive structures.[31]

The vacuum on the Left created out of the move to the right (and disintegration) of the Labour Left and the Eurocommunists, and the demise of groups, such as Militant, CND, and the Anti-Apartheid Movement were increasingly filled in the 1990s by the radical environmental movement, and in the 2000s by anti-globalisation and anti-capitalist activism. Left trade unionists and revolutionary socialists thus began to recognise the importance of engagement with these movements and made tentative connections over issues where mutual agreement existed. The Stop the War Coalition, a movement whose president is Tony Benn and whose membership includes socialists, trade unionists, peace activists and muslim groups for instance, joined thousands of anti-capitalist activists at the G20 protests in London in March 2009.

Left Construction of the Late 1960s and 1970s

Hall is instrumental in two major reassessments of the Left at two different points in the period this chapter covers. The first is the establishment of the New Left in the mid-1960s, and the second is the New Times project, which came to published fruition in 1989.[32] Of 1956, when Britain invaded Suez and the USSR sent 2000 troops to suppress the Hungarian uprising, Hall stated, "it crystallised what we were saying about imperialism not being finished, and the Soviet Union being a totalitarian power. We were against both."[33] Thereafter, Hall became a founding editor of what would be *New Left Review.* In 1967, Hall, along with Williams and Edward Thompson wrote,

---

[30] Idealism is discussed in more detail in Chapter 2, page 39.
[31] Having said that, there have been examples of productive interaction, such as the Liverpool Docks Strike of 1995-1997, where marches and demonstrations saw traditional labour movement activists, revolutionary socialists, and radical environmentalists forming what seemed to be an effective coalition.
[32] Hall and Jacques, eds., *New Times.*
[33] Hall, quoted in Maya Jaggi, "Stuart Hall, Prophet at the margins," *The Guardian* (8 July 2000).

it is our basic case, in this manifesto, that the separate campaigns in which we have all been active, and the separate issues with which we have all been concerned, run back, in their essence, to a single political system and its alternatives. We believe that the system we now oppose can only survive by a willed separation of issues, and the resulting fragmentation of consciousness. Our own first position is that all the issues–industrial and political, international and domestic, economic and cultural, humanitarian and radical–are deeply connected; that what we oppose is a political, economic, and social system; that what we work for is a different whole society.[34]

Hall and other New Left contributors sought to develop a political movement that was anti-Stalinist, as well as anti-capitalist, and while there was already at this early stage a move away from class politics ("I had a debate with Raphael Samuel about class which we had for the rest of his life; the class system no longer explained a time of modern consumer-oriented capitalism"[35]) there was, nevertheless, a solidity and stability of position in relation to opposing the capitalist system in its entirety, and an emphasis on the importance of the solidarity and unity of forces in order to achieve this goal. There was also a classical Marxist identification of the inextricable link between property and power and the need for those relations to be transformed.

Twenty years on, however, this promotion of unity and solidarity, and of attacking one whole system as the source of exploitative and oppressive power, had atrophied. Hall welcomed the "proliferation of new points of antagonism" and the "new social movements of resistance organised around them," and with this, a distribution of focus to areas assumed previously to be less worthy of political attention, such as "a politics of the family, of health, of food, of sexuality, of the body." He identified the absence of "any overall map of how these power relations connect and of their resistances," and thus concluded that "perhaps there isn't, in that sense, one 'power game' at all, more a network of strategies and powers and their articulations–and thus a politics which is always positional."[36] These two positions, separated by twenty years, are useful coordinates within which to explore the conditions that are the terrain of such a change in political perspective.

---

[34] Stuart Hall, Raymond Williams and Edward Thompson, "From *The May Day Manifesto*," in *The New Left Reader*, ed. Carl Oglesby (New York: Grove Press, 1969), 111-43, 113-14.
[35] Hall, quoted in Jaggi, "Stuart Hall, Prophet at the Margins."
[36] Hall, "The Meaning of New Times," 130.

Hall considered the "newness" of the New Left to result from its opposition to both capitalism and Stalinism. This is against a background of crisis in the Communist Party, which, in the aftermath of the uprising in Hungary, found its membership reduced to about two-thirds of what it had been.[37] While there had been a certain synonymy between Marxist theory and the political positions of the Communist Party, after the Hungarian uprising there was a proliferation of different socialist groups making claims to *the* Marxist tradition. Hence, "the Marxist Left" started to be to be talked about.[38] The significance of various internationalist struggles and regimes claiming Marxism as their basis was influential within the eclectic positions of the New Left. However, the New Left's eclectic approach kept it relatively aloof from revolutionary *party* politics. The Leninist tradition of the strong, democratically centralist, vanguard party was considered stifling and anachronistic.[39]

There was a disinclination to engage with the Trotskyist revolutionary tradition; indeed Callaghan states that "the intellectual leadership of the dissident communists," such as Thompson, appear "never to have even considered the Trotskyist option," and "for this reason made little headway in understanding Stalinism and the Soviet Union." The priority for Thompson and others involved in the *New Reasoner* was to emphasise socialism's attractions, move away from what they saw as the economically deterministic preoccupations of both Leninist and Trotskyist approaches, and engage instead with "the cultural, experiential and ideological facets of life," which it perceived the Leninist tradition to have neglected almost completely. Callaghan describes the *New Reasoner* as heading "closer to a Gramscian Marxism," seeing "insurrectionary Leninism as unable to meet the needs of socialists in advanced capitalist societies."[40] Coterminous with this thinking, Hall remembers orthodox Marxism relegating culture to "a decorative addendum to the 'hard world' of

---

[37] Callaghan, *The Far Left in British Politics*, 69.

[38] Williams, "Notes on Marxism in Britain since 1945," *New Left Review* 100 (November 1976-January 1977): 81-94, 82.

[39] See V. I. Lenin, *What is to be done?* (Beijing: Foreign Languages Press, 1978; first published in 1902); "Party Organisation and Party Literature," in *Lenin: Selected Works* (Moscow: Progress Publishers, 1968; first published in 1905). Critics of Leninist approaches to party organisation include Ralph Miliband, who argues, "democratic centralism ... has always served as a convenient device for authoritarian party structures." "The Future of Socialism in England," *Socialist Register* (1977): 38-50, 50.

[40] Callaghan, *The Far Left in British Politics*, 71.

production and things."[41] Of course, it should be noted that Antonio Gramsci's commitment to class struggle, his unwavering focus on capitalist economics, and his support of the Comintern right up until his death, was overlooked by Hall and others in favour of his work on culture and his theory of hegemony.

The dearth of a Marxist tradition of cultural theory and aesthetics provided the New Left with the impetus and space to develop theories and criticism in this area. The ideological uncertainty resulting from engaging with such a subject as "culture" led predictably to criticism of the political signification of some of this work.[42] Eagleton accuses Williams's *Culture and Society* of failing to recognise "culture" as an ideological term.[43] Williams's work tended to conflate aesthetics, politics, and ethics with modes and social relations of production, and in so doing produced the precariously depoliticised and politically indistinct subject of "culture." This over-subjectification of culture was also accompanied by a zealous resistance to "economistic Marxism." The desire to move outside of deterministic economic frameworks was accompanied by an under-theorising of economic class relations in whatever "lived experience" was the focus of enquiry.

Another indictment of this move of the New Left towards cultural theory is one of academicism. Williams, himself, demonstrated awareness of this:

> while academic theory, at its best, gives us the necessary foundations for any operative theory, it can, at its worst, be quite quickly incorporated–the unlooked-for recognition of the untouchable becoming, rather smoothly, the invitation to stay–within the fluid eclecticism now characteristic of academic institutions, until even Marxism becomes a "subject."[44]

As well as pursuing theory at the expense of practice, the academic expression of Marxism and socialism, particularly in the form of cultural studies, made it peculiarly susceptible to commoditisation. Moyra Haslett claimed that "unlike other marxist approaches, cultural studies has no accompanying political form, and its international interests, its curiosity

---

[41] Hall, quoted in Jaggi, "Stuart Hall, Prophet at the margins."

[42] Williams increasingly recognised the ambiguities of the term "culture": "the number of times I've wished that I had never heard of the damned word. I have become more aware of its difficulties, not less, as I have gone on." *Politics and Letters* (London: Verso, 1981), 154.

[43] Williams, *Culture and Society* (London: Hogarth, 1958).

[44] Williams, "Notes on British Marxism since 1945," 85.

about other cultures, have ironically made it a product which can be sold on a global scale." She concluded that from a Marxist perspective, "cultural studies is suspiciously complicit with contemporary advanced capitalism."[45]

Of course, academics are not alone in their interest in Marxism in the universities. Representations of students as radicals and as the predominant agents of social change dominate the way that the 1960s and particularly 1968 has been constructed. The upsurge in student radicalism prompted debate over the location of students in the struggle against capitalism. Anthony Barnett claimed in 1969,

> until this year the English debate on the student movement was concerned with two problems: whether students can be revolutionaries, and whether struggle in the universities can be revolutionary struggle. It is now widely accepted that the answer to both these questions is yes. Yes, students in student struggle can be revolutionaries; yes, the universities are strategic and vulnerable elements of late bourgeois society.[46]

Of course, the traditional, syndicalist measure of pre-revolutionary resistance was insufficient for the assessment of student struggle, and student activists were clearly self-conscious in their attempts to refashion elements of Marxist theory in the image of their own revolutionary agency.

This emphasis on counter-organisation and revolutionary culture echoed throughout the New Left, the new social movements, as well as student activism.[47] Gorz moved the emphasis of insurgency away from productive labour, viewing instead the production of the self to be the arena of interest, and seeing this taking place in all spheres of life. He concluded,

> this production takes place not only in the work situation but just as much in the schools; cafés, athletic fields; on voyages; in theatres, concerts,

---

[45] Moyra Haslett, *Marxist Literary and Cultural Theories* (London: Macmillan, 2000), 127.

[46] Antony Barnett, "A Revolutionary Student Movement," *New Left Review* 53 (January-February 1969): 43-53, 43.

[47] The attractions of this emphasis on "culture" for the women's and civil rights movements were partly to do with the facilitation within this approach of pursuing consciousness and consciousness-raising, as well as the deconstruction of traditional divisions between private and public spheres. This wider application of the political thus enabled women and black activists, for example, to analyse, confront and critique sexism and racism in new, exciting, and liberating ways.

newspapers, books, expositions; in towns, neighbourhoods, discussion and action groups–in short, wherever individuals enter into relationships with one another and produce the universe of human relationships.[48]

Therefore, with this growing emphasis on, and politicisation of, culture, resistance became increasingly encapsulated in one's whole lifestyle, as opposed to one's struggle in the workplace.

This is accompanied by the work of French neo-Marxist Louis Althusser, whose concepts of "overdetermination" and the "relative autonomy" of the superstructure were immensely influential, both inside and outside the academy.[49] Considered to be useful tools that provided a more nuanced engagement with the Marxist model of base and superstructure, these were simultaneously identified as helpful in guarding against "vulgar Marxism." However, in his *Poverty of Theory*, Thompson described Althusserianism as an "unmeasured assault upon 'historicism,'" examples of which he considered were its tendency to reduce history to ideology, and its propensity to privilege structures at the expense of processes. He defended what he saw as the "growing self-confidence" of English empiricism in the pursuit of "the materialist conception of history," against a French philosophical tradition, particularly Althusserian structuralism, which immobilised agency in the context of pre-existing structures of power.[50]

Throughout this period, Gramsci's theories of hegemony and the "war of position" co-dominated, albeit uncomfortably with the ideas of Althusser

---

[48] Gorz, "From Strategy For Labour," in *The New Left Reader*, ed. Oglesby, 41-42.

[49] Althusser described overdetermination as referring to the "general contradiction" (between the forces and relations of production) as well as to the necessity for "an accumulation of circumstances and currents" which will "*fuse* into a *ruptural unit*." This multiple process of contradiction–overdetermination–is indivisible from the "total structure" of the "social body"; "it is radically affected by them, determining and determined in one and the same movement by the various *levels* and *instances* of the social formation it animates." "Contradiction and Overdetermination," in *The New Left Reader*, ed. Oglesby, 57-83, 67; 68-69. Williams described overdetermination as "an attempt to avoid the isolation of autonomous *categories* but at the same time to emphasise relatively autonomous yet of course interactive *practices.*" *Marxism and Literature* (Oxford: Oxford UP, 1977), 88.

[50] Edward Thompson, "The Poverty of Theory," in *The Poverty of Theory and Other Essays* (London: Merlin, 1978), 193-397, 194; 196. As well as Althusser, Ernesto Laclau, Étienne Balibar, Gaston Bachelard, Jean Cavaillès, Georges Canguilhem and Michel Foucault are all objects of attack, the last four in particular pejoratively characterised as existing within "a particular French tradition of epistemology and idealist structuralism." "The Poverty of Theory," 387.

in the New Left, the universities, as well as the Communist Party. For Gramsci, the predominance of the ruling class rests not merely in its ability to deploy the resources of physical coercion afforded by the state apparatus but also relies on consent.[51] This consent or spontaneous unquestioning loyalty is fostered within the realms of civil society by institutions such as the church, trade unions, universities and through the direction of intellectual and cultural life in general.[52] An un-Gramscian implication of this ideology-oriented direction during this period was, however, the decentring of the working class as the predominant agent of socialist transformation. Orthodox Marxist strategies of revolutionary class struggle were seen by some as more appropriate to the Victorian period. American sociologist, C. Wright Mills, claimed not to comprehend why some New Left contributors held "so mightily to 'the working class' of the advanced capitalist societies as *the* historic agency, or even as the most important agency."[53] Part of the reason for this thinking appeared to arise from the view that the working class had been bought off by capitalist reforms and was effectively undergoing a process of "embourgeoisement." This is clearly illustrated in Thesis 27 of "The Appeal from the Sorbonne" from the Open Assembly of June 13-14 1968,

---

[51] This idea resurrects Niccolo Machiavelli's "centaur": "half-animal and half-human. They are the levels of force and of consent, authority and hegemony, violence and civilisation." Antonio Gramsci, *Selections from the Prison Notebook* (London: Lawrence and Wishart, 1976), 170.

[52] The main task of counter-hegemony is to break the ideological bond based on consent between the ruling class and the exploited. Stripping the former of its spiritual and intellectual prestige and power is to banish illusion and lay bare the real economic-corporate interests of the bourgeoisie. The "organic intellectuals" are not identified as individuals of a certain type but are defined by function, a much broader, non-elitist interpretation. For, just as all take part in human social activity, so all are to some extent intellectual producers. The organic intellectual lives the life of the worker, and guides, teaches and inspires, rousing workers out of passivity to combat the oppression of everyday existence and dominant ideologies. S/he represents the values of the proletariat but only as a mediator. The workers themselves are the ultimate bearers of revolutionary change and not the vanguard or party elites. Gramsci's organic intellectuals aim to achieve unity between the working class and the intellectuals. To tip the balance in favour of the revolutionary movement prior to the "war of manoeuvre," the organic intellectuals are engaged in synthesising dichotomies in the "war of position," and building the maximum possible unity in a new historical bloc.

[53] C. Wright Mills, "The Politics of Responsibility," in *The New Left Reader*, ed. Oglesby, 23-31, 28.

the proletariat, like the bourgeoisie in its time, has been revolutionary in knowing that it could have a dialogue only by radically transforming the society. The proletariat has lost this power everywhere in the world. A new ruling class has been born, a synthesis, in fact, of the proletariat and the bourgeoisie. This 'association of interests' seeks to conserve the ideology of the last century in its entirety as a guarantee of its new privileges.[54]

This stance can also be seen as a reflection of the ambiguity of location of these new agents of social change (students, women, black civil rights activists, gay liberation campaigners, and those resisting colonialism) with regards to the classical Marxist tradition.

Culture, counter-culture, aestheticism, utopianism, a destabilisation of Marxist theory, particularly with regards to the base/superstructure model, and the decentring of the working class as the primary lever of historical change were all dominant preoccupations of various Left groupings in the 1960s–but not, of course, of all Left organisations. The International Socialists (IS) was one of the first revolutionary organisations involved in the student protests of the late 1960s.[55] The Vietnam Solidarity Campaign (VSC) and CND were two of the focal campaigns for intervention and mobilisation and this was illustrated by the involvement of IS in the VSC and the Revolutionary Socialist Students' Federation. But whilst resistance to, and campaigning against, imperialist war was viewed as an essential component of the international opposition to capitalism, the IS was simultaneously wary of a politics that substituted these activities for class struggle. In his book on the revolutionary Left, Peter Shipley described IS

---

[54] "The Appeal from the Sorbonne," in *The New Left Reader*, ed. Oglesby, 267-73, 272.

[55] IS emerged in the late 1940s from a tiny group of Marxist revolutionaries involved in the (Trotskyist) Revolutionary Communist Party (RCP). IS proposed that the USSR was "state capitalist" as opposed to a "degenerated workers' state," and thus a social revolution was needed to transform it into a socialist society. In their view, socialism did not exist anywhere, and workers' control in the USSR, was not maintained after Lenin's era. In 1950 they founded a journal called *Socialist Review*; they became known as the Socialist Review group, and were effectively led by Tony Cliff. At the end of the 1950s, the group's activities expanded with the emergence of CND, and an agitational newspaper entitled *Industrial Worker*, which then became *Labour Worker* in 1964 and *Socialist Worker* in 1968. By 1964 the group had become known as IS and claimed over 200 members. They withdrew from the Labour Party in 1965-66 and after two years of coming out their sales were 10,000. By 1968 they had doubled their membership from below 500 to over 1000. See Callaghan, *The Far Left in British Politics*; and Peter Shipley, *Revolutionaries in Modern Britain* (London: The Bodley Head, 1976).

as snubbing "the anti-proletarian content of many of the ideas associated with the student movement."[56] Hence, far from abandoning faith in workers as primary agents of change, IS responded positively to the huge upsurge in class struggle in 1972-74, and the industrial militancy that continued 1974-79. IS viewed the primacy of working-class agency as an essential principle of which student struggle should support, and in fact it is seemingly non-coincidental, that whilst student and New Left directions were retreating from class politics, IS organised a "turn to the class." Hence, student membership of IS decreased, and the beginning of the 1970s saw the building of an industrial network.

The International Marxist Group (IMG) was another revolutionary organisation that intervened with some significance in the events and issues discussed.[57] Of all the revolutionary Left groupings, the IMG seem most to have reproduced eclectically the political ideologies and strategies that moved in and out of fashion during the 1960s and 1970s. While IS involved itself in the liberation campaigns with caution because of the increasing distance of the campaigns from class politics, IMG activists immersed themselves wholeheartedly in struggles over Ireland, feminism, racism, Vietnam, CND, youth campaigns, the organisation of school students and the unemployed. The numerous front organisations that the IMG set up resulted in dispersed groupings of activists, groupings that lacked stability and coherence. A theoretical justification for this was represented by the slogan "from the periphery to the centre," a slogan that embraced the idea that revolutionary development was proceeding from the "third world" to the advanced capitalist countries. Although it attempted to promote Leninism through its youth organisation, the Spartacus League, it remained predominantly a student and intellectual grouping.

In contrast, the almost exclusive focus on class of other Left (particularly Leninist) groups resulted in the subsuming and de-prioritising

---

[56] Shipley, *Revolutionaries in Modern Britain*, 134.

[57] IMG emerged from a split in the Revolutionary Socialist League, which worked within the Labour Party. A group of six people started a Fourth International journal entitled *The Internationalist* in 1961, from which the IMG emerged. Pat Jordan and Tariq Ali were removed from the leadership in 1972 as both were considered accountable for the lack of working-class recruitment, and were viewed as more aligned to the student perspectives of 1969. In 1978 the IMG membership was 750. The early 1980s saw the IMG promoting the Tony Benn campaign to democratise the Labour Party, and by now it was totally submerged in entrism and CND. It re-named itself the Socialist League and in 1983 it brought out *Socialist Action*, which replaced *Socialist Challenge*.

of other identities, those based around gender, race, ethnicity, and sexuality. The historian, Sheila Rowbotham, herself an ex-member of IS, asserts that within revolutionary parties that organise on Leninist lines,

> there is no conscious commitment to struggling against the forms of relationship which are created by the division of labour under capitalism as part of the effort to make socialism. ... It is assumed that the existence of a revolutionary party itself can transcend the particular interests of sections within the working class.[58]

In response to both the unwillingness of Marxist groups to engage with a feminist critique, as well as in rejoinder to the class-neglectful character of liberal and radical feminism, Marxist-feminists throughout the 1970s and early 1980s attempted to pursue a materialist and revolutionary theory, which repositioned the conventionally subsumed category of gender to a more significant and prominent location within a Marxist approach.[59] Similarly, American black activists, such as the Black Panther party member, Huey Newton, saw the contradiction between liberation from racist oppression and the continuance of capitalism, "we realise that this country became very rich upon slavery and that slavery is capitalism in the extreme. We have two evils to fight, capitalism and racism."[60] Malcolm X, too, positioned the civil rights fight within a broader perspective, "you can't operate a capitalistic system unless you are vulturistic; you have to have someone else's blood to suck to be a capitalist."[61] However, these activists tended to be criticised by the revolutionary Left for ceding too much ground to (bourgeois) radical feminism or Black Nationalism, and ignored or rejected by sections of feminist and black consciousness

---

[58] Sheila Rowbotham, Lynne Segal and Hilary Wainwright, *Beyond the Fragments: Feminism and the Making of Socialism* (London: Merlin Press, 1979), 96.

[59] Juliet Mitchell, *Woman's Estate* (Harmondsworth: Penguin, 1971); Zillah Eisenstein, ed., *Capitalist Patriarchy and the Case for Socialist Feminism* (London: Monthly Review Press, 1979); Michèle Barrett, *Women's Oppression Today: Problems in Marxist Feminist Analysis* (London: Verso, 1980); Lydia Sargent, ed., *The Unhappy Marriage of Marxism and Feminism: A Debate of Class and Patriarchy* (London: Pluto Press, 1981); and Lise Vogel, *Marxism and the Oppression of Women: Toward a Unitary Theory* (New Jersey: Rutgers University Press 1983).

[60] Huey Newton, "A Prison Interview," in *The New Left Reader*, ed. Oglesby, 223-40, 225.

[61] Malcolm X, "I Don't Mean Bananas," in *The New Left Reader*, ed. Oglesby, 207-22, 212.

movements who had a characteristic indifference or hostility to class politics.

These debates became more polarised in a post-boom context with the increasing economic crises of the 1970s. The right-wing Labour government of 1974-79 saw Dennis Healey capitulate to the International Monetary Fund, the loans from which were predicated upon substantial cuts in the public sector. The Social Contract was drawn up with the Trades Union Congress (TUC), which curbed pay claims for three years to below 5%, but which was increasingly eroded by the pressure from rank and file trades unionists, who experienced ever deteriorating pay and conditions. It can thus be argued that the all too frequently eclipsed struggles of the working classes in the late 1960s and early 1970s were predominantly ones of advance and attack, whereas with the erosion of gains and reforms in the context of recession, the conditions of the IMF and the social contract, the industrial militancy of the mid- to late 1970s became rather more defensive. David Purdy argued in *Marxism Today* that what most "characterised the decade from 1966-1975 was that the ruling class was unable decisively to impose a new strategic course on the working class" but at the same time the working class "failed to advance beyond the bounds of corporate defencivism to mount an offensive political struggle around a credible alternative economic programme of its own."[62] This was not helped by the shift of many 1960s radicals away from (mild) concern for workers and production towards a preoccupation with consumption and cultural practices. Roland Muldoon of Cartoon Archetypal Slogan Theatre (CAST) admitted,

> by the time the working class became active and placed a demand on theatre, CAST had become enmeshed in its self-importance. Rich situations like Heath versus the miners went untouched by us. We were being sidetracked into the Rock culture argument.[63]

The conspicuous deficiency in unified action and reciprocal solidarity between the new liberation campaigns and working-class struggle was clearly a detrimental position for all challenging capitalism in whatever form.

Radical Left activity peaked dramatically in the late 1960s, and particularly in 1968; however, its subsequent deterioration and implosion

---

[62] David Purdy, "British Capitalism Since the War: Part 2," *Marxism Today* (October 1976): 316.
[63] Roland Muldoon, "Cast Revival," *Plays and Players* 24.4.279 (January 1977): 40-41, 41.

were equally severe. Student activists, the new social movements, and the
New Left's celebration of "difference" and "diversity" were a source of
strength during a time of high levels of political and economic struggle.
However, the downturn in working-class resistance took place during
increasing economic catastrophe: the collapse of the post-war economic
system based on the Bretton Woods agreement (the dollar was no longer
convertible to gold), the oil crisis in 1973, and the government's
subsequent clawing back of the gains and reforms previously won,
particularly in terms of the Incomes Policy and Social Contract in 1975.[64]
Therefore, the earlier, and seemingly productive, coalition of diverse
groups and campaigns that made up the "movements," now tended–in this
new economic context–to turn in on themselves with positive diversity
leading instead to negative fragmentation and division. An illustration of
this tendency can be seen in the increasingly divisive development of the
WLM (Women's Liberation Movement), whose last formal conference in
Birmingham in 1978 witnessed acrimonious debates over, in Janelle Reinelt's
words, "the question of men and their place in a feminist struggle."[65]

By identifying key authors of this historical construction, and the
contexts within which they exist, it has been possible to understand ways
in which the move away from Marxism towards neo- or post-Marxism,
poststructuralism, and postmodernism became the new orthodoxy. Rustin,
in his critique of New Times emphasised the problems of academicism,

> in so far as mental labour does become more central to the production
> process, it is not surprising that those who live by it gain in social power,
> just as the depopulation of the countryside earlier had its consequences for
> class relations. It is understandable that in this environment, the new
> intelligentsia should develop an optimistic view of its leading role.[66]

---

[64] The nature of the "downturn" is a contentious issue. Dave Lyddon argues that it
was "the introduction of incomes policy in the summer of 1975 at the time of the
highest inflation for nearly sixty years, and rising unemployment, that led to the
fall in strike activity. ... Statistically ... the drop has been exaggerated. But, of
course, there *was* a serious downturn in workers' struggle in its character–less
offensive, and more defensive; less victories and more defeats; not the absence of
solidarity action, but the absence of successful solidarity action. And yet it is
important to realise that industrial action at the workplace, whether defensive or
combative, carried on right through the 1970s– much of it not recorded, and almost
invisible to outside observers." "Demythologising the downturn," *International
Socialism* 25 (Autumn 1984): 91-107, 99; 100.
[65] Janelle Reinelt, "Beyond Brecht: Britain's New Feminist Drama," in *Feminist
Theatre and Theory*, ed. Helene Keyssar (London: Macmillan, 1996), 35-48, 37.
[66] Rustin, "The Trouble with 'New Times,'" 313.

In this way, the official history of the Left can be viewed as an act of self-fashioning on the part of its authors. A problem faced by Left academics is the isolation from organised political practice. In relation to the attempts of Williams, Hall, and Thompson to establish a more formal kind of Left unity in the late 1960s, Rustin describes this grouping as having a "primarily intellectual membership," who "will not, for reasons of inclination and professional commitments, give sufficient priority to the needs of politics and organisation over those of ideas."[67] Privileging cultural discourses inevitably resulted in the (perhaps inadvertent) location of these as primary determining elements of the social formation, which in turn led to the economic becoming endlessly deferred.

Implications for Socialist Theatre

Contention over the relationship between theory and practice is also applicable to theatre. In one sense theatre is both theory and practice, or theory in practice; it is conceptualised and/or written (theorised), as well as performed (practised). The historical tendency to view plays as literary texts, as opposed to performances, has prompted the question of whether language-based theories alone produce the most fruitful framework within which to negotiate theatrical modes of signification. Mark Fortier claims "theatre and theory are both contemplative pursuits, although theatre has a practical and sensuous side which contemplation should not be allowed to overwhelm."[68] This tension is also present in the material production of theatre. The theatrical event is subject to economic and political criteria, and yet masks this relationship through its location as "leisure," "entertainment," and "the arts." Theatre *workers* are presented as *players,* theatre's economic base concealed, and the division between work and play blurred.

Predictably the late 1960s and early 1970s saw an explosion in political theatre.[69] Counter-cultural, revolutionary Left, and student protest

---

[67] Rustin, "The New Left and the Present Crisis," 70.

[68] Mark Fortier, *Theory/Theatre* (London: Routledge, 1997), 6.

[69] See Catherine Itzen, *Stages in the Revolution: Political Theatre in Britain Since 1968* (London: Eyre Methuen, 1980); Edgar, *The Second Time as Farce;* Sandy Craig, ed., *Dreams and Deconstructions: Alternative Theatre in Britain* (Ambergate: Amber Lane Press, 1980); A. Davies, *Other Theatres: The Development of Alternative and Experimental Theatre in Britain* (London: Macmillan, 1987). I do not provide an extensive overview of theatre produced in this period, but rather offer a few examples in order to give a sense of the way in which Left theatre related to the socialist contexts I have outlined.

provided a fertile environment for political creativity. Several Left playwrights and theatre companies demonstrated commitment to, and engagement with, the counter-culture, and there were also plays performed by groups such as Red Ladder about rent rises, housing, and workplace issues. Director Chris Rawlence described this latter activity in the following way,

> by 1970 we were taking our shows into the trade union movement. It was recognised by many shop stewards and other workers that theatre could fulfil an important educational function within their union. This involved invitations to Red Ladder to make and perform short plays about such questions as collective bargaining, the Industrial Relations Act, the role of advancing technology, the question of amalgamation in the AUEW, and unemployment.[70]

Hence, there was an overtly functional dimension of political theatre, the aim of which was to express a situation or a message in the clearest possible way. The dominant form in use was agitprop, which confirmed workers in their class struggle; however, agitprop was not considered suitable during a period of "class retreat," thus the mid-late 1970s saw other forms emerge, forms that drew on popular culture, music hall, folk music, Brechtian theatre, techniques of shock and disruption, as well as the more conventional mode of social realism.

Alongside a more class-based oriented theatre, were anarchic and agitational plays such as those influenced by the Situationists, examples of which are Howard Brenton's *Christie in Love* (1969), and *Magnificence* (1973).[71] Situationist theory informed the "happening" wherein the consumer spectacle was disrupted with a resulting momentary blurring of the division between art, happening and life, which intended to shock the audience into a heightened state of consciousness. These plays drew on the Situationist idea of pervasive alienation, which cut across social class. Alternatively there was the use of historical narratives as a way of intervening in contemporaneous politics, such as Pam Gems' *Queen Christina* (1977) and Roger Howard's *Siege* (1980).[72] Towards the end of the 1970s there were plays in mainstream theatre that subverted the traditional (bourgeois) theatrical forms of social realism and naturalism, an

---

[70] Chris Rawlence, "Political Theatre and the Working Class," in *Media, Politics and Culture*, ed. Carl Gardner (London: Macmillan, 1979), 61-70, 65.
[71] Howard Brenton, *Christie in Love* (London: Methuen, 1970); *Magnificence* (London: Methuen, 1973).
[72] Pam Gems, *Queen Christina* (London: St. Luke's, 1982); Roger Howard, *Siege* (Colchester: Theatre Action Press, 1981).

example of which was David Hare's *Plenty* (1978).[73] Edgar describes political theatre of the late 1970s as becoming "more analytical, more discursive, more about worrying contradictions than amplifying great blasts of anguish or triumph."[74]

In mainstream theatres, the condition of England play tended to explore public dissatisfaction through social and historical, rather than economic perspectives. Alternative theatre was also producing plays that were less likely to meet the central tenets of the political economy head on, and focused rather on the destructive implications of the socio-economic system. This was accompanied by the emergence of a feminist theatre, which approached theatre, as Edgar states, "as a laboratory for the testing, under various conditions, of new ways of relating to each other and the world, often through forms that stood at perversely oblique angles to the content they sought to embrace."[75] However, notwithstanding the positive development of feminist theatre, Left theatre in general reflected the demise of counter-cultural excitement and the rapidly emerging and pervasive pessimism that accompanied the Thatcher era.

Another significant issue during this period was the debate over the medium in which socialist playwrights should be working. With television reaching an increasingly large number of working-class viewers, socialist playwright, Trevor Griffiths, proposed it as the most effective medium for engaging with an immediate mass audience, seeing it as "thunderingly exciting to be able to talk to large numbers of people in the working class."[76] However, Edgar claimed television audiences did not experience television "en masse," and that the family living room was "the place where people [were] at their least critical."[77] Rawlence agreed, adding that television audiences did not have a self-awareness of themselves as audiences; "less still do viewers–a passive term–feel they have power to shape the image."[78]

Indeed, two decades later, Griffiths displayed his frustration with television's increasing commercialisation, complaining of almost "the removal of political drama from television."[79] Commercial pressures had an increasingly profound effect on the theatre too, of course. For political

---

[73] David Hare, *Plenty* (London: Faber, 1978).

[74] Edgar, *The Second Time as Farce*, 130.

[75] Edgar, *The Second Time as Farce*, 130.

[76] Griffiths, Interview, *Leveller*, quoted in Edgar, *Second Time as Farce*, 37.

[77] Edgar, "Political Theatre," *Socialist Review* (April/May 1978), quoted in Itzen, *Stages in the Revolution*, 167.

[78] Rawlence, "Political Theatre and the Working Class," 63.

[79] Trevor Griffiths, Interview, *Socialist Review* 185 (April 1995): 22-23, 22.

playwrights, the arguments for and against theatre, and for and against performing in mainstream venues, have remained relevant issues. A further question arising from this debate has been the extent to which art contributes towards political change. Griffiths claims, "it's very difficult to make political art, to make art out of politics, at a time when people aren't making politics out of politics."[80]

Funding crises dominated theatre in the 1980s. In response to CAST's cut in funding, their founder, Muldoon believed this was because they were "being too dangerous" and so "had to be stopped because of the ideology of the Conservatives."[81] John McGrath of 7:84 England and Scotland claimed that by the end of the 1980s, alternative theatre "was effectively shut down in England."[82] Out of a "Theatre in Crisis" conference at Goldsmith's College in 1988 emerged a declaration signed by several playwrights (including Churchill), actors and directors, condemning the funding situation, claiming theatre as a basic cultural right, which should be accessible to all, and calling for the theatre to be funded by public money, the organisation of which should be democratic and devolved.[83] In subject matter, there was a general shift away from the public forum to private settings and a tendency towards less overtly political subject matters.

The 1990s seemed to confirm what had been a gradual shift towards, or a slow surrendering to, a postmodern sense of the ubiquity and fluidity of political signification. Theatre director and academic Baz Kershaw embraced what he identified as a paradigm shift away from modernism to postmodernism, interpreting this move as bringing with it a "semiosis of protest tended towards greater polyphony and heteroglossia," which involved "multiple referenced images" adjoined to "monologic slogans," slogans that in turn became "more aphoristic and punning." Kershaw evaluates "this kind of deep cultural shift" as having a tendency to render "traditional forms of 'political theatre' redundant" since "civil radicalism could, as it were, reshape itself through the postmodern, shaking itself

---

[80] Griffiths, quoted in Sarah Hemming, "Caught in the Crossfire," *Independent* (8 January 1992).
[81] Roland Muldoon, Interview, *Fringe First: Pioneers of Fringe Theatre on Record*, ed. Roland Rees (London: Oberon Books, 1992), 68-76, 75.
[82] John McGrath, *The Bone Won't Break* (London: Methuen, 1990), 30.
[83] The declaration was signed by Caryl Churchill, Max Stafford-Clark, David Edgar, Howard Brenton, Trevor Griffiths, Peter Hall, John McGrath, Harold Pinter, Sheila Hancock, Verity Lambert, Jane Lapotaire, Juliet Stevenson, Jonathan Pryce, Janet Suzman, Timberlake Wertenbaker and Arnold Wesker. See D. Keith Peacock, *Thatcher's Theatre* (London: Greenwood, 1999), 57.

increasingly free of the meta-narratives that had given those earlier forms their meaning and utility."[84] However, this celebratory account seems not to recognise the hostile economic and political context that was the framework within which political theatre entered into decline. Severe cuts in funding to most socialist and alternative theatre groups accompanied by a changing ideological public discourse made it especially difficult for political theatre to maintain itself. Furthermore, the extent to which postmodern performance could be understood as a contemporary version of political theatre is highly questionable. The tendency of postmodern performance towards political relativism, along with its interest in the mechanisms of meaning and the constructed nature of discourses were not automatically equivalent to an anti-capitalist art.

Placing Churchill

Situating Churchill's plays within socialist contexts enriches readings of her work, but it also acts as an acknowledgment of Churchill's active political commitment. This book does not focus on Churchill's personal engagement with socialist politics; her plays are considered to be illuminated through their own, self-evident reflection of, and engagement with, a variety of Left debates. However, it is useful to acknowledge that Churchill's political interest extends beyond the stage. As a middle-class, Oxford-educated, mother of three, Churchill, perhaps, does not possess a conventional socialist identity. This outsider status might well contribute towards the oblique perspectives of her plays. Nevertheless, although not renowned for membership of political parties, and, for long periods of time, caring for children in the domestic sphere, Churchill still has a notable record of political commitment.

This commitment is illustrated not only by her support and sponsorship of the contemporary Stop the War Coalition, but also by her participation in the less popular anti-war activity during the Nato bombing of Kosovo in 1999.[85] She has also actively supported the Palestinian struggle, which is demonstrated by an extra performance of *Far Away* at the Albery Theatre, London, in 2000, ticket sales from which were donated to two theatres in the Occupied Territories, Al Kasaba and Inad. This support has continued

---

[84] Baz Kershaw, *The Radical in Performance: Between Brecht and Baudrillard* (London: Routledge, 1999), 122.
[85] See the joint letter by Howard Barker, Howard Brenton, Jonathan Chadwick, Caryl Churchill, Charlotte Cornwell, David Edgar, Adrian Mitchell, Alan Plater, Maggie Steed and twenty-three others, Letter to the Editor, *The Guardian* (10 April 1999).

with her public opposition to the Israeli offensive in Gaza, which has taken the form of letters to newspapers and promotion of the demonstration that took place in London on 10 January 2009.[86] Most famously, of course, Churchill wrote a ten-minute play, *Seven Jewish Children: A Play for Gaza* which was staged at the Royal Court Theatre in February 2009.[87]

As well as participating in traditional expressions of political activism–including protesting against the Vietnam War, campaigning for nuclear disarmament and opposing Apartheid in South Africa–Churchill has also been involved in less visible and less conventionally political activity. A good example is her collaboration in the mid-1970s with the then director of the Royal Court's Young People's Theatre Scheme, Joan Mills. Together they initiated a drama project at the William Tyndale Junior School, Islington, where they facilitated twice-weekly workshops resulting in the pupils' production of the play, "Strange Days." Philip Roberts notes that the school "became the focus of a heated debate the same year (1975) about 'progressive' versus 'traditional' teaching methods."[88] Another notable act was in relation to Churchill's Northern Ireland documentary play for BBC 1, *The Legion Hall Bombing*, which was transmitted 22 August 1978.[89] It was about the Diplock courts, which were introduced in 1973 to try paramilitary activity. The voiceover, which provided an account of the Diplock courts, including explaining the absence of a jury and presence of only one judge, was substituted by the BBC for their own "objective" version as the original was considered to be "political comment." Churchill says, "we took our names off the credits as a protest."[90] This was a particularly brave action, since the late 1970s constituted a period of intense hostility to Irish republicanism on the part of the British state and in public discourse.

---

[86] The letter reads: "we speak out for the people of Gaza. What is happening there is a crime against humanity. We are asking everyone to be at Speaker's Corner in London at 12.30pm on Saturday 10 January, and join the march to the Israeli embassy." It is a joint letter signed by Tony Benn and Andrew Murry (President and Chair of the Stop the War Coalition), along with many other signatories, including Churchill, Samuel West, Tariq Ali, Timberlake Wertenbaker, Linton Kwesi Johnson, and John Pilger. Letter to the Editor, *The Guardian*, (8 January 2009).

[87] Churchill, *Seven Jewish Children: A Play for Gaza* (London: Nick Hern, 2009). The play was free to attend and is free to download from the internet. http://www.royalcourttheatre.com/files/downloads/SevenJewishChildren.pdf

[88] Roberts, *About Churchill*, 165.

[89] Churchill, *The Legion Hall Bombing* (transmitted 22 August 1978 BBC1).

[90] Churchill, quoted in *Interviews with Contemporary Women Playwrights*, eds. Kathleen Betsko and Rachel Koenig (New York: Beech Tree Books, 1987), 81.

Churchill also has an honourable political record of resisting the increasing commercialisation of the theatre. At the British Theatre in Crisis conference, held at Goldsmith's College in 1988, Churchill warned of "a recognisable impetus by the government towards the privatisation of theatre," and called for "a concerted rejection of private sponsorship because of the intrinsic inequalities which the system promotes, and to the level of control which it gives to business organisations whose values are ultimately those of Thatcherism."[91] Churchill's opposition to commercial sponsorship ultimately led to her resignation as a Royal Court Council member; her arguments against Barclays' sponsorship of the Royal Court were not heeded. In November 1990 she sent a resignation letter explaining that she "[couldn't] accept the Royal Court being used to launder the image of a bank." She put on record that she did not "feel happy with any company sponsorship," since she considered this to sanction both the product as well as "the government's policy of privatising the arts, along with medicine and water."[92] In the same letter she states, "there's been a lot of talk in the building about 'the times' as if they were a force of nature–we are part of them just as much as the government, the city and business interests, and our opposition can be part of them."[93]

---

[91] Churchill, "British Theatre in Crisis," *New Theatre Quarterly* 5.19 (August 1989).

[92] Churchill, Letter to the Chairman of the English Stage Company, 116.

[93] Churchill, Letter to the Chairman of the English Stage Company, 116.

CHAPTER TWO

THE POLITICS OF UTOPIA

You should be entirely different.
Everything. Everything.
(*Fen*, 157)

There were no words in Romanian or English
for how happy I was.
(*MF*, 131)

Introduction

Although rather amorphous, a utopian theoretical framework, once more clearly delineated, can offer a stimulating apparatus through which a politics of Churchill's plays can be dynamically reframed.[1] The initial connections between utopian studies, socialist contexts traced in the previous chapter, and Churchill's plays illuminate such areas as individual and collective desire, images of an unalienated future, and transcendent moments where a sense of liberation is fleetingly experienced. The expression of degenerative utopian, anti-utopian, and dystopian fears is additionally a tangible mode of political signification in Churchill's work. Political scientists, Barbara Goodwin and Keith Taylor introduce their influential study of utopia with the following question,

> the essentially contested nature of the concept of utopia and the chequered history of utopian thought can be traced back to the paradox at the heart of the pun which More coined: is the good place (eutopia) by definition *no*

---

[1] For general studies and histories of utopia, see: Ruth Levitas, *The Concept of Utopia* (Hemel Hempstead: Philip Allan, 1990); Barbara Goodwin and Keith Taylor, *The Politics of Utopia* (London: Hutchinson, 1982); Krishan Kumar, *Utopia and Anti-Utopia in Modern Times* (Oxford: Basil Blackwell, 1987); Frank E. Manuel and Fritzie P. Manuel, *Utopian Thought in the Western World* (Cambridge, Massachusetts: Harvard UP, 1979).

place (utopia)? Differently put, is utopia necessarily unrealisable because of its ideal nature?[2]

This question exemplifies the difficulty in reaching a consensus over defining utopia.[3] Is utopia an escapist fantasy, a fantasy that circumvents the material world by way of its complete otherness? Or is utopia an objectification of a politicised form of hope, serving to drive (sections of) society forward, and critiquing the existing ideological formation by way of envisioning alternatives? It could also be, as Catherine Belsey suggests, "not necessarily a goal, but a hypothesis, a possibility, which clarifies the present by denaturalising its practices."[4] Is it necessarily Left-wing, emancipationist, or even progressive? And is it an object situated in time (the golden age of the past espoused by classical myth or a future society), place (a utopian space or an existing intentional community), or process (the free movement of capital advocated by Adam Smith or class struggle espoused by Karl Marx)?

However, this semantic complexity can provide a productive, albeit protean, conceptual framework within which to explore the political signification of multifarious cultural practices. Ruth Levitas's *The Concept of Utopia* locates desire, "desire for a better way of being and living," as one constant feature of utopianism in the context of a ceaseless variability in content, form, and function, which helps to provide conceptual continuity.[5] The political approaches to which an emphasis on desire gives rise, have meant that utopianism has been both celebrated and treated with suspicion from within anti-/counter-capitalist quarters. Feminists, anarchists, and radical environmentalists have applauded utopian transcendence of the dominant order and found useful the privileging of the imagination that accompanies utopian political practice. The prevailing thinking within traditional Marxism, in contrast, has displayed anxiety over what it sees as the inability of utopian activity to undermine the dominant order precisely because of its escape from it. Marxists have emphasised instead the importance of pursuing a rigorously materialist approach to political analysis and activity, one that locates the destruction of the system as

---

[2] Goodwin and Taylor, *The Politics of Utopia*, 15.
[3] For a brief but insightful discussion of the lack of agreement between scholars over defining utopia and utopianism, see Lyman Tower Sargent, "Is there only one utopian tradition?" *Journal of the History of Ideas* 43.4 (1982): 681-89.
[4] Catherine Belsey, *Desire* (Oxford: Blackwell, 1994), 195.
[5] Levitas, *The Concept of Utopia*, 7.

dependent upon critique from within and of the social formation, as opposed to what is considered to be utopian idealism.[6]

Doubts expressed by Karl Marx and Frederick Engels over the (idealist) utopian practices of nineteenth-century utopian socialists, Henri de Saint-Simon, Charles Fourier, and Robert Owen precipitated the suspicion of utopianism that exists within the Marxist tradition. The charge was that the utopian socialists responded to the unjust system with "reflective reason," and that they sought to create "a new and more perfect social order," and implement it "from without, by propaganda and wherever possible by the example of model experiments." Engels's evaluation was that "these new social systems were foredoomed to be Utopias; the more they were worked out in detail, the more inevitably they became lost in pure fantasy."[7] The utopian socialists disregarded the economic circumstances of society and thus ignored the historical specificity of their own environment. Engels refuted as non-materialist and hence doomed as a political project, the privileging of the idea at the expense of confronting the economic and material relations of the existing social context. Nevertheless, political theorist, Vincent Geoghegan argues that once read in context, the ideas of Marx and Engels concerning the utopian socialists did not necessarily refute utopian approaches in principle.[8] The early socialist critique of capitalism championed by Saint-Simon, Fourier, and Owen was welcomed by Marx and Engels as containing "the most valuable materials of the enlightenment of the working class."[9] However, the later followers of the utopian socialists

---

[6] As well as providing theoretical arguments against what are seen as idealist utopian political practices, the Marxist tradition is also suspicious of the seemingly middle-class nature of these activities. The luxuries of time, money, and cultural capital appear to be helpful in facilitating the activist to occupy trees, join intentional communities, or participate in transcendent political practices. Working-class activists, it is argued, are more likely to join a trade union and participate in work-based militancy, and for Marxists, of course, the conflict between labour and capital is of *primary* importance.

[7] Frederick Engels, *Socialism: Utopian and Scientific* (Peking: Foreign Languages Press, 1975), 51-52.

[8] Vincent Geoghegan, *Utopianism and Marxism* (London: Methuen, 1987). Geoghegan points out that Engels's *Socialism: Utopian and Scientific* was originally entitled *Die Entwicklung des Sozialismus von der Utopie zur Wissenschaft*, which translates as the development, or even the evolution, of socialism from utopia to science. This changes the emphasis from an oppositional relationship to a productive one.

[9] Karl Marx and Frederick Engels, *The Communist Manifesto*, intro. A. J. P. Taylor (London: Penguin, 1967; first published in 1848), 116.

continued to promote utopian community against the background of the accelerating development of the proletariat, and were therefore, in effect, disregarding and even competing against the growth of class struggle,

> in proportion as the modern class struggle develops and takes definite shape, this fantastic standing apart from the contest, these fantastic attacks on it, lose all practical value and all theoretical justification.[10]

Jennifer Burwell reframes this tension in terms of what she calls the utopian and critical impulses, the former of which she sees as positing "a self-contained and inaccessible ideal 'elsewhere' where social contradiction has always already been resolved," and the latter, which she thinks limit "themselves to a negative hermeneutics of exposure."[11] In this proposition, the utopian is without a critical relationship with the contemporary material world, and the critical impulse fails to envisage an alternative to it. Burwell considers the weakness of the critical impulse to lie in its seeming inability to dislodge itself from the object of its denigration. This failure to move outside of the discursive parameters of the dominant order inadvertently re-authorises the very system that it seeks to challenge. In contrast, in the utopian impulse's tendency to escape from the non-utopian context, in its interest in the (barely conceivable) absolute state of otherness, it fails to confront existing conditions and in so doing, leaves these conditions undisturbed. This dichotomy between critical and utopian poles can be mapped on to the differing positions, strategies, and tactics exercised by various groupings on the British Left in the 1970s and beyond, where utopian political practices of the counter-culture on the one hand contrasted with class struggle of revolutionary socialists and trade unionists on the other.

Of course, Marxists were not alone in displaying unease over utopian approaches. Indeed, utopian fiction was in crisis by the beginning of the twentieth century. The optimistic and structurally integrated utopias, such as Edward Bellamy's *Looking Backward* (1888), William Morris's *News from Nowhere* (1890), and H. G. Wells' *A Modern Utopia* (1905), were in demise in the wake of world war, the degeneration of post-revolutionary Russia, the rise of Nazism, and a seemingly unstoppable capitalist trajectory.[12] Anti-utopias and dystopias such as E. I. Zamyatin's *We* (1920-

---

[10] Marx and Engels, *The Communist Manifesto*, 117.
[11] Jennifer Burwell, *Notes on Nowhere: Feminism, Utopian Logic, and Social Transformation* (London: University of Minnesota Press, 1997), ix.
[12] Edward Bellamy, *Looking Backward* (Harmondsworth: Penguin, 1982; first published in 1888); William Morris, *News from Nowhere: Or an Epoch of Rest:*

21), Aldous Huxley's *Brave New World* (1932) and George Orwell's *Nineteen Eighty-Four* (1949) emerged as dominant forms.[13] In addition to the growth of dystopia, utopianism became appropriated by commercial discourses and the ideal state of happiness was re-categorised as the fetishisation of commodity consumption in the Western capitalist imagination. Tom Moylan describes utopia as "reduced to the consumption of pleasurable weekends, Christmas dreams, and goods purchased weekly in the pleasure-dome shopping malls of suburbia." Alternative forms of desire, desire for experiences other than the commercially-defined, became treated increasingly with suspicion and reformulated as "psychologically or socially aberrant."[14]

Dystopias depicting a negative image of society, often authoritarian as in *Nineteen Eighty-Four*, or determined by technology as in *Brave New World*, frequently served as warnings or satirical projections of existing conditions or tendencies. In this way, dystopia's political force lay in its critique, a critique that in turn was foreground through the effacement of alternatives. Dragan Klaić, whose study explores plays in which the future is the dramatic time, describes dystopia as a "gloomy paraphrase of utopia" and the "last refuge of utopian hope." He identifies a paradox in dystopian drama: the greater success the dystopia has in signifying "its own bleak vision, the more effectively it calls for its rejection–confirming that dystopia carries the critical and subversive functions of utopia."[15] In this reading, then, it might be said that in representing a total vision of negativity, the silenced space of possible alternatives necessarily articulates itself.

The psychological dimensions of human motivation were taken up by the Frankfurt School in their attempt to re-engage with the utopian in the 1940s, 1950s and 1960s.[16] Theodor Adorno's conviction that ideology overwhelms social discourses prevents him from locating the utopian

---

Being Some Chapters From a Utopian Romance by William Morris (Cambridge: Cambridge UP, 1995; first published in 1890); H. G. Wells, *A Modern Utopia* (London: Penguin, 2005; first published in 1905).

[13] E. I. Zamyatin, *We* (Bristol: Bristol Classical Press, 1994; first published in 1921); Aldous Huxley, *Brave New World* (London: Flamingo, 1994; first published in 1932); George Orwell, *Nineteen Eighty-Four* (London: Penguin, 1990; first published in 1949).

[14] Tom Moylan, *Demand the Impossible: Science Fiction and the Utopian Imagination* (London: Methuen, 1986), 8.

[15] Dragan Klaić, *The Plot of the Future: Utopia and Dystopia in Modern Drama* (Michigan: The University of Michigan Press, 1991), 7.

[16] For a brief, critical introduction to the Frankfurt School, see Goran Therborn, "The Frankfurt School," *New Left Review* 63 (September-October 1970): 63-96.

impulse either spatially or in processes, but he glimpsed the utopian in the formal properties of works of art, recalling the idea of the good place/no-place. He claimed, "it is not the office of art to spotlight alternatives, but to resist by its form alone the course of the world, which permanently puts a pistol to men's heads." He also identified the work of art as offering "temporary freedom from the compulsion of practical goals."[17] In Herbert Marcuse's engagement with the utopian he combined Hegelian Marxism with Freudian theory in his consideration of fantasy as an enabling medium, a medium speaking "the language of the pleasure principle, of freedom from repression, of uninhibited desire and gratification." This, he argued, can gesture towards post-capitalism in a way that theory (due to its inextricable connection with the irrational present) fails to achieve.[18] Walter Benjamin's fusion of elements of Marxist and Talmudic theory produced an engagement with the utopian that combined notions of the ancient past with modernity. He states, "to articulate the past historically does not mean to recognise it 'the way it really was,'" but rather, "it means to seize hold of a memory as it flashes up at a moment of danger."[19]

In an attempt to recover what Perry Anderson described as "a generosity and confidence of vision missing from the mainstream of historical materialism ...–whose very definition as a science has restricted its human range,"[20] Ernst Bloch devised his own utopian theory in *The Principle of Hope*. Bloch's thesis was dependent upon the notion of a Marxist synthesis of cold and warm streams, the cold signifying Burwell's critical impulse, or the Marxist notion of a materially grounded critique, the warm signalling the utopian, imaginative receptivity to alternative ways of being. Bloch explains, "only coldness and warmth of concrete anticipation together therefore ensure that neither the path in itself nor the goal in itself are held apart from one another undialectically and so become reified and isolated."[21] Bloch destabilised what he saw as the closed fields of bourgeois discursive modes by exploding the compartmentalisation of time and substituting it with a dynamic dialectical

---

[17] Theodor Adorno, "Commitment," in *Aesthetics and Politics: The Key Texts of the Classic Debate Within German Marxism*. ed. Frederic Jameson (London: Verso, 1977), 177-95, 180; 193.

[18] Herbert Marcuse, *Eros and Civilisation* (Boston: Beacon Press, 1966), 142.

[19] Walter Benjamin, "Theses on the Philosophy of History," in *Illuminations*, trans. Harry Zohn (London: Fontana Press, 1992), 245-55, 247.

[20] Perry Anderson, *Arguments Within English Marxism* (London: Verso, 1980), 159.

[21] Ernst Bloch, *The Principle of Hope*, Volume One, ed. and trans. Neville Plaice, Stephen Plaice and Paul Knight (Oxford: Blackwell, 1986), 209.

process. This was the commencement of a theory that moved away from focusing on the more static realms of contemplation and interpretation. Bloch states, "the rigid divisions between future and past thus themselves collapse, unbecome future becomes visible in the past, avenged and inherited, mediated and fulfilled past in the future." The past is no longer assumed to be separate and isolated, "a reified Factum without consciousness of its Fieri."[22] "Contemplation" is the activity of reflecting on an enclosed field of the past, which Bloch viewed as an expression of the bourgeois enforcement of existing conditions. In contrast, the utopian impulse drawn from the "anticipatory consciousness" is the basis for exploring the "Not-Yet-Conscious," "that is: a relatively still Unconscious disposed towards the side of something new that is dawning up, that has never been conscious before."[23] Historical contemplation was placed alongside philosophical interpretation as a bourgeois discursive mode in need of explosion in order to prise open and change the stasis of the past, the present, and the future.

Although dystopia competed more vigorously with utopia as a dominant cultural form in the twentieth century, there was a revival of interest in utopianism, both as an aesthetic mode, and as political practice in the aftermath of May 1968. The counter-culture defined itself largely in terms of its immediate transcendence of the dominant culture as well as against more traditional expressions of Left culture. As part of this development there was the resurgence of "critical" (often feminist) utopian art.[24] The critical utopia can be seen as a response to the repudiation of utopianism in the twentieth century. The radical utopian imagination was maintained in the critical utopia, but the traditional utopian society, one conceived as a wholly perfect and integrated system was no longer present. Indeed, in the critical utopia the boundary between the utopian and non-utopian world became less rigid both structurally and ideologically. Protagonists moved in and out of the utopian space, both affecting and being affected by it, and instances of discontent were accommodated within the utopian terrain. The development of the feminist

---

[22] Bloch, *The Principle of Hope*, Volume One, 8-9. In relation to "a reified Factum without consciousness of its Fieri," Bloch uses the Latin forms of "fact" to distinguish the finalised and closed objectification (factum) from the emphasis on the process of becoming (fieri).

[23] Bloch, *The Principle of Hope*, Volume One, 11.

[24] See Ursula Le Guin, *The Dispossessed* (London: Harper Collins, 1996); Joanna Russ, *The Female Man* (London: Women's Press, 1985); Marge Piercy, *Woman on the Edge of Time* (London: Women's Press 1979); Sally Miller Gearhart, *The Wanderground* (London: Women's Press, 1988).

utopia since the 1970s was predominantly preoccupied with the reconstruction of an active agency in the context of the postmodern fragmentation of the subject, as well as with confronting the problem of locating a stable position from which a critique could be voiced. Confronted with the stasis of older utopian models, post-1960s critical utopias explored innovative ways of engaging with current political and theoretical concerns, whilst at the same time retaining the demonstrable and aspirational features of the genre.

The popularity of the utopian form for feminist writing was partly due to its facilitation of non-traditional modes, both literary and political. An array of marginal political practices were explored and celebrated in feminist utopianism, including such (usually trivialised) acts of individual and collective processes of remembering, the projection of fantasy and desire, and the elevation and prioritisation of the imagination, all of which have been associated with the subject's struggle to find alternative means of asserting her agency and communicating within a hostile signifying system. Utopianism additionally spoke to women's traditional association with domestic and private spaces. Utopian elevation of desire and the imagination facilitates what Frigga Haug has argued is an overlooked form of utopian resistance, that of daydreaming.[25] According to Frances Bartkowski, "feminist fiction and feminist theory are fundamentally utopian in that they declare that which is not-yet as the basis for a feminist practice, textual, political, or otherwise."[26]

There was a resurgence in the 1990s of utopian forms of political struggle by activists, such as the radical environmental movement, who utilised Henri Lefebvre's notion of "moments" of "presence," as well as strategies of pre-figuration as key political practices. Lefebvre applies Marx's theory of alienation to every aspect of life.[27] Alienated from our work, our activities, from each other and from ourselves, we barely experience authenticity in life. He developed a "theory of moments" where "moments" of "presence" interrupt the banality of alienated everyday life. As Rob Shields explains, "moments" are "those times when one recognises or has a sudden insight into a situation or an experience beyond the merely empirical routine of some activity." He describes a "moment" as "a flash of the wider significance of some 'thing' or event—its relation to the whole,

---

[25] Frigga Haug, "Daydreams," *New Left Review* 162 (March/April 1987): 51-66.
[26] Frances Bartkowski, *Feminist Utopias* (London: University of Nebraska Press, 1989), 12.
[27] Henri Lefebvre's use of "alienation" is with reference to space and spatiality, and emphasises displacement and distance.

and by extension, our relation to the totality."[28] However, Lefebvre considered each everyday activity or experience as potentially moment-bearing, and used dialectical materialism to propose a dialectic of "absence" and "presence" in everyday practices.

Lefebvre's theory concerning the production of space was also in dialogue with utopian approaches. He considered social space to be of primary importance–as part of both the means and forces of production. Space was theorised as a means of renewing the hegemony of the capitalist class through spatial segregation and through that class's exclusive ownership of the means to design spatiality. For Lefebvre, the freedom to create our own spatiality is the key signifier of an emancipated existence.

French theorist, Michel de Certeau, is similarly interested in the production of utopian creative moments in everyday practices. He states,

> many everyday practices (talking, reading, moving about, shopping, cooking, etc.) are tactical in character. And so are, more generally, many 'ways of operating': victories of the 'weak' over the 'strong' (whether the strength be that of powerful people or the violence of things or of an imposed order, etc.), clever tricks, knowing how to get away with things, 'hunter's cunning,' manoeuvres, polymorphic simulations, joyful discoveries, poetic as well as warlike.[29]

de Certeau moves on to discuss "la perruque," which he describes as a worker's own personal activity pursued during work hours and/or with the employer's materials: "*la perruque* may be as simple a matter as a secretary's writing a love letter on 'company time,'" or as complex as a cabinetmaker's "borrowing a lathe to make a piece of furniture for his living room."[30] Notwithstanding the gender stereotyping, de Certeau usefully theorises the creative, playful, and subversive interventions in everyday practices. He illustrates ways in which ideologies inscribed in cultural spaces, work structures, and everyday practices are resisted and rebelled against frequently by ordinary people.

As discussed in Chapter 1, utopian pre-figuration involves the performance of acts of liberation in the immediate here and now–rather than using conventional political tactics of campaigning for something that is hoped will be achieved at a future time. This utopian vision of political praxis recalls the susceptibility of utopian transcendence to

---

[28] Robert Shields, *Lefebvre, Love and Struggle* (London: Routledge, 1998), 58.

[29] Michel de Certeau, *The Practice of Everyday Life*, trans. Steven Randall (London: University of California Press, 1984), xix.

[30] de Certeau, *The Practice of Everyday Life,* 25.

dissipate into escapism because it disengages from the dominant order, leaving the system unaffected. Furthermore, the alternative discourse of critique, or conventional socialist strategy, offers no reconstruction, and therefore finds it difficult to escape the terms of that which it denounces. However, the two approaches display an inter-relationship. In response to what she identifies as the anticipatory/utopian pole and the critical/diagnostic pole, Burwell states,

> these two poles already imply one another: utopia implicitly critiques existing conditions by explicitly thematising a set of wishes and hopes for an alternative society; critique implicitly draws upon the utopian impulse to establish the 'outside' of existing conditions upon which our notion of critical distance rests.[31]

However, although the two approaches "imply one another," a more challenging intervention is for both utopian and critical poles to operate in a dialectic, what Bloch argues as neither reifying the goal nor the path in isolation but appreciating the dynamic consequences that result from the interaction of the two.

Space, Distance, and Postmodernity

Frederic Jameson argues that multinational capitalism's appropriation of all spheres of human life represents a new phenomenon that erodes the relative autonomy of the cultural field, dissolving critical distance. He claims that "distance in general (including 'critical distance' in particular) has very precisely been abolished in the new space of postmodernism."[32] This is due to our total entrapment in the terms of dominating discourses. What follows is the seeming impossibility of resistance to, and transcendence of, the system, the attempts at which Jameson says "are all somehow secretly disarmed and reabsorbed by a system of which they themselves might well be considered a part, since they can achieve no distance from it."[33] Attempts have been made to reconstruct an active critical agency through rejecting a unified and transcendental subject in favour of utilising the contradictions produced out of different subject positions. Judith Butler, for example, identifies the gap between the interpellation of a subject and the non-identification of the subject with

---

[31] Burwell, *Notes from Nowhere*, 3.
[32] Frederic Jameson, "Postmodernism, or The Cultural Logic of Late Capitalism," *New Left Review* 146 (July-August 1984): 53-92, 87.
[33] Jameson, "Postmodernism," 87.

that inscribed position.[34] Critical distance is therefore reconstructed, not from a utopian space that is distant or external to ideology, but from a location that is produced out of the misrecognition of, and contradictions between, different subject positions. This space of criticism is not divorced from ideology but not overwhelmed by it either.

As if in recognition of the problems for critical agency outlined by Jameson and responded to by Butler, utopian space in fictional representation became more fluid, self-critical, and dialectical. Indeed, the metaphor of utopian space is itself contradictory, for utopia's linguistic definition refuses spatial coordinates; it is located *nowhere*. This internal tension contributes to its semantic multi-dimensionality, as well as reinforcing its political force since its aspirational character is unstoppable precisely because it is situated *nowhere*. This benefits contemporary theories of social transformation that struggle to resist the colonisation of space by capital, such as de Certeau's identification of "tactics," "ruses," "trickery," and "deception" as utopian modes of non-compliance and resistance, modes that are enacted by "consumers" and "users" in everyday life. He describes the "innumerable ways of playing and foiling the other's game" that form part of the "subtle, stubborn, resistant activity of groups which, since they lack their own space, have to get along in a network of already established forces and representations."[35] He also refers to cultural practices, such as songs, folklore, and stories of miracles, providing specific examples from the Brazilian peasants of Pernambuco, who respond to the dominant discourse "'from aside' with irrelevance and impertinence in a different discourse, a discourse one can only *believe*."[36] Songs, folk stories, and wishful iconography are considered to be resistant to diffusion or cooption by the dominant discourse, for their terms of production remain outside of the communication system that structures the articulation of the dominant order.[37]

Theatrical Space

Utopian theory offers an illuminating framework for thinking about theatrical space. Theatrical space has no spatial permanence. The

---

[34] Judith Butler, *Bodies that Matter: On the Discursive Limits of Sex* (London: Routledge, 1993).

[35] de Certeau, *The Practice of Everyday Life*, 18.

[36] de Certeau, *The Practice of Everyday Life*, 17.

[37] Of course, this brings us back to the problem of critical distance and the difficulty of establishing a locus, language-based or otherwise, that is situated *outside* of the dominant order.

performance of theatre is temporary and ephemeral, and thus the utopian "good place" that is at the same time "nowhere" or "no-place" has a rich resonance in the transitory production of theatre. The theatrical space, in the form of a physical building, hosts plays temporarily at different times and on different days, and often the play tours a variety of theatres–moving from space to space, across the country or countries–an activity that further exemplifies its spatial fluidity. Indeed the theatre groups, Joint Stock and Monstrous Regiment, groups with which Churchill worked on several of her plays, were touring companies interested in experimenting with space. Most obviously they challenged the static spatial configuration of (bourgeois) drawing-room theatre's presentation of a seemingly natural and trans-historical reality at the same time as deconstructing a similarly conventional use of space in the social realist and kitchen sink drama of The Angry Young Men in the 1950s.

Diana Knight describes theatre as "a sort of laboratory for constructing the liberated social space of utopia."[38] The theatrical space is a liminal zone, a zone that places the audience in a liminal role. Drawing on the anthropologist Victor Turner, Baz Kershaw compares the position of the theatre audience with the role of participants in ritual. Kershaw describes theatre as placing "the participant 'betwixt and between' more permanent social roles and modes of awareness." He considers theatre's primary feature to be its inducement of the audience "to accept that the events of the production *are both real and not real.*"[39] As a consequence the audience is able to participate in the manipulation of regulations and conventions that make up the social framework. Such a liminal space that oscillates between the real and fictional can be interpreted as a momentary utopian break in the signification of the dominant order. Kevin Hetherington discusses this in relation to rite of passage rituals wherein the transitional and unstable liminal place and phase is then superseded by an ideological consolidation and a reintegration of the subject into society as a new person, with a new identity.[40] Drawing on Epic Theatre, Churchill's Brechtian plays, such as *Light Shining* and *Vinegar Tom*, seek to remove the refuge of neutrality and indecision that is coterminous with an

---

[38] Diana Knight, *Barthes and Utopia: Space, Travel, Writing* (Oxford: Clarendon Press, 1997).

[39] Baz Kershaw, "Performance, Community, Culture," in *The Routledge Reader in Politics and Performance*, eds. Lizbeth Goodman and Jane de Gay (London: Routledge, 2000), 136-42, 138-39.

[40] Kevin Hetherington, *Expressions of Identity: Space, Performance, Politics* (London: Sage, 1998).

audience's apathetic reception, inducing an audience instead to participate in a politicised, transformational experience.

In his essay, "Of Other Spaces," Michel Foucault outlines his theory of "heterotopias" as places that are "something like counter-sites, a kind of effectively enacted utopia in which the real sites ... found within the culture, are simultaneously represented, contested, and inverted."[41] These spaces are situated outside of all other spaces but still contain an identifiable locality. He proposes that "between utopias and these quite other sites, these heterotopias, there might be a sort of mixed, joint experience, which would be the mirror." A mirror exists independently but it also "exerts a sort of counteraction on the position" of the viewing subject.[42] Heterotopias are sites where a diversity of discourses are at play but are also sites that provide a refuge from authoritarian systems of control. With its facilitation of the performance of differing and contradictory representations, and the stage's reflectional characteristics, the theatre clearly meets the criteria of a heterotopia. The theatrical space produces a convergence and interaction of many spaces, spaces that ordinarily are mutually exclusive. The theatrical space oscillates between the real and not real; it is an identifiable site (if only temporarily) but in its transient nature as well as its reference to other fictional sites, it gestures towards the imaginary and the utopian.

Certain expressions of theatrical language can be regarded as producing a non-assimilable mode of signification: what Antonin Artaud describes as the "language of symbols and mimicry ... silent mime-play ... attitudes and spatial gestures ... objective inflection."[43] These theatrical expressions produce a multiplicity of signification, the meaning of which is not easily appropriated or absorbed by dominant discourses. de Certeau's reference to the Brazilian peasants, who respond to the dominant discourse from aside for example, can be likened to the theatrical "aside" so frequently used in renaissance drama as an expression of subversion, transgression, and parody. Indeed, Churchill frequently uses the full breadth of theatrical language in her plays. Examples include historical documentation, contemporary songs, surreal monologue, and Brechtian episodic scenes in *Light Shining* and *Vinegar Tom*; the manipulation of linear narrative and the appearance of ghosts in *Top Girls* and *Fen*; the inclusion of verse, song, dance, mime, and fairies in *Serious Money* and *The Skriker*; moving between speaking English and speaking Romanian,

---

[41] Michel Foucault, "Of Other Spaces," *Diacritics* 16.1 (Spring 1986): 22-27, 24.
[42] Foucault, "Of Other Spaces," 24.
[43] Antonin Artaud, "Mise en scène and Metaphysics," in *The Routledge Reader in Politics and Performance*, eds. Goodman and de Gay, 98-101, 99-100.

the staging of bizarre nightmares, and the appearance of a vampire and angel in *Mad Forest*; and a gruesome pre-execution fashion parade of prisoners wearing flamboyant hats in *Far Away*. This dynamic use of dramatic montage contributes to the formation of a plurality of theatrical languages, a plurality that is not easily neutralised by prevailing political discourses.

Although non-utopian in the modes of hierarchy and exclusivity that are inscribed in the economic, cultural and institutional forms of mainstream theatre, the social relations of theatre also embody utopian features. The utopian is located in the joint experience of performance, an experience that embodies a shared exchange between actors and audience in the production of the event, an event that in turn takes place in a collective space. In *The Empty Space*, Peter Brook expresses a utopian vision of the collective production of theatre. He describes the theatre as "a very special place" and as "different from everyday life":

> it is always hard for anyone to have one single aim in life–in the theatre, however, the goal is clear. From the first rehearsal, the aim is always visible, not too far away, and it involves everyone. We can see many model social patterns at work: the pressure of a first night, with its unmistakable demands, produce that working-together, that dedication, that energy and that consolidation of each other's needs that governments despair of ever evoking outside wars.[44]

The potential for a utopian working practice has of course been explored by socialist and feminist theatre groups, such as Joint Stock and Monstrous Regiment in the 1970s. These groups worked as collectives, using collaborative working methods with playwrights, and doubling up in acting roles in order to avoid the hierarchical divisions that can be produced by the separation of actors into major and minor roles. Additionally, theatre collectives often employed a form of pay parity as an economic recognition and reinforcement of equality and unity. Hence, while the novel is the form of the traditional utopia (where the narrator is usually the guest who is guided around the utopian literary space), the multi-dimensionality of theatrical space, the multiplicity of theatrical languages, the cooperative nature of producing plays, and the utopian

---

[44] Peter Brook, *The Empty Space* (London: MacGibbon & Kee, 1968), 98.

possibility of performance make theatre a potentially vibrant utopian form.[45]

Utopianism and Churchill's Plays

Light Shining in Buckinghamshire

Light Shining is interested in the destabilisation of established historical narratives and the utopian potential of historical space in its representation of English revolutionary activity on the part of the Ranters, Levellers, and Diggers during the English Civil War and revolution of the 1640s.[46] Max Stafford-Clark directed the Joint Stock actors in the original production and a three-week workshop involving Churchill, Stafford-Clark, and the actors was followed by a nine-week script-writing period where Churchill worked alone. This was the first time Churchill had worked with actors except in rehearsal, and the excitement this produced is exemplified by her comments:

> I was constantly amazed by their skills, and fascinated by the idea of working in this way. We had to learn about something remote and then find out how we related to it. There was a lot of reading history, and then finding similar things in our own lives.[47]

Churchill's reading included A. L. Morton's *The World of the Ranters* and Christopher Hill's *The World Turned Upside Down*.[48] Her engagement with communist and New Left historicism serves as a defence and reinforcement of the type of working-class history "from below" produced in Britain by History Workshop and the Workers' Educational Association (WEA). It does so in the context of revisionist challenges to it, particularly

---

[45] For a rare engagement with the relationship between utopia and performance, see Jill Dolan, *Utopia in Performance: Finding Hope at the Theater* (Ann Arbor: University of Michigan Press, 2005).

[46] For an earlier version of this discussion, one that examines *Light Shining* and *Vinegar Tom* as utopian history plays, see Siân Adiseshiah, "Utopian Space in Caryl Churchill's History Plays: *Light Shining in Buckinghamshire* and *Vinegar Tom*," *Utopian Studies* 16.1 (Spring 2005): 3-26.

[47] Churchill, Interview by Geraldine Cousin, *New Theatre Quarterly* 4.13 (February 1988): 3-16, 6.

[48] A. L. Morton, *The World of the Ranters* (London: Lawrence & Wishart, 1970); Christopher Hill, *The World Turned Upside Down* (London: Penguin, 1991). See also H. N. Brailsford, *The Levellers and the English Revolution*, ed. Hill (London: Cresset Press, 1961).

directed at Hill, from historians, such as J. C. Davis in his *Fear, Myth and History* and Conrad Russell in his editorship of *The Origins of the English Civil War*. Davis and Russell sought to substitute the Marxist explanation– a Bourgeois revolutionary destruction of monarchical and feudalist systems of power–with a contingency-based historiography, emphasising instead the role of chance and political infighting as explanations for the causes of the Civil War (which is not classed as a revolution in this formulation).[49] Churchill's contribution to this debate is one that is in broad alliance with Marxist historiography but is also one that places women and gender relations at the centre of the representation of socialist history.

The play is in two acts that are constructed out of short scenes where, as Churchill describes, "each scene can be taken as a separate event rather than part of a story."[50] In the original production that opened in the Traverse Theatre, Edinburgh in September 1976, and, after touring, played at the Royal Court Theatre Upstairs in London, six actors played twenty-five parts but also swapped roles. Churchill explains that this

> seems to reflect better the reality of large events like war and revolution where many people share the same kind of experience. ... When different actors play the parts what comes over is a large event involving many people, whose characters resonate in a way they wouldn't if they were more clearly defined. [51]

The sense of shared experience within the play is reproduced outside of it too because the division of labour among the actors is one that encourages parity and unity. Hence, the working conditions in the production of the play coalesce with the play's utopian impulses, and aptly lend themselves to the representation of silenced plebeian and feminist histories.

It is also of significance that *Light Shining* was written and performed in 1976: just after the upsurge in working-class and student struggle, but also at the start of disillusionment and pessimism that set in with a more

---

[49] J. C. Davis, *Fear, Myth and History: The Ranters and the Historians* (Cambridge: Cambridge UP, 1986); Conrad Russell, ed., *The Origins of the English Civil War* (Basingstoke: Palgrave Macmillan, 1973). Other examples include: Hugh Trevor-Roper, *Catholics, Anglicans and Puritans: Seventeenth Century Essays* (London: Secker & Warburg, 1987); G. E. Aylmer, *Rebellion or Revolution: England 1640-1660* (Oxford: Oxford UP, 1987); and Peter Laslett, *The World We Have Lost: Further Explored* (London: Methuen, 1983).
[50] Churchill, A Note on the Production, *Light Shining in Buckinghamshire*, in *Caryl Churchill Plays: 1* (London: Methuen, 1985), 184-85, 184.
[51] Churchill, A Note on the Production, *Light Shining*, 184; 185.

defensive political activism in the context outlined in the previous chapter. Churchill comments, "the revolutionary hopes of the late sixties and early seventies were near enough that we could still share them, but we could relate too to the disillusion of the restoration and the idea of a revolution that hadn't happened."[52] Her comments in the introduction to the play implicate the duality of the two historical moments:

> for a short time when the king had been defeated anything seemed possible, and the play shows the amazed excitement of people taking hold of their own lives, and their gradual betrayal as those who led them realised that freedom could not be had without property being destroyed.[53]

The recreation of (utopian) emancipatory space and its subsequent expropriation in both historical moments is a significant political parallel in the play. Another is 1970s personal politics and spiritualism and the activities of the Ranters, "whose ecstatic and anarchic belief in economic and sexual freedom was the last desperate burst of revolutionary feeling before the restoration."[54]

Informed by Brecht's Epic Theatre, *Light Shining* is a play comprising twenty-one self-contained scenes, which produce an episodic sequence of events and contain dramatic styles and devices that break up a naturalistic narrative. Set in 1647, the play dramatises key moments in the lives of plebeians and radical sect members of the Levellers, Ranters, and Diggers. The views of these radical sects are suppressed under the emerging dominance of Oliver Cromwell and the leadership of his New Model Army, who have become synonymous with the Parliamentarian cause, and have eclipsed other, more challenging, republican voices. The title of the play comes from a pamphlet written by a group of radical Levellers from Buckinghamshire who promoted the idea of the abolition of property, which in turn prompted the Digger pamphlet written in 1649, "More Light Shining in Buckinghamshire." Churchill includes a quotation from the pamphlet in her introductory notes to the play: "you great Curmudgeons, you hang a man for stealing, when you yourselves have stolen from your brethren all land and creatures."[55]

There are competing versions of utopia in the play. Star, who recruits for Cromwell's army, uses the language of Fifth Monarchism to encourage

---

[52] Churchill, "Caryl Churchill," in *The Joint Stock: The Making of a Theatre Collective*, ed. Rob Ritchie (London: Methuen, 1987), 118-21, 119.
[53] Churchill, Introduction to *Light Shining*, 183.
[54] Churchill, Introduction to *Light Shining*, 183.
[55] Churchill, Introduction to *Light Shining*, 183.

soldiers to sign up. Jerusalem is appealed to as the land of freedom and plenty, which will be established on earth with the coming of Christ as King once the current King has been disposed:

> life is hard, brothers, and how will it get better? ... When parliament has defeated Antichrist then Christ will come. Christ will come in person, God and man, and will rule over England for one thousand years ... When Christ came, did he come to the rich? No. He came to the poor. ... Now is the moment. ... Some will be cast into the pit, into the burning lake, into the unquenchable fire. And some will be clothed in white linen and ride white horses and rule with King Jesus in Jerusalem shining with jasper and chrysolite (194-95).

The military necessity of the Parliamentarian army to recruit the poor in large numbers gives rise to a Christian liberationist language, which appeals to justice and freedom, constructing the poor as Christ's Saints. A utopian fantasy of heaven on earth informs the figurative rhetoric through which political agitation is conducted. This millenarian utopian discourse is drawn on again in Cobbe's vision (a character based on the historical Ranter, Abiezer Coppe). The vision is a cataclysmic experience, full of apocalyptic imagery that culminates in Christ's directive, "go to London, to London, that great city, and tell them I am coming" (206).

There are different spatial modes of utopianism in the play. One that seems to employ, in Burwell's terms, both a utopian and critical intervention comes from the Diggers who reclaim the land at St. George's Hill, Surrey, for common usage. Gerrard Winstanley announces (his words taken from an edited version of "The True Levellers Standard Advanced, Or the state of the Community opened, and presented to the Sons of Men," written in 1649),

> a declaration to the powers of England and to all the powers of the world, showing the cause why the common people of England have begun to dig up, manure and sow corn upon George Hill in Surrey. Take notice that England is not a free people till the poor that have no land have a free allowance to dig and labour the commons. It is the sword that brought in property and holds it up, and everyone upon recovery of the conquest ought to return into freedom again, or what benefit have the common people got by the victory over the king? (219)

Utopia is located in the free and common access to, and usage of, the land. This contrasts with the previous scene—the Putney Debates—wherein ownership of private property is endorsed as a basic natural right, and suffrage granted only to those with an interest (property) in case the majority without an interest abolish interests altogether. It is noteworthy that the activity of the Diggers–an activity that undermines the very basis of capitalism (property relations)–occurs *off-stage*, which is, a kind of "no-place." Again, the significance of "the good place" that is at the same time "no place" resonates as the audience experiences the Diggers' reclamation of land indirectly (through its reporting) and thus imaginatively. In this way it might be said that there is something characteristic of utopian activity that is resistant to conventional forms of representation.

Utopian space is also produced out of the destabilisation of passive subject positions, a process that informs the increasing empowerment of many of the characters in the first act. In the scene entitled, "Two Women Look in a Mirror," the audience sees two women, experiencing for the first time the reflection of their whole bodies in a large mirror, looted from a Royalist mansion. Frances Gray usefully identifies the evocation in this scene of the Lacanian mirror stage, an event that is radically subverted by Churchill who images female solidarity in the mirror as opposed to an individual and alienated Other.[56] The absence of stable spatiality for the mirror's reflection also alludes to Foucault's heterotopia with its image of the ideal lacking spatial grounding. The surrounding dialogue–"we're burning his papers, that's the Norman papers that give him his lands. ... There's no one over us. There's pictures of him and his grandfather and his great great–a long row of pictures and we pulled them down" (207)– additionally suggests an image of the potentiality of what Marx termed "a class for itself." "A class in itself" develops a politicised consciousness of its location in production relations and becomes "a class for itself," a process that stimulates revolutionary activity. Typically of Churchill, she subverts the traditional masculinist configuration of class politics generally espoused by mainstream Marxism by foregrounding women as central agents of class struggle.

Act 1 is full of utopian drive, containing several spaces of possibility where a growing sense of active agency develops in a number of characters. Hoskins, a female vagrant preacher, begins to reclaim the bible as she challenges the Calvinist preacher's reference to St. Paul in his attempt to silence her. She retorts, "Joel. Chapter two. Verse twenty-eight. 'And it shall come to pass that I will pour out my spirit upon all flesh; and your sons and your daughters shall prophecy. ... And also upon the servants and upon the handmaids in those days will I pour out my spirit" (201). Briggs, "a working man," is recruited by the corn merchant, Star,

---

[56] Frances Gray, "Mirrors of Utopia: Caryl Churchill and Joint Stock," in *British and Irish Drama Since 1960*, ed. James Acheson (London: Macmillan, 1993), 47-59.

into the army and quickly becomes politicised, joining the Levellers, and becoming elected as an agitator by his regiment. He rapidly attempts to secularise the discourse of revolution and recognises that war in Ireland serves only colonial interests. Claxton (a character based loosely on the historical figure Laurence Clarkson or Claxton) moves towards the Ranters, and this journey is coterminous with his growing insight into ways in which ideology permeates sexuality, relationships, and property. He says, "my body is given to other women now for I have come to see that there is no sin but what man thinks is sin. ... Sometimes I lie or steal to show myself that there is no lie or theft but in the mind" (221). Several characters repudiate their subordinated subject positions and progressively locate themselves as dynamic agents, taking hold of language and political discourse in empowering and creative ways.

The spaces of possibility begin to close, however, as Act 2 proceeds. In the penultimate scene, Hoskins, Cobbe, Brotherton, Briggs, and Claxton meet in a tavern and discuss what has happened after the betrayal at the Putney Debates. Pathos threatens to usurp the more radical utopian impulses as the coming of Christ is frenziedly and ecstatically appealed to by all except Briggs, who is the lone secular voice. Utopian struggle is relegated to modes of non-compliance, the "tactics," "ruses," "trickery," and "deception" outlined by de Certeau. Cobbe repeatedly swears, and asks, "is it nothing but a lifetime of false words, little games, devil's tricks, ways to get by in the world and keep safe?" (230).

The last scene, entitled "After," explains the circumstances of these characters after the Restoration. The speeches have become brief, flat, and monologic. Claxton speaks the last few lines of the play, lines that indicate the disappearance of the utopian impulse; the audience is told there is an "end of perfection" (241). Claxton reports that he went to Barbados, another utopian terrain, an "exotic" island, which was soon to be appropriated by imperialist enterprise. His final line is, "my great desire is to see and say nothing" (241). The utopian impulse has gone and the previously empowering rejuvenation of language is now curtailed by political defeat and censorship. Seeing (something) and saying nothing becomes the primary (in)activity. Whether Claxton is in exile or is now aligned with the new system, or whether his silence is due to repression or complicity are left critically unanswered at the end of the play.

Light Shining stages competing versions of utopia, utopian spaces, and utopian processes. These competing versions reflect the debates over theory, tactics, and strategies that took place within Left and counter-cultural circles. Donald Campbell in *Plays and Players* comments, "parallels with our own time exist in plenty–the scene depicting the Putney debates reminded me very much of the squabbles of the British Labour Party,"[57] and Irving Wardle wrote in *The Times*, "numerous points of contact with the modern world, such as the treatment of vagrants and squatters, crop up naturally."[58] Meenakshi Ponnuswami additionally points to the connections between the transgressive, carnivalesque practices of the Ranters in their performativity of liberation–their swearing, drunkenness, practice of free sexuality–and these utopian tendencies within the contemporaneous counter-culture.[59] The Diggers' practice of reclaiming the land, contrasting with the Levellers' negotiation with the Parliamentarians, is similarly resonant of the competing strategies and tactics that dominated the British Left in the 1970s. *Light Shining* explores a range of differing forms of the utopian, representing weaknesses as well as strengths of a variety of utopian modes of political activity. The limitations of the performativity of immediate liberation–such as the Ranters' final outburst of millenarianism–are exposed, but so the restrictive range of the critical impulse of the Levellers is similarly shown to be vulnerable to absorption by the system. *Light Shining* contributes towards the construction of socialist history with its celebration of the courage, political enlightenment, and activism of radicals during the English revolution. Although it dramatises their political defeat, the utopian aspirations of collective revolution combined with individual freedom are represented positively through an amalgamation of various utopian and critical practices. Churchill undertakes what Bloch's *Principle of Hope* proposed, for *Light Shining* wrenches open the past, both to support the re-construction of silenced histories, and to intervene in the present in the hope of changing the future.

Vinegar Tom

Written in the same year as *Light Shining* and first performed a month after, under the direction of Pam Brighton at the Humberside Theatre, Hull, in October 1976, then on tour, and at the ICA and Half Moon Theatres, London, *Vinegar Tom* was also a collaborative venture (this time with the socialist-feminist theatre collective Monstrous Regiment) and was

---

[57] Donald Campbell, "Traditional Movement," *Plays and Players* (November 1976): 20-21.
[58] Irving Wardle, *The Times* (28 September 1976), repr. in *File on Churchill*, by Fitzsimmons, 30.
[59] Meenakshi Ponnuswami, "Fanshen in the English Revolution," in *Caryl Churchill: Contemporary Representations*, ed. Sheila Rabillard (Winnipeg: Blizzard Publishing, 1998), 41-59.

again set in the seventeenth century. The work on *Vinegar Tom* began before *Light Shining*, and Churchill completed a first draft during this period, but she left the play at this stage to work with Joint Stock, and then returned to *Vinegar Tom* after the completion of *Light Shining*. Hence, there seems to be an explicit inter-textuality and inter-theatricality between these two plays, which reinforces their overlap, as Churchill says, "both in time and ideas."[60]

The sense of excitement Churchill expressed over working with Joint Stock is also displayed in this initial period of working with Monstrous Regiment. She describes her feelings after meeting the company,

> I left the meeting exhilarated. My previous work had been completely solitary–never discussed my ideas while I was writing or showed anyone anything earlier than a final polished draft. So this was a new way of working, which was one of its attractions. Also a touring company, with a wider audience; also a feminist company–I felt briefly shy and daunted, wondering if I would be acceptable, then happy and stimulated by the discovery of shared ideas and the enormous energy and feeling of possibilities in the still new company.[61]

Churchill conveys the sense of thrill at the newness of this way of working and the stimulation produced by the "discovery of shared ideas" and the opening up of "possibilities," utopian terms expressive of hope and inspiration.

While the sense of utopian possibility appears as tangible in the account on the making of *Vinegar Tom* as it was on *Light Shining*, *Vinegar Tom* is nevertheless more complex in its relationship with the expression of utopian modes. Churchill describes *Vinegar Tom* as

> a play about witches, but none of the characters portrayed is a witch; it's a play which doesn't talk about hysteria, evil or demonic possession but about poverty, humiliation and prejudice, and the view which the women accused of witchcraft had of themselves.[62]

The play makes explicit the patriarchal connections among the institutions of church, state, and family and illustrates the formation of misogynist myth-making by using a mixture of historical and religious documentation

---

[60] Churchill, Introduction to *Vinegar Tom*, in *Caryl Churchill Plays: 1*, 129-31, 129.
[61] Churchill, Introduction to *Vinegar Tom*, 129.
[62] Churchill, "A Woman's Point of View," Interview by Maggie Rose, *Sipario* (November-December 1987): 99-100, 99.

and references. These can be seen in the repeated citation of the witch hunt bible *The Malleus Maleficarum: The Hammer of Witches* written in 1484 by the Reverends Heinrich Kramer and James Sprenger, which was in use for three centuries.[63] The play also includes the characters, Kramer and Sprenger, who in the original production were played by women dressed as Edwardian music-hall gents in top hats and tails.

Although there is explicit employment of historical material, Churchill explains in the introduction to *Vinegar Tom* that she "didn't base the play on any precise historical events, but set it rather loosely in the seventeenth century." This was "partly because it was the time of the last major English witch hunts, and partly because the social upheavals, class changes, rising professionalism and great hardship among the poor were the context of the kind of witchhunt" in which she was interested.[64] Unlike *Light Shining*, *Vinegar Tom* additionally incorporates modern songs by actors out of character and in contemporary dress, the intervention of which breaks up the dramatic narrative. Gillian Hanna of Monstrous Regiment, who played Alice in the original production, explains this intervention in terms of the company's wish to "smash that regular and acceptable dramatic form," since they "didn't want to allow the audience to get off the hook by regarding it as a period piece, a piece of very interesting history."[65] In this sense, it is a more confrontational play, one that seeks to arrest the audience with a belligerent mode of representation, a representation that removes "neutral" space in which spectators may wish to reside. It thus offers an alternative to Jameson's characterisation of the postmodern obliteration of distantiation, or the effacement of critical space.

The play may not engage straightforwardly with utopian modes and seems to depend more on the critical impulse as its driving force, but there are some powerful utopian representations. Firstly, as Hanna mentioned, the smashing of conventional theatrical form that *Vinegar Tom* so explicitly enacts, recalls Bloch's focus on history and utopianism: the enclosed historical narrative is disassembled and blast through with contemporary provocative moments. There is a reconstruction of predominantly poor and unconventional women's histories, a destabilisation of liberal historiography, as well as a counter-balancing of other (male)

---

[63] Heinrich Kramer and James Sprenger, *The Malleus Maleficarum: The Hammer of the Witches*, ed. Montague Summers (New York: Dover, 1971).
[64] Churchill, Introduction to *Vinegar Tom*, 30.
[65] Gillian Hanna, "Feminism and Theatre," *Theatre Papers* 8, 2nd Series (1978): 9-10, 9.

socialist narratives, such as Arthur Miller's *The Crucible* (1953).[66] While the girls in Salem in 1692, similarly, are not witches and are represented in the main as victims of patriarchal hegemony; nevertheless, the profundity of the parable for McCarthyism is located in the flawed but essentially good *male* figure of John Proctor, with Abigail Williams displaying the qualities of beauty, lust, guile, fickleness, and deviousness–typical constructions that comprise the object of the male gaze.

Vinegar Tom relegates the central male consciousness of *The Crucible* to the scarcely drawn and unnamed Man in Scene 1, together with surly Jack (the tenant farmer, who induces little more than hostility from the audience), and stereotypes of the sadistic and authoritarian Doctor (an off-stage character), the witch hunter Packer, and the fathers of witch hunting, Kramer and Sprenger. Female characters dominate the dramatic landscape and form the focus of a fully rounded community. The differences between the women are not idealistically veneered, and, indeed, serve as an obstacle to survival and change; however, a common utopian thread of female desire reverberates throughout the play and connects the female characters in a network of gendered subjectivity.

The poor village girl, Alice, and the landowner's daughter, Betty, for example, are irreconcilably differentiated in class terms–so much so that it becomes a life and death distinction as Betty is saved from hanging solely because of her class status–but they nevertheless parallel each other in a utopian yearning to transcend their immediate environments. Alice's repeated request in Scene 1 to the unnamed Man to take her with him to Scotland or London is matched in the following scene by Betty's articulation of her longing to escape the estate and–by implication–her role: "on my way here I climbed a tree. … I could see the other side of the river. I wanted to jump off. And fly" (140). Even Jack's self-righteous wife, Margery, reveals intimations of utopian yearning, intimations that are reflected in the insinuation of repressed sexual desire as she sings a song to accompany her struggle to churn butter, "Johnny's standing at the gate waiting for a butter cake. Come butter come, come butter come" (143). This gathers more significance from its location in the scene immediately after the song that mournfully narrates the development of women's sexuality, "Nobody Sings."

As in *Light Shining*, there are attempts to formulate a more self-empowered subject position, particularly by Alice, who in her conversation with the Man just after they have had sex at a roadside, endeavours to articulate herself as a subject, as opposed to an object, of

---

[66] Arthur Miller, *The Crucible* (London: Penguin, 2000; first published in 1953).

desire, "I don't like a man too smooth" (135). Further on in the scene, she echoes the discourse of the Ranters in *Light Shining*, "any time I'm happy someone says it's a sin" (136). Initially the Man collaborates with this by alluding to the utopianism of the political culture of radical sects in London:

> there's some in London say there's no sin. Each man has his own religion nearly, or none at all, and there's women speak out too. They smoke and curse in the tavern and say flesh is no sin for they are God themselves and can't sin. The men and women lie together and say that's bliss and that's heaven and that's no sin. (136)

But Alice's struggle to construct herself as an autonomous subject is thwarted by the Man, who, when asked if he will take her with him, retorts, "take a whore with me?" He scoffs, "what name would you put to yourself? You're not a wife or a widow. You're not a virgin. Tell me a name for what you are" (137). His power to switch swiftly from camaraderie to misogyny is made clear. This dialogue also demonstrates that Alice requires a man's "generosity" if she is to locate a wider range of modes of self-assertion.

A space that signifies a pro-female or "womanist" utopia–in Alice Walker's use of the term–is Ellen's cottage.[67] Ellen, the cunning woman, tries to support other women in their self-determination. She says to Alice's friend Susan, who is pregnant for the sixth or seventh time after miscarrying several times and almost dying during childbirth, "take it or leave it, my dear, it's one to me. If you want to be rid of your trouble, you'll take it. But only you know what you want" (154). Unlike the male doctor who administers discipline, Ellen promotes choice. Betty also enjoys Ellen's unconventional space. She asks, "can I come again sometimes just to be here? I like it here" (156). Ellen's cottage becomes a counter-site, a Foucualdian heterotopia, where women come to enjoy a brief period away from the patriarchal domination of their everyday lives.

---

[67] As well as relating specifically to black feminists, "womanist" also refers, more generally, to any woman "who loves other women, sexually and/or nonsexually. Appreciates and prefers women's culture, women's emotional flexibility ... and women's strength. Sometimes loves individual men, sexually and/or nonsexually. Committed to survival and wholeness of entire people, male *and* female. Not a separatist, except periodically for health. Traditionally universalist ... and capable. Loves music ... dance ... the moon ... the Spirit ... struggle ... the folk ... herself. Regardless. Womanist is to feminist as purple is to lavender." Alice Walker, *In Search of Our Mother's Gardens* (London: Women's Press, 1984), xi-xii.

There are two utopian parodies in the play. A fascistic utopia is
ironically signified in the song "Something to Burn":

> Sometimes it's witches, or what will you choose?
> Sometimes its lunatics, shut them away.
> It's blacks and it's women and often it's Jews.
> We'd all be quite happy if they'd go away.
> Find something to burn.
> Let it go up in smoke.
> Burn your troubles away. (154)

As well as referring to the activity of scapegoating, this song also
sardonically imagines a far right utopian fantasy with women in their
place, "lunatics" locked up, and no Jewish or black troublemakers
"infecting" a white male vision of social perfection. A further ironic
utopian image is Ellen's depiction of Betty's life as a rich wife:

> your best chance of being left alone is marry a rich man, because it's part
> of his honour to have a wife who does nothing. He has a big house and
> rose garden and trout stream, he just needs a fine lady to make it complete
> and you can be that. You can sing and sit on the lawn and change your
> dresses and order the dinner. (169)

This description functions paradoxically as a reminder of Betty's class
privilege (Ellen continues, "what would you rather? Marry a poor man and
work all day?"[68] [169]), and serves as an acknowledgement of the lack of
self-determination that complicates female class "dominance."

As part of its implication of the duality of past and present, *Vinegar
Tom* explores the dystopian impulse that informs both a patriarchal
configuration of systemic structures and the complicit behaviour with
these structures of some female characters, such as the bitter tenant
farmer's wife, Margery, and the witch hunter's assistant, Goody. Despite
this complicity though, both the critical and utopian impulses are
manifested in characters, such as Alice, and her mother, Joan, who, when
faced with hanging for witchcraft, remain defiant to the end. Joan's pre-
hanging speech (in which she performs the role of a witch, claiming to be
the cause of trouble, misfortune, and accidents in the village over the last
ten years) provides her with a momentary space from where she assumes
an active and commanding persona. She fleetingly transcends the
ideological parameters imposed upon her as she temporarily occupies the

---

[68] A similar rhetorical question re-emerges in *Top Girls* during the argument
between Joyce and Marlene. See Chapter 4, page 145.

demonised but powerful role that she has been accused of, claiming omnipotently, "the great storm and tempest comes when I call it" (173). The utopian yearning for a wholly different social landscape is played out amidst a dystopian setting where fear, division, and poverty form the material conditions of this community. Hence, although the political signification of the play seems to function predominantly at the critical pole, there are traces of utopia that exist in a specifically female matrix of space, language, and consciousness, which in turn is figured as a mode of survival and local resistance.

Top Girls

Top Girls, which was written in 1980-82, performed in 1982 and directed, like *Light Shining*, by Stafford-Clark, is similarly concerned with specifically female engagements with power, subjectivity, and space, and is again firmly grounded in a discourse of class politics. This is the first of the plays discussed that requires an all-female cast; sixteen female characters were played by seven actors in the original production. The all-female productive context thus gestures towards a feminist utopian practice, locating women at the centre of both production and representation. Unlike the previous two plays, however, *Top Girls* was not a collaborative venture, and the sense of collectivity that joint projects tend to produce is perceptibly (and appropriately given the subject matter) lacking.

It is also written, performed, and set in the aftermath of Margaret Thatcher's election victory; hence, a gloomy sense of the dystopian dominates the material relations of the play's production as well as its content. As discussed in Chapter 1, the economic and political assaults had begun to take effect in Thatcher's first term on public and municipal bodies including the National Health Service, Local Government, trade unions, and law centres, and the rapid intensification of monetarism had also started to affect the economic structure, and to a debatable extent, the ideological freedom of theatre. David Edgar argues that these cuts in the arts in conjunction with "gentle but consistent political pressure prised open the cracks sufficiently to let the sap of Thatcherism seep through."[69] Stafford-Clark, at the Royal Court Theatre, comments in the mid-1980s, "I now run a commercial business that occasionally puts on plays."[70]

---

[69] David Edgar, *The Second Time as Farce: Reflections on Drama in Mean Times* (London: Lawrence and Wishart, 1988), 19.
[70] Max Stafford-Clark, quoted in *Thatcher's Theatre: British Theatre and Drama in the Eighties*, by D. Keith Peacock (London: Greenwood Press, 1999), 50.

Gray regards *Top Girls* as expressive of the dystopian: "language is not charged with the potential to embody and achieve a better world but a rigid discourse imposing as well as expressing monetary values."[71] The language in Acts 2 and 3 of *Top Girls* is characterised by a sense of limitation and restriction. An expression of dissatisfaction at the loss of an idiom of emancipation is a key articulation. Act 1, however, as Gray notes, offers a "far more complex" language from historical, literary, and mythical women, and it is this Act that complicates what might be a more straightforwardly negative play.[72]

Top Girls lacks the aspirational vision of *Light Shining* and the political confidence that inspires the campaigning force of *Vinegar Tom*. It is more self-critical. In part it critiques the neglect of class politics within the feminist movement. In this way it speaks directly to feminists and socialists about the importance of pursuing anti-capitalist and feminist goals in tandem. It is not, however, an introspective play; it equally addresses a wider audience both in its astute representation and critique of Thatcherite Britain and the depiction of the strained relationship between two sisters, their choices or lack of them, and their relationship with their niece/daughter. While, perhaps, politically defensive, *Top Girls* simultaneously contains a formidable energy that gestures forward in its sustained and forceful demonstration of the unacceptability of the political status quo. It may not offer tangible alternatives but in its representation of the absolute intolerability of the (non-utopian) socio-economic landscape, it intimates that change is essential.

The first Act complicates what might have been a more straightforward and naturalistic rendering of a particular set of political and social circumstances. Act 1 is both hyper-realist in its staging of overlapping speech, which more naturally reflects dinner party conversation, and fantastically contrived with its hosting of historical, mythical, and literary female figures from different historical periods. It is Marlene's fantasy of a trans-historical, all-female space where female achievement can be appreciated and celebrated. Indeed, this act powerfully connotes a utopian space of femininity with its representation of a genealogy of women resisting their banishment to private spaces and no longer discrete from history. The carnivalesque characterises the undulating movement of the polyphonic exchanges, with heightened moments of carnival release illustrated in such instances as the stage directions' imperatives, "*they are quite drunk*" and "*they get the giggles*" (73).

---

[71] Gray, "Mirrors of Utopia," 56.
[72] Gray, "Mirrors of Utopia," 56.

As with *Vinegar Tom* a feminist utopian impulse is located to some extent in the desire to travel and escape. Marlene confesses she finds it difficult to sit still, and has moved from the Fens to London in order to escape her restrictive environment, leaving her daughter, Angie, to be brought up by her sister, Joyce. The Victorian Scottish traveller, Isabella Bird, comments, "I always felt dull when I was stationary," with Lady Nijo (a thirteenth-century Japanese Emperor's courtesan turned Buddhist nun) concurring, "yes, that's exactly it. New sights. The shrine by the beach, the moon shining on the sea" (67). There are also utopian moments of anarchic release in the humorous recognition of the social construction of gender roles: "he found it interesting, I think, that I could make scones and also lasso cattle" (63). The story of Pope Joan (who is thought to have disguised herself as a man and been Pope in the ninth century) describes giving birth, which comically de-naturalises pregnancy; she explains, "I didn't know what was happening. I thought I was getting fatter, but then I was eating more and sitting about, the life of a Pope is quite luxurious," to which she adds the caveat that she "wasn't used to having a woman's body" (70). These comical instances indicate a momentary break in the dominance of patriarchal signification and could be likened to Lefebvre's "moments" of "presence," where a utopian flash of non-alienation is fleetingly experienced.

As several critics have observed, however, this act is not an idealised and uncritical celebration of female solidarity. The all-female utopian space is more akin to Burwell's discussion of critical utopias where dystopian moments occur within the utopian space, and a structural and ideological permeability characterises the boundary between utopia and dystopia. The limitations of a commonality of female subjectivity are gently but explicitly established. Isabella's expression of independence and autonomy is articulated through a colonial discourse. Her identification with the colonial imagination blights the romanticism of a trans-historical/cultural/racial and classless female solidarity: "I said, Hennie we'll live here forever and help the natives" (55). Griselda, similarly, remarks in response to Marlene's criticism of her submissiveness to her husband that she would "rather obey the Marquis than a boy from the village," to which Marlene concurs, "yes, that's a point" (75). Hence, the tension produced in the canonisation of a genealogy of extraordinary women is unapologetically suggested within this utopian projection. The historical specificity of each character's subjective context is shown not to be easily assimilable to a progressive feminist identity.

However, the commonly made claims that the women do not listen to each other, talk over each other, and are competitive are overstated. Roger

Cornish and Violet Ketels claim, "they chatter on about their lives, their dialogue overlapping, their words often indecipherable since they rarely listen to each other."[73] Janet Brown describes the act as "almost a parody of feminist glorifications of women's community," representing "egoists who interrupt one another continually."[74] Certainly, the dialogue does not reflect a (middle-class) valorisation of equally distributed and sensitively managed exchanges, and seems to signify an element of disjunction between the characters, a disjunction indicating, as Joseph Marohl states, "differences in ideology and practice."[75] However, the overlapping exchanges are, in Churchill's description, at "the level of amusing anecdotes, of sharing stories and entertaining each other with them."[76] Multiple conversations overlap with one another, which is illustrative of enthusiasm, excitement, and the pursuit of giving, as well as receiving, pleasure, at least as much as it is a symptom of self-centredness and competition.

This Act includes a sophisticated and intricate matrix of paradoxical and contradictory sites of struggle and submission over gender, class, and racial identities. It also postures towards utopian transcendence through the pooling together of uneven historical subjectivities and thus threatens to supersede existing terms of categorisation. It teeters on the brink of utopia and dystopia as it holds in the balance an exuberant celebration of feminist space as well as an unapologetic critique of the idealisation of the category "woman." Elaine Aston reads the complex ending of the scene as a climactic revulsion at the (dystopian) symbolic order.[77] But the sense of deterioration and chaos suggested by the drunkenness, crying, and vomiting are also poised against the triumphant speech of Dull Gret, the significance of which is magnified since it is the first time the audience hears her speak more than a few words. The last line of her account of leading the fight against devils in hell is: "oh we give them devils such a beating" (82). She finishes her speech in a triumphant register. The battle's occurrence in a mythical place (no-place) and its representation in a

---

[73] Roger Cornish and Violet Ketels, *Landmarks of Modern British Drama* (London: Methuen, 1986), 529.

[74] Janet Brown, "Caryl Churchill's *Top Girls* Catches the Next Wave," in *Caryl Churchill*, ed. Phyllis Randall (London: Garland Publishing, 1988), 117-30, 127.

[75] Joseph Marohl, "De-realised Women: Performance and Identity in *Top Girls*," *Modern Drama* 30.3 (September 1987): 376-88, 378.

[76] Churchill, Interview by Lizbeth Goodman, repr. in "Overlapping Dialogue in Overlapping Media," in *Essays on Caryl Churchill*, ed. Rabillard, 69-101, 80.

[77] Elaine Aston, *An Introduction to Feminism and Theatre* (London: Routledge, 1995), 47-48.

painting recall Marcuse's location of the utopian in art. Hence, the potential pathos induced by the actions of other characters does not necessarily colonise the final interpretative possibilities of the Act, and the audience is left instead with the dynamism of contradictory postulations.

Acts 2 and 3 foreground as counter-utopian the relations that construct the everyday spaces of work and home in late capitalist society. The Thatcherite values of Marlene become increasingly evident in the employment agency scenes through a subtle satire on the glorification of individualism and monetary and managerial success. Comparatively, Joyce's defence of her working-class identity and understanding of the perniciousness of class privilege is represented as politically necessary. However, the absence of a specifically gendered critique within class-focused politics not only underlines the fact that Joyce's life (like her mother and father's) seems to have been wasted, but also that her political discourse falls short of offering alternatives that might make a difference to a new generation of working-class women, such as her niece/daughter Angie.

In this sense *Top Girls* operates predominantly along the lines of the critical pole of political analysis; a muffled anger perceptibly informs the dissatisfaction with the restrictive and non-utopian terms of contemporaneous political debate, and is only counteracted by the impact of Act 1, an act that offers a wider range of interpretive modes. This does not result, however, in surrender to a cynical complicity with the contemporary political moment. Rather it implies that the question of whether Marlene is morally abhorrent for gaining her independence at the expense of her sister (or sisters generally) is only partially relevant and that the equally pertinent silent absence that demands consideration is the question of how do both sisters (all sisters), as well as their niece/daughter achieve full emancipation.

Fen

Another collaboration with Joint Stock, *Fen*, written following workshops in the Fens in 1982, was first performed at the University of Essex in January 1983 and was directed by Les Waters. It then opened at the Almeida Theatre in London the following month. Churchill describes it as "a play with more direct quotes of things people said to us than any other I've written," and one where she has "a particularly lively sense of how much it owes to other people."[78] It overlaps in its political preoccupations

---

[78] Churchill, Introduction to *Caryl Churchill Plays: 2*, ix-x, ix.

with the concerns of the other three plays so far discussed, particularly in its representation of the rural working class (already staged in the figures of Joyce and Angie in *Top Girls*), and its reconstruction of predominantly female relations in the family, workplace, and wider social context. It also continues to interweave naturalist representation with the surreal, supernatural, and mythical in the form of folklore, the staging of ghosts, the supranormal appearances of Shirley ironing the field, and Nell, "a fully realised Fen tiger," crossing the stage on stilts.[79] It is, however, starkly dissimilar to the other plays, and particularly to *Top Girls*, in its political engagement with utopian modes. Although its construction of the conditions of the characters' lives is represented through dour and gloomy imagery, the characters in *Fen* simultaneously embrace utopian expression as a mode of survival and cathartic release in the context of a dearth of oppositional discourses.

The play's depiction of an unyielding sense of a harsh environment is conveyed more acutely through the repeated representation of poverty and hard manual labour. The physically strenuous, low paid, and exploited work undertaken by the women on stage relays the set of production relations that largely frames the "choices" available to them. This was reinforced dramaturgically in the first London production wherein the uncomfortable experience of watching–in a middle-class space of leisure– the endemic unhappiness pervading the community and the backbreaking labour performed by these women was heightened by the impact on the senses of a cold Almeida theatre. In his review of *Fen*, Michael Coveney states, "the penetrating cold of the fens is appropriately, if uncomfortably, complemented by the temperature in the Almeida's auditorium."[80] Rob Ritchie explains,

> the Almeida Theatre, still in the process of refurbishment, hosted the London run. Bare walls, freezing temperatures and a mist that slowly engulfed the auditorium were conditions that would not have suited many plays ... but they were splendidly apt for *Fen*. ... It was, in all senses, a chilling evening.[81]

Sharing this peculiarly difficult environment with the audience in this sensory way worked to encourage spectators to empathise with the women's plight. In addition, by removing the usually snug conditions of

[79] Gray, "Mirrors of Utopia," 56.
[80] Michael Coveney, *Financial Times* (17 February 1983), repr. in *London Theatre Record* 3.4 (12-25 February 1983): 112-13, 113.
[81] Ritchie, ed., *The Joint Stock Book,* 27-28.

the theatre, it was made more difficult for audiences to dwell in a comfortable state of apathy.

Out of this unforgiving landscape a utopian dramatic discourse emerges that takes several forms. Story-telling and the reproduction of oral history passed down generations through the act of re-membering is one such form. A poetic utopianism characterises the somewhat mystical register of communication in which characters at times participate. May (the mother of the central protagonist Val) tells her grandchildren, "when the light comes down from behind the clouds it comes down like a ladder into the graveyards. And the dead people go up the light into heaven" (158). Non-verbal performances form part of a utopian language; Val and Frank dance together in Scene 5, "*old-fashioned, formal, romantic, happy*" (153), and May sings at the end of the play; the Production Note reads, "she stands there as if singing and we hear what she would have liked to sing. So something amazing and beautiful–she wouldn't sing unless she could sing like that."[82] A utopian moment of perfection and fulfilled desire is ephemerally signified.

Utopian desire is a repeated articulation in *Fen*. It informs the crux of Val's tragic inability to choose between her lover, Frank, and her children. After Frank kills her, Val's ghost consoles him with the assurance that she wanted him to kill her, but he replies, "you should have wanted something different" (189). She did, of course, want something different but what she wanted was not possible in the circumstances within which she was trapped. Recalling Moylan's recognition that desire in excess of commodity fetishism is considered to be socially aberrant, Val's yearning for something different is viewed as subversive in the village and her mother churlishly taunts her for presuming to want more, "what you after? Happiness? Got it have you? Bluebird of happiness?" (159). May's challenge is both an attempt to trivialise Val's desire and a pessimistic acknowledgement that Val's pursuit of happiness is doomed. Val retorts, "don't start on me. Just because you had nothing" (159). For May, repressing her desires and rejecting the pursuit of happiness are necessary strategies for survival; hence, her refusal to sing signifies her awareness of the unlikelihood that someone like her–a poor woman from the Fens– could make it as a successful singer; Val says, "my mother wanted to be a singer. That's why she'd never sing" (190).

The most militant character, Nell, a single woman in her forties, also expresses utopian desire. In response to the young girls, Becky, Deb, and

---

[82] Churchill, Production Note to *Fen*, in *Caryl Churchill: Plays 2* (London: Methuen, 1990), 145.

Shona, who taunt her for being a witch or a hermaphrodite, she counters, "nasty, nasty children. ... You should be entirely different. Everything. Everything" (157). Nell's intimation of the possibility of an alternative to the existing socio-political context is informed by a utopian yearning, but one that is accompanied too by a politics of critique and confrontation. However, her understanding of trade union principles is not matched by her fellow friends and workers, and thus leads to her frustrated but insightful interrogative, "am I crazy? Am I crazy? Am I crazy?" (150). This is an ironic insight, a kind of Lefebvrian moment of presence wherein to experience social relations objectively, produces a brief and paradoxical flash of insanity at the very moment of non-alienation.

However, Nell is not the only site of political and economic struggle in *Fen*. Val's grandmother, Ivy, tells jumbled stories at her ninetieth birthday party, which include glimpses of a more class-conscious past:

> fellow come round on his bike and made his speech in the empty street and everybody'd be in the house listening because they daren't go out because what old Tewson might say. 'Vote for the blues, boys,' he'd say and he'd give them money to drink. They'd pull off the blue ribbons behind the hedge. Still have the drink though. ... 'You join that union, Jack', I said. Nothing I couldn't do then. (178)

This undocumented history provides the farmer, Tewson's, earlier anti-union comment to Miss Cade ("you want to watch the Transport and General Workers" [162]) with greater significance; it also opens up the potential for a re-emergence of militancy. Furthermore, May's speech reveals that the workers engaged with low-levels of non-compliance, recalling de Certeau's everyday tactics and ruses; in this example the workers accept the bribe from the boss without fulfilling their end of the bargain.

However, the utopian impulse competes with Thatcherite discourses, discourses represented most clearly in the characters of Tewson and Geoffrey, the latter of whom, states, "everything's changing, everything's going down. Strikes, militants, I see Russians behind it" (16). More politically ambiguous are the modes of resistance narratives, such as Shirley's account of her ancestors' ritual exorcism of emotional frustration. She recounts,

> my grandmother told me her grandmother said when times were bad they'd mutilate the cattle. Go out in the night and cut a sheep's throat or hamstring a horse or stab a cow with a fork. ... 'What for?' I said. They felt quieter after that. (189)

Gray evaluates this positively, interpreting it as a description of "a past when labourers killed the owner's cattle instead of working with icicles on their faces."[83] Perhaps this action evokes Luddite rebellion, but what seems more plausible is that labourers killed cattle as cathartic release in order to be able to continue to work with icicles on their faces.

This political ambiguity extends to the play's engagement with other utopian modes of dreaming, folklore, and the presence of ghosts. For instance, the intervention of the ghost in nineteenth-century rags, the purpose of which is to admonish Tewson's exploitative role, is both symbolic of the non-traditional forms of resistance in the village, as well as forming part of the collective consciousness of the agricultural workers, who–unlike the urban working class–do not fit easily into a conventional characterisation of the proletariat. The physical presence of the ghost from the past on stage destabilises the Enlightenment narrative of progress and rebuffs the hasty retreat from theorising social class in the 1980s, through its exposure of the similarities in working conditions of past and present labourers. While this gestures towards a radical critique of existing structures, a possibility remains, however, that the subversive potential is prone to evaporation. In response to Gray's evaluation of fantasy as "a real force with the possibility of accomplishing real change,"[84] Ann Wilson views it as one of "the community's powerful mechanisms of regulation, including self-regulation," and symptomatic of "a failure to imagine life other than the one being lived," the repression of which results in "violence which pervades the community and frequently erupts as self-abuse."[85] However, although Wilson is wisely alert to the negative connection between fantasy and self-regulation, she nevertheless neglects the more nourishing aspects of this politically ambivalent and contradictory culture.

This political ambivalence can be located in the contradictory applications of different utopian strands. Memory, for example, is used to keep alive a radical history but it simultaneously operates as a conservative mechanism that is resistant to change. Shirley's husband, Geoffrey, recalls, "we had terrible times. If I had cracked tomatoes for my tea I thought I was lucky. So why shouldn't you have terrible times?" (170). Although this is articulated by one of the explicitly reactionary characters, it resonates in others, such as May and Shirley, and competes

---

[83] Gray, "Mirrors of Utopia," 56.
[84] Gray, "Mirrors of Utopia," 56.
[85] Ann Wilson, "Hauntings," in *Drama on Drama: Dimensions of Theatricality on the Contemporary British Stage*, ed. Nicole Boireau (London: Macmillan, 1997), 152-67, 162-63.

against the more subversive discourses of Nell, Val's grandmother, Ivy, and the ghost. The characters dream and imagine through the media of songs and stories but this is also a prominent source of tension in the village. May's desire not to desire is the circular and paradoxical force that simmers beneath the surface and erupts in the climax of the play with the uncontrollable spilling over of emotion.

Fen dramatises utopian modes within a grim landscape and in this sense challenges the conventional construct of the countryside as an idyllic panacea to the ills of the city. Churchill describes *Fen* in the following terms,

> it's a complicated world ... incredibly remote and backward in some ways–in the way the workers are very badly paid and yet still feel loyal to the farmers, at the same time that it's entirely of the present, because the land they're loyal to is owned by multinational corporations. The English have an idea that the real England is the countryside, and that it's a beautiful retreat, completely separate from the corrupt values of people living in cities. ... But it's a pastoral fantasy.[86]

Fen successfully deconstructs the Arcadian utopia projected onto rural locations. However, it also stages a community to a large extent devoid of the critical impulse that so powerfully informs the political signification of *Top Girls*. The utopian modes located in the play become a means to survive, a network of ruses, in the context of a harsh and casualised working community, but they also threaten to discourage change by means of the escapist space they offer.

Serious Money

Written in the same year as its first performance at the Royal Court Theatre, London, in March 1987, and once again directed by Stafford-Clark, *Serious Money* develops further the astringent register of *Top Girls* in its complete elimination of the utopian and its use of satire. With its obliteration of the conventional signifiers of community, solidarity, altruism, and human kindness, *Serious Money* can simultaneously be likened to a 1980s yuppie utopia with its sardonic celebration of the accumulation of money for its own sake. Sociologist, Barry Richards, states,

---

[86] Churchill, Interview by Laurie Stone, "Making Room at the Top," *The Village Voice* XXVIII.9 (1 March 1983): 80-81, 80.

whereas in the 1960s and 1970s it was almost always the Left that was the architect of utopian features and that gave voice to utopian impulses in the national consciousness, now it seems as if it is the New Right that has placed before us the most compelling agendas for social transformation.[87]

Serious Money, in this sense, reflects the post-1960s/1970s demise of Leftist utopian vision and represents, instead, a New Right utopia in the form of a satirical or anti-utopia.

Manifestly different from Churchill's other work, the representation of a corporate take-over in the City of London in *Serious Money* moves the focus of drama away from the conditions of the oppressed subject and into the world of stock brokers and financial speculation. This reconstruction of an impenetrable space of commercial totality incited controversy over its political effectiveness. Brighton, who had directed *Vinegar Tom*, states,

> one of the things I find singularly depressing is that plays like *Serious Money* have borrowed the rhetoric of being progressive political plays, when they're really comedies of manners that feed into the bourgeois sense of wanting to see itself reified in a way the working class very rarely get reified on stage. It's just the fucking yuppies going, 'Whoopee, we're real, we exist, we're on stage.' ... So far from moving in the same direction as socialist theatre, it's in total conflict with it.[88]

The play presents a precariously satirical celebration of the amorality of an exclusive world to an audience whose make-up, both at the Royal Court and in the second run at the Wyndham theatre in July 1987, frequently consisted of City stock brokers. However, British Telecom was not seduced, clearly viewing the play as subversive, as "a production with which no public company would wish to be associated," and refusing "to provide the telephones for the Wyndham's production."[89]

While some, such as Brighton, voiced anxiety over the politics of *Serious Money* and refused to call it socialist, or even a political play, others considered its satire to be politically sharp and persuasive. Theatre critic, Ros Asquith, comments,

---

[87] Barry Richards, "Enterprise, Omnipotence and Dependency," in *The Values of the Enterprise Culture*, eds. Paul Heelas and Paul Morris (London: Routledge, 1992), 194-213, 199.

[88] Pam Brighton, "Theatre in Thatcher's Britain," *New Theatre Quarterly* 5.18 (May 1989): 113-23, 121.

[89] British Telecom, quoted in Introduction to *Caryl Churchill Plays: 2*, x; Churchill, Introduction to *Caryl Churchill Plays: 2*, x.

international capitalism is a cesspit, as Caryl Churchill's brilliant, unforgiving and furiously funny *Serious Money* (Royal Court) keeps reminding us. ... It is rare to enjoy a play without a single appealing character, but such is the case here. It's a fault of agitprop, but this is agitprop of Brechtian dimensions, it's so high class you forgive the flaws in favour of the flow.[90]

The degree of balance in the combination of dramatic genres, forms, and styles, including most obviously city comedy, but also, as Asquith mentions, agitprop and Brecht, to some extent informs the political signification of the play.

The short scene from Thomas Shadwell's *The Volunteers, Or, The Stock-jobbers* of 1693 that forms the opening of *Serious Money* situates the play within a tradition of city comedy that dates back to the century of the emergence of capitalism.[91] As well as confirming Janelle Reinelt's ascertainment that "the play's foundation, then, is the Brechtian historicisation of finance," the Shadwell scene also raises the question of how the play is to be read in terms of the comic.[92] Klaus Peter Müller argues that the polarisation in audience reception of *Serious Money* is based on the spectator's choice of responding to the play as either a comedy or a satire; the former represents a new order which is "life-enhancing, fertile and positive in almost all of its aspects," and the latter allows an "old order to prevail" with "the dominating negative society ... not overcome by a more idealistic new system, but ... shown to be absurd," and signifying "clear moral norms against which it is measured unfavourably."[93] Müller judges the play to be satirically forceful, like "a dance macabre," which is "intended to be disturbing."[94] In this way, the City spectators' reception of *Serious Money* as comedy is interpreted as reading against the grain. In contrast, Ruby Cohn sees the satire as threatened by the "energetic rhymes" which "pound home the repetitive quality of corruption, unredeemed by any direct or honest statement."[95]

---

[90] Ros Asquith, *City Limits*, repr. in *London Theatre Record* (26 March–22 April 1987), 369.

[91] Thomas Shadwell, *The Volunteers, Or, The Stock-jobbers* (London: James Knapton, 1693).

[92] Janelle Reinelt, "Caryl Churchill," *After Brecht* (Ann Arbor: University of Michigan Press, 1994), 81-107, 97.

[93] Klaus Peter Müller, "A Serious City Comedy," *Modern Drama* 33. 3 (September 1990): 347-62, 348.

[94] Müller, "A Serious City Comedy," 356.

[95] Ruby Cohn, *Retreats from Realism in Recent English Drama* (Cambridge: Cambridge UP, 1991) 91.

Aston makes a further contribution,

> while those inside the markets may easily read the signs encoded in the different coloured blazers (uniforms) of the traders and understand the language of 'moneyspeak,' the non-City spectator is alienated by visual and linguistic sign-systems; is positioned as 'outsider,' as critical observer.[96]

The rhyming verse that Cohn considers susceptible to an uncritical comedic reception can be viewed rather as buttressing the alienation effects of an unfamiliar commercial discourse and the estranged performance of City manipulators. Aston argues that while the non-City spectator will respond to the satirical force of the play with respect to her/his critical position as distanced observer from the projection of a foreign world, the City spectator engages "in the pleasure of identification, refusing to 'see' the signs which position her or him as the satirical subject."[97]

Meaning is not stable, unified, or uniformly received by all spectators of course, and this applies to all plays, and yet *Serious Money* is exceptional in the Churchill canon for the controversy caused by its polarised reception. Churchill was generally untroubled by the fact that some of the City enjoyed the play, stating that she would have been worried "if *only* people from the City liked it" or "if *all* people from the City liked it," and if they "failed to see that it was getting at them at all." She found the evenings of block bookings from the City less effective than a more integrated audience, as a majority City audience made "them rather self-conscious, and unsure about whether it was alright to laugh at things or not." Churchill also points to "quite a few people who would be opposed to a good deal of what goes on in the City who've come out with renewed vigour for the things that they believe in after seeing the play." She locates part of the cause of the unexpected reception in the fact that "people confuse attractiveness and goodness."[98]

This quality of attractiveness threatens to problematise the play's socialist character. The play's setting is a New Right utopia, where city swindlers live in an enclosed world of shares, money, and trade, but unlike characters in a dystopia, the City dwellers are driven by a tremendous vitality that while analogised to (and determined by) the exploitative logic of the market, are nevertheless represented as playful and energising.

---

[96] Aston, *Caryl Churchill* (Plymouth: Northcote House, 1997), 74.

[97] Aston, *Caryl Churchill*, 75.

[98] Churchill, Interview by Geraldine Cousin, 15-16.

Dystopian characters, such as Winston Smith in Orwell's *Nineteen Eighty-Four* suffer intensely under the bleakness and oppression of the "bad place"; or, like the characters in Huxley's *Brave New World*, they are kept passively content, in this example by the hallucinogen, soma. In contrast, the brokers, dealers, arbitrageurs, traders, and bankers of *Serious Money* drink champagne, snort cocaine, make financial deals, and view their "work" as "a cross between roulette and space invaders" (244). Although Graham Saunders is right to point out that the City perpetrators' "avaricious trickery" lacks the "wit of gentleman rogues" of the seventeenth century city comedies, *Serious Money*, nevertheless remains a sharp and dynamic play.[99] The play's effervescence is frequently mentioned in reviews, such as Victoria Radin's, which describes it as "hectic and exuberant," and Clive Hirschhorn's, which calls it a "dazzler."[100]

Churchill explains her understanding of the attractive qualities of the play thus,

> of course it's attractive to do lots of fast deals and make lots of money. Obviously there's an energy and attraction to that, which doesn't mean that you think it's a good thing. We wanted to create that paradox in the play—that tension between it being an attractive world and a dangerous one.[101]

Part of the attraction is also due to the liberating exposé of the absence of a tangible referent for the signifier "money." Scilla states, "on the floor of Liffe the commodity is money. You can sell money, you can buy and sell absence of money, debt, which used to strike me as funny" (244). This fetish of money is a liberating representation because it peels away the Victorian moral codes that usually validate unequal distributions of wealth, codes frequently utilised in Thatcherite discourses. Moreover, no character attempts to justify his or her actions with reference to an ethical framework. The ideological façade of neoliberalism (that presents itself as ultimately the most ethical system) is treated as a well-known and shared joke that everyone recognises as a charade.

---

[99] Graham Saunders, "The Tradition of City Comedy in Contemporary British Drama," in *Adaptations: Performing across Media and Genres*, eds. Monika Pietraz-Franger and Eckart Voigts-Virchow (Trier: Wissenschaftlicher, 2009), 19-30, 22; 23.

[100] Victoria Radin, *New Statesman* (3 April 1987); Clive Hirschhorn, *Daily Express* (29 March 1987), both repr. in *London Theatre Record* (26 March-22 April 1987): 369; 371.

[101] Churchill, Interview by Geraldine Cousin, 16.

The characters reject conventional bourgeois ethics (as well as socialist and liberal morality) and in the process expose as a myth the socially responsible appearance of capitalism. The Big Bang of October 1986 that saw the deregulation of the London Stock Exchange precipitates the increase in trading free from the pretence of moral codes. Frosby, who tips off the Department of Trade and Industry about Jake's dealings, complains of the changes since deregulation,

> The stock exchange was a village street.
> You strolled about and met your friends.
> Now we never seem to meet.
> I don't get asked much at weekends. (215)

The dismantling of an old, established network is compounded for Frosby by the class make-up of traders in the London International Financial Futures Exchange, "those barrow boys in Liffe you'd expect to see on a street corner selling Christmas paper and cheap watches" (215). While Scilla says, "there's a lot of power still held by men of daddy's class," Jake is considered by Grimes to be "the only public schoolboy what can really deal" (205). Grimes' educational attainment of one CSE does not prevent him from earning "a hundred grand, plus the car and that, and fifty in [his] hand" (204).

Serious Money is careful, however, not to intimate the presence of moral differences between the new petty-bourgeois appropriation of "serious money" and the old capitalists. Duckett, the Chair of Albion, a company considered to be "old-fashioned" and "a good English firm that has the loyalty of its employees and the support of the local community" is equal in greed and ruthlessness to Corman. Duckett complains,

> it's very unfair to be attacked like this. I run a highly efficient company. I've sacked the finance director and the chief of marketing who'd both been with the company ten years. I've closed two factories and made five hundred people redundant. No one can say I'm not a hardhitting management. (235)

His desire to plunder new markets and to accumulate ever-increasing profit dominates his libidinal economy; he confesses, "what I dream of you know is cornering the coffee market. Brazil needs to be hammered into the ground and the price kept right down low" (235). Utopian desire is reproduced satirically in Duckett's yearning aspiration to corner the coffee market. No sense of philanthropic altruism and paternalistic industrial responsibility tempers Duckett's adherence to the logic of the accumulation of profit.

Liberation from responsible and ethical behavioural codes is also expressed through the crude register that dominates the dialogue of the play. The repeated use of "fuck" and "cunt" is momentarily shocking; however, a (hypocritically) polite register is discarded for a raw but more truthful idiom, which communicates through a range of commercial imagery. Even the most private relationships are expressed financially; Jacinta tells Zac, "you're so charming, I'm almost as fond of you as I am of a Eurobond" (300). Recalling the jaunty satire on colonialism in Churchill's *Cloud Nine* (1979),[102] Ghanaian importer, Nigel Ajibala announces,

> One's based in London so one's operation
> Is on the right side of exploitation.
> One thing one learned from one's colonial masters,
> One makes money from other people's disasters. (261)

A lampooning celebration of the exploitation that informs capitalist agency, a celebration expressed through bracing, energetic verse produces sustained moments of anarchic pleasure.

Serious Money might be considered as politically constricted in its sardonic representation of a commercial totality, which precludes the presence of oppositional voices. In this reading, its political assault works through a critical, rather than utopian, politics, confronting the systemic centre but offering no glimpse of an alternative in its silencing of utopian impulses. This, in turn, risks re-affirming the object of attack because of its declination to move beyond this critical paradigm. But then again, the logic of the political satire in the play simultaneously necessitates an engagement with alternative possibilities. The exposure of neoliberal ethical codes to be nothing more than the values pertaining to swindlers, cheats, and parasites in effect obfuscates the trajectory of capitalist reform, and the entire system of capitalist economics is put into question. The play relies upon a shared perspective of the deplorability of this anti-utopian world and an alternative to it is the suppressed utopian other that necessarily insists upon itself.

---

[102] Churchill, *Cloud Nine* (London: Nick Hern, 1989; first published in 1979).

Mad Forest

Students at the Central School of Speech and Drama, London, first staged *Mad Forest* in June 1990. It was directed by Mark Wing-Davey and was subsequently performed at the National Theatre, Bucharest, in September 1990. It opened at the Royal Court Theatre, London, in October 1990 with the same cast. In many ways it can be paralleled with *Light Shining* in terms of its engagement with the subject of revolution. The competing versions of utopia in *Light Shining* are similarly drawn in *Mad Forest* but the committed socialist stance that informs the drama of the former is sifted through a more politically uncertain and exploratory filter in the latter. *Mad Forest* engages with the political ambiguities of Left responses to the fall of the communist bloc and Eastern European revolutions, but it seems to offer little sign of a distinct political alignment. It appears to reflect instead the sense of destabilisation of political binaries and the resulting uncertainty that was perceived by sections of the British Left. Nonetheless, Churchill is careful not to represent Western democracy as transparently knowable or to allow capitalism to appear as a desirable alternative to Stalinist communism.

There are a range of utopian representations in *Mad Forest*. The play opens with the struggle to articulate and communicate. Churchill writes in the Production Note, "since the play goes from the difficulty of saying anything to everyone talking, don't be afraid of long silences."[103] The scenes' headings are spoken first in Romanian and then in English as if from a phrasebook, an action that places language and translation at the forefront of the play's interests. This action works as a reminder that access to others' events and histories must be negotiated by way of a cross-cultural dialogue as opposed to appropriation or assimilation. In addition, the language of the phrasebook is not sufficiently broad and sophisticated to express the content of the scene. It thus adds to the general suggestion in Part 1 that verbal expression and communication between ordinary Romanians has been curtailed and repressed to the extent that audible speech has become functional with more significant exchanges occurring in whispers and in non-verbal communication. Indeed, the audience is often interpellated as the authorities because spectators are prevented from hearing the Vladu family's whispering, whispering that is masked by the loud radio to guard against surveillance.

---

[103] Churchill, Production Note to *Mad Forest*, in *Caryl Churchill Plays: 3* (London: Nick Hern, 1998), 104.

A Stalinist utopia of socialist realism is the subject of Flavia's class in Scene 4 as she tells her pupils, "today we are going to learn about a life dedicated to the happiness of the people and noble ideas of socialism." In great contrast to the opening scene, the stage directions indicate that she addresses her class "*loudly and confidently*" (110). Flavia exclaims, "the new history of the motherland is like a great river with its fundamental starting point in the biography of our general secretary" (110). Paradoxically from a Marxist perspective, Ceauşescu is constructed as the author of socialism and the creator of communism; the presence of "bourgeois individualism" in this supposedly communist narrative is ironically left unrecognised. Flavia continues by explaining that this new history,

> flows through the open spaces of the important dates and problems of contemporary humanity. Because it's evident to everybody that linked to the personality of this great son of the nation is everything in the country that is most durable and harmonious, the huge transformations taking place in all areas of activity, the ever more vigorous and ascendant path towards the highest stages of progress and civilisation. (110)

Ceauşescu is referred to as utopian subject and object, utopian process and goal. Flavia describes him as not only "the founder of the country," but "the founder of man" (110). The Marxist celebration of grassroots, collaborative activity and its critique of privileging personalities and individuals is replaced in the Romanian context by the construction of an impenetrable historical totality, the locus and logos of which is Nicolae Ceauşescu.

Part 1 reverberates with de Certeau's tactics and ruses, which are utopian practices of non-compliance in everyday life. The whispering masked by increasing the volume of the radio is one such instance. Lucia communicates her wish for an abortion to the Doctor by note passing and bribery while at the same time conversing aloud in a contrary strain (the Doctor says "there is no abortion in Romania. I am shocked that you even think of it" [113]). Jokes are used in Scene 8 to disguise a more political exchange in what appears, at first, to be a tale of a car crash between a civilian and a Securitate where a third party starts bashing the Securitate's car. This then turns into a prefigurative expression of the uprising, exemplified by the punch line of the driver, "sorry, I thought it had started" (114).

There are moments when these surreptitious modes of communication are abruptly flouted, as when Radu, who is standing in a queue for meat whispers loudly, "down with Ceauşescu" (111). The queue itself is a transitory space, a sort of fluid no-place with different people moving in and out of it. The ephemeral and transient nature of the space of the queue inscribes it with a glimmer of utopian possibility, which a permanent or more established space lacks. Other characters in this scene pretend not to hear him, and Radu in return looks "round as if wondering who spoke" (111), an action that unites the queue somewhat subversively in its unified performance of ignorance.

A further utopian representation is the spiritual transcendence to which the church purports to provide access. The Angel says to the Priest,

> when people come into church they are free. Even if they know there are Securitate in church with them. ... Even if you say Ceauşescu, Ceauşescu, because the Romanian church is a church of freedom. Not outer freedom of course but inner freedom. (115)

"Inner freedom" is depicted as a utopian state in the context of the authoritarianism that characterises the material world. The Priest says,

> I go out into the blue and I sink down and down inside myself, and yes then I am free inside, I can fly about in that blue, that is what the church can give people, they can fly about inside that blue. (115)

However, this is a precariously escapist utopian prospect. In fact the Romanian Church's political passivity–and in this instance its utopian escapism–extends to its complicity with the Ceauşescu regime. This spiritual access to utopia is revealed to be a deception, a deception that is accompanied by the deliberate neglect of the repressive practices of the Ceauşescu system.

Part 2 is the section of the play informed most by the utopian impulse. Like the Diggers' reclaiming of land in *Light Shining*, the revolution is not acted out but rather reported. Characters that do not appear elsewhere in the play recount their experiences of the few days beginning 21 December. The revolution's indirect dramatisation–through the use of reporting–reflects the resistance to representation that characterises revolution, at the same time as emphasising the revolutionary narrative as a site of contestation. Revolutionary space is figured as liminal, where, through a dynamic process, new identities are refashioned. A student says, "I see a friend and at first I don't know him, his face has changed and when he looks at me I know my face is changed also" (124). The utopian transformation occurs through a collective experience–the student recognises her/his own changed self through the presence and confirmation of the other. The translator, well versed in language-use, declares, "there were no words in Romanian or English for how happy I was" (131). The revolutionary experience is unspeakable; it defies representation, and in so doing, invests fully in the most transcendent spirit of utopia.

The utopian potential begins to disperse towards the end of this section as confusion develops over the details of what has occurred. A struggle over authorship of the revolutionary narrative becomes a dominant site of disputation, as illustrated by the Securitate's report, "in the night the army cleaned the blood off the streets and painted the walls and put tar on the ground where there were stains from the blood so everything was clean" (128). One of the students says, "there were leaflets thrown down from helicopters saying, Go home and spend Christmas with your family" (131). A faction has already established itself as an authority and attempts to take control of the revolution by assuming leadership. Another student reports, "on the 25 we hear about the trial and their deaths. It is announced that people must return their weapons so we go to the factory and give back our guns" (135), and the bulldozer driver says, "I stay home with my family till the 28, then I go to work. They say the time I was home will be off my holidays" (136). Revolutionary possibilities recede as power is rescinded from the thousands of revolutionists.

The opening scene to Part 3 confirms the curb of the utopian with a disquieting dramatisation of a vampire's conversation with a dog. The vampire says, "I came here for the revolution, I could smell it a long way off" (137). This image resurrects Romania's mythical past and in doing so resounds with Marx's comments in "The Eighteenth Brumaire of Louis Bonaparte,"

> the tradition of all the dead generations weighs like a nightmare on the brain of the living. And just when they seem engaged in revolutionising themselves and things, in creating something that has never yet existed, precisely in such periods of revolutionary crisis they anxiously conjure up the spirits of the past to their service and borrow from them names, battle-cries, and costumes in order to present the new scene of world history in this time-honoured disguise and this borrowed language.[104]

Marx makes special reference to the use of imagery from the Roman Empire in the French revolution in order to construct a heroism and tragic dimension that was lacking. Here, however, the vampire is not actively

---

[104] Marx, "The Eighteenth Brumaire of Lous Bonaparte," in *Karl Marx Selected Writings*, ed. David McLellan (Oxford: Oxford UP, 1977; first published in 1852), 300-25, 300.

summoned up, but comes instead uninvited to feed, its presence serving to highlight the absence of post-revolutionary direction and the seduction of tradition.

Mad Forest dramatises the empowerment of people quickly gaining a liberating articulacy through the process of revolution, an articulacy previously suppressed. The appropriation of the revolution thwarts the utopian impulse in the play but the play does not capitulate entirely to a defeatist or cynical sensibility. The limitations of revolutionary consciousness are made explicit in anti-Hungarian chauvinism and racism towards gypsies; however, in what is figured as another kind of utopian space–Florina and Lucia's grandparents' house in the countryside–Florina, Radu, Lucia, and Ianoş talk freely and share their desires:

> LUCIA: A holiday by the sea.
> *Pause.*
> FLORINA: Sleep late in the morning.
> *Pause.*
> RADU: Paint what I see in my head.
> FLORINA: Go into work tomorrow and everyone's better.
> LUCIA: Gabriel walking.
> IANOŞ: Rodica talking.
> *They laugh.* (156)

Hence, although the revolution has been stolen, and re-emerging divisions threaten to undermine the reconstituted solidarity between people, there is nevertheless a renewed openness and confidence that exists alongside the sense of disappointment that revolutionary failure brings.

The Skriker

The Skriker was first performed at the National Theatre, London, in January 1994 and was directed by Les Waters. A notoriously difficult play to make sense of, *The Skriker* nevertheless benefits from being considered in relation to concepts of utopianism. The closure of the play presents the audience with a disturbing dystopian vision of a polluted wasteland. One of two protagonists of the play, Lily (a girl in her late teens) has gone with the Skriker (an ancient and damaged fairy) to what she thinks is the underworld in an attempt to make things better. Instead she finds herself 100 years hence and is faced with an old woman and deformed girl,

> Lily appeared like a ghastly, made their hair stand on endless night, their blood run fast. 'Am I in fairyland?' she wandered. 'No,' said the old crony, 'this is the real world' whirl whir wh wh what is this? Lily was solid flash.

If she was back on earth where on earth where was the rockabye baby gone the treetop? Lost and gone for everybody was dead years and tears ago, it was another cemetery, a black whole hundred yearns. Grief struck by lightning. And this old dear me was Lily's granddaughter what a horror storybook ending. (290)

This "horror storybook ending" is accompanied by the stage directions' instructions: "*the passerby stops dancing*" (291). The passerby has been dancing continuously throughout the play ("*the passerby never stops dancing*" [253]), the movement of which is expressive of energy, vibrancy, and most importantly, continuity. Stopping so suddenly reinforces more acutely the sense of finality of this last scene.

Although closing with a dystopian vision of the future, *The Skriker's* preceding narrative is more complex in its relationship with utopian and dystopian impulses. The first scene is set in the fairy underworld, itself a site of mythical significance, a site that intersects with both notions of the "good place/no place" and the "bad place." In one sense this is a fairyland utopia, an unreal world populated by a fair fairy, a brownie, and the green lady, all benign nymphs, spirits, and fairies. At the same time, however, there are numerous malignant child-drowning and child-eating goblins, fairies, and giants, and, of course, the death portent and shape-shifting Skriker itself. The fairy underworld can be read as a projection of the human imagination or the human collective unconscious and simultaneously as a world external to human experience, a world that exists outside of human morality and one that pertains more to the non-human natural environment. It shimmers with utopian appeal, but is simultaneously forbidding and dangerous. The stage directions describe the underworld as follows,

As Skriker and Josie arrive it springs into existence. Light, music long table with feast, lavishly dressed people and creatures, such as Yallery Brown, Nellie Longarms, Jenny Greenteeth, The Kelpie, Black Dog, Rawheadandbloodybones, The Radiant Boy, Jimmy Squarefoot, Black Annis (with a blue face and one eye). It looks wonderful except that it is all glamour and here and there it's not working–some of the food is twigs, leaves, beetles, some of the clothes are rags, some of the beautiful people have a claw hand or hideous face. But the first impression is of a palace. Skriker is a fairy queen, dressed grandiosely, with lapses. As they arrive the rest burst into song. Everyone except Josie and the Skriker sings instead of speaking. They press food and drink on Josie, greet her, touch her. (268-69)

The self-conscious performativity of fairyland (*"it springs into existence"*) and the emphasis upon singing give it a musical theatre quality. Or rather this is a parody of a musical. The utopian space of the perfect world of the musical is tinged here in the underworld with the grotesque, the grotesque emphasised particularly in the presence of clawed hands and hideous faces.

Music, singing, dancing, and extravagant costumes are forms that particularly lend themselves to utopian expression. They pose an alternative to the more regulatory discourses of speech and writing, and in doing so gesture towards something other, towards something beyond the contemporary moment. These artistic forms appeal to the senses, an appeal that resides in the non-rational, and thus serves to offer an alternative idiom within which to communicate. This alternative idiom can be understood in Marcuse's terms as a glimpse of uninhibited desire that implicates a post-capitalist world in a way more rational modes of communication find difficult to achieve. The fairy underworld can be likened to Julia Kristeva's concept of the chora, "a nonexpressive totality formed by the drives and their stases in a motility that is as full of movement as it is regulated." In many ways Kristeva's chora displays utopian features in its expression of the pleasure drives as well as in its non-locatable nature. Kristeva writes,

> although our theoretical description of the *chora* is itself part of the discourse of representation that offers it as evidence, the *chora,* as rupture and articulations (rhythm), precedes evidence, verisimilitude, spatiality, and temporality.[105]

Indeed, the underworld does precede evidence, verisimilitude, spatiality, and temporality. The problem is, however, that because of the malign behaviour of humans, the fairy underworld suffers from environmental poisoning. Hence, the captivating first impression of this world soon disappears as the audience realises this utopian vision is contaminated. After the first flush of enchantment is over "*a hag rushes in shrieking*" (269). She sings: "where's my head? Where's my heart? Where's my arm? Where's my leg? Is that my finger? That's my eye?" (269). The hag has been chopped to pieces by the spirits. A lost girl warns Josie, "don't eat. It's glamour. It's twigs and beetles and a dead body. Don't eat or you'll never get back." (270). The utopian and dystopian collide in this world;

---

[105] Julia Kristeva, *Revolution in Poetic Language*, trans. Margaret Waller (New York: Columbia UP, 1984), 25-26.

what appears at first to be a charming space of magic and possibility turns out to be a brutal prison of decay and carnage.

The Skriker itself is a difficult figure to locate within a utopian framework. A feminine figure–played by a woman, Kathryn Hunter, in the original production and one that shape-shifts into mostly female characters–she is an immensely powerful presence. As a manifestation of a feminised/ist chora-like underworld, the Skriker seems to bear utopian possibility. Josie talks of being "impressed by the magic" (250) of the Skriker, who can make money appear from Lily's mouth (252) and "*flowers fall from above*" (263). The Skriker's metamorphosis from one human form into another, again, promises utopian possibility because of its participation in the act of complete transformation. Changing into something utterly other, something wholly outside of and different to the self resonates with utopian possibility. A stable and unified self is replaced by a fluid and changeable set of identities that take part in an endless process of transmutation. The transgression of the temporal and spatial (where and when does the Skriker reside?) similarly recasts the figure of the Skriker with utopian potential.

The language used by the Skriker also seems to overlap with utopian linguistic modes. Its opening speech begins as follows,

> heard her boast beast a roast beef eater, daughter could spin span spick and spun the lowest form of wheat straw into gold, raw into roar, golden lion and lyonesse under the sea, dungeonesse under the castle for bad mad sad adders, and takers away. (243)

This resembles the avant-garde characteristics of modernist prose, a prose that also comprises characteristics of Hélène Cixous' notion of l'écriture féminine. Like Cixous' call for a subversion of phallocentric rhetorical structures in "The Laugh of the Medusa"–for women to write their bodies–the Skriker's speech reconfigures the conventional sentence into a pluralistic non-linear articulation.[106] The writhing serpents that constitute Medusa's hair produce an appropriate metaphor for the non-structured fluidity Cixous looks for in a model for women's writing. L'écriture féminine's pursuance of non-stasis in writing and its escape from the rules of logic and rationalism lend it a utopian desire, which threatens to surpass the phallocentric order. The Skriker's speech ("chop chip pan chap finger chirrup chirrup cheer up off with you're making no headway. Weeps seeps deeps her pretty puffy cream cake hole in the heart operation" [243])

---

[106] Hélène Cixous, "The Laugh of the Medusa," trans. Keith Cohen and Paula Cohen, *Signs* 1 (1976): 875-93.

embodies an open-endedness absent in conventional writing. Its sense of the unfinished, along with its dream-like qualities, push constantly at the limitations of realism, and in doing so carry with it a utopian impulse to move beyond contemporary representations.

At the same time, however, much of the Skriker's speech ("slit slat slut. That bitch a botch an itch in my shoulder blood. Bitch botch itch. Slat itch slit botch. Itch slut bitch slit" [243]) lacks the *jouissance*–the pleasure of the eruption of the feminine libidinal economy in writing–that characterises l'écriture féminine. Instead of a sense of enjoyment and bliss that the multiplicities of feminine erogenous zones produce, the Skriker's speech conveys a distinct absence of sensuality, "better butter bit of better bitter but you're better off down here you arse over tit for tattle, arsy versy, verse or prose or amateur status the nation wide open wide world hurled hurtling hurting hurt very badly" (271). The Skriker's speech is joyless, and in being so it falls short of producing a mode of utopian communication characterised by a yearning for an alternative, an alternative beyond the symbolic order of the contemporary social landscape. Joylessness is a pertinent feature because, as Josie suspects, the Skriker is sick, sick from years of environmental pollution inflicted upon the natural world by humankind. Again then, in similar terms to the signification of the fairy underworld, the Skriker's speech resembles a site of collision between the utopian and dystopian.

The Skriker is a complex play that utilises both utopian and dystopian modes. Although it closes in the realm of dystopia, the play as a whole does not reside solely in the dystopian. In fact, in many ways it can be seen to dwell in utopian possibility. *The Skriker* is full of singing, dancing, mime, bright costumes, fantastical images, and magic. All of these form part of a utopian figurative language in the play, a language that circumvents regulatory modes of realism. That said, the play is at the same time a warning of the impending probability of a futureless world if environmental destruction continues. Hence, *The Skriker* dramatises competing modes, representations, and impulses of utopia and dystopia, showing utopian desire to be ailing in an intensely dystopian context.

Far Away

Whilst the climax of *The Skriker* provides us with a glimpse of the future as wasteland because of our destruction of the environment, *Far Away*, first performed at the Royal Court Theatre, Upstairs, in November 2000, dramatises an apocalyptic dystopia of global war with all constituents of the world–including the non-human natural world–participating. Theatre critics concur over its dystopian nature. Michael Coveney from the *Daily Mail* described *Far Away* as "about the end of the world."[107] Sam Marlowe from *What's On* writes, "Churchill's dystopian vision of a world turned against itself is … filled with horror and disgust," he identifies "the Holocaust, environmental issues, ethnic cleansing and the everyday brutality of humanity's disregard for humanity" to be the play's concerns.[108] Kate Bassett from the *Independent on Sunday* describes the play as "politically acerbic" with a "brutally fragmented structure," the fragmentation of which "reflects the irrational social schisms that keep opening up in Churchill's near-apocalyptic terrain."[109] *Time Out's* Jane Edwardes thinks *Far Away* "recalls Pinter's *Party Time*, as well as Orwell's *1984* and *Animal Farm*."[110] However, some critics bemoan the play's opacity. Rhoda Koenig of the *Independent* asks, "is this a play about totalitarianism or ecology and, if so, what is it saying about them?"[111] The *Guardian's* Michael Billington complains, "while I am willing to accept Churchill's thesis that we are sliding into barbarism, I would prefer the case to be argued rather than presented as a dramatic given."[112]

Not unlike *The Skriker*, *Far Away* concludes with a dystopian vision of apocalyptic terror. A long speech from the adult Joan (Harper's young niece from Act 1) closes the play, some of which is quoted here:

> there were thunderstorms all through the mountains. … The rats are bleeding out of their mouths and ears, which is good, and so were the girls by the side of the road. It was tiring there because everything's been recruited, there were piles of bodies and if you stopped to find out there was one killed by coffee or one killed by pins, they were killed by heroin, petrol, chainsaws, hairspray, bleach, foxgloves, the smell of smoke was where we were burning the grass that wouldn't serve. (38)

---

[107] Michael Coveney, *The Daily Mail* (8 December 2000) repr. in *Theatre Record* (18 November 2000): 1574.

[108] Sam Marlowe, *What's On* (6 December 2000) repr. in *Theatre Record* (18 November 2000): 1574.

[109] Kate Bassett, *Independent on Sunday* (3 December 2000) repr. in *Theatre Record* (18 November 2000): 1577.

[110] Jane Edwardes, *Time Out* (6 December 2000) repr. in *Theatre Record* (18 November 2000): 1576.

[111] Rhoda Koenig, *Independent* (2 December 2000) repr. in *Theatre Record* (18 November 2000): 1575.

[112] Michael Billington, *Guardian* (1 December 2000) repr. in *Theatre Record* (18 November 2000): 1578.

Thunderstorms, rats, and girls bleeding from the ears and mouth, piles of bodies, and burning grass form the landscape within which Joan journeys in order to be reunited with her husband, Todd at her aunt, Harper's, house. The final section of the speech recounts Joan's strangely evocative encounter with the river ("when you've just stepped in you can't tell what's going to happen [38]"), the mythical significance of which recalls the abode of the dead, Hades. The rivers Acheron (sorrow or woe) Cocytus (lamentation), Phlegethon (fire), Lethe (forgetfulness), and Styx (hate) make up the five rivers of Hades, by way of which, according to Greek myth, the dead reach the underworld.[113] Sorrow, lamentation, fire, forgetfulness, and hate–the characteristics of the five rivers of Hades–aptly describe the setting of *Far Away's* final act. This Act is a reproduction of Hades, the underworld, a place akin to hell, or at least where the dead await judgement. Whereas the fairy underworld in *The Skriker* is a parallel place, a place that, at times, impinges dangerously onto the human world, in *Far Away* human society has degenerated into a Hades-like dystopia where the dead accumulate and await judgement.

Indeed a deliberate act of forgetting–associated with the river Lethe from where the dead drink to forget past lives–seems to be much to blame for the deterioration of the social order. The exchange between Todd and Harper is focused on the make-up of factions in the war, the changing of alliances, and the necessary ideological adjustments to suit alliance-changing. Deer transform from vicious beasts that "burst out of parks and storm down mountains" (33) into friendly animals with "natural goodness," which is evidenced in their "soft brown eyes" (35) once they form a more acceptable alliance. Political disconnection–the negation of the relationship between causes and effects within the social landscape–pervades the world of *Far Away*, a pervasion that leads to the final apocalyptical nightmare of the third Act. The demise of the collective and neglect of social responsibility have led to a dystopian world dominated by individualism and political severance, the violent effects of which have resulted in a perverse environment where "horses [go] galloping by screaming with their heads made of wasps" (29).

The final Act represents the complete breakdown of cooperation both between and within nature and humanity. Una Chaudhuri insightfully points to Michel Serres's *The Natural Contract* as a possible source for Act 3;[114] she says, "the breakdown of the social contract in the course of the genocidal century leaves us confronting *a different order of violence*

---

[113] See Robert Graves, *The Greek Myths* (London: Penguin, 1992).
[114] Michel Serres, *The Natural Contract* (Ann Arbor: University of Michigan Press, 1995).

than ever before, that of the natural world that we have so long abused."[115] Whereas utopian images, impulses, and processes are merely glimpsed, desired, or imagined in plays such as *Light Shining*, *Vinegar Tom*, *Top Girls*, and *Fen*, the violent reality of dystopia is concretised in *Far Away*. It is brought into view as an all-consuming apocalypse that once materialised, is (like Hades) the final phase of human history. Imperialist war and the incessant misuse of nature have brought with it–not Francis Fukuyama's idea of the end of history where capitalist economics and liberal democracies are proved to be the best systems–but rather the annihilation of human society and the natural world as we know it.[116]

Although *The Guardian's* theatre critic, Billington, complained that the case for barbarism is not made in the play, the sinister characteristics of the first and second Acts lead credibly to the dystopian climax of the third. These sinister features are primarily expressed through a strong sense of social and political disconnection. The setting of the first Act is ambiguous; the stage directions read, *"Harper's house. Night"* (3). Information about Harper and her husband, an off-stage character, is scarce and no reason is provided for why Harper's niece, Joan, is staying there. This absence of an explanatory narrative within which to make sense of the Act is reinforced further in the strange exchange between Harper and Joan, an exchange that produces a sinister sense, although not a clear account, of what is going on. The vision is of a disjointed world bereft of an ethical discourse, the absence of which produces large disjunctions within human social practices. Joan's continual quest for certainty ("why did you have me to stay if you've got this secret going on?" [13]) and moral integrity ("why was uncle hitting them?" [13]) seem to be the last acts of probity in this unsettling environment.

As a child, Joan shows concern for others but as an adult hat maker in Act 2, she seems morally oblivious to the ritualised killings of the prisoners in the weekly parades. Her concern is rather with the wasted hats that are burnt with the prisoners. The audience is denied a coherent sense of the social context in Act 1 although what it does gain, it gains through the young Joan's persistent questioning. However, in Act 2, the adult Joan seems totally disconnected from aspects of her immediate environment. Yet, while Todd stays "up till four every morning watching the trials" (18), Joan does not "like staying in in the evenings and watching trials" (20). This might suggest Joan's distaste for the trials, but elsewhere in the

---

[115] Una Chaudhuri, "Hell in the Heartland," in *Mapping Uncertain Territories*, eds. Thomas Rommel and Mark Schreiber (Trier: Wissenschaftlicher, 2006), 49-60, 52.
[116] Francis Fukuyama, "The End of History," *The National Interest* 16 (summer 1989): 3-18, 3.

Act she shows exclusive concern for the aesthetics of hat-making and for her own working conditions; she says to Todd, "you make me think in different ways. Like I'd never have thought about how this place is run and now I see how important it is" (26). This is a fragmented, disintegrative, and atomised society where events and activities are detached from their wider social implications.

Of all Churchill's plays, *Far Away* is unique in its dystopian character. The glimmer of optimism embodied in the child of Act 1 is in demise in the second and extinguished by the third. Here, the dystopian impulse has triumphed. The atomisation of society has produced a violent world lacking in social and political coherence, a world where disconnection is the dominant social trait. Grand narratives are long gone, but even micro-narratives–modest attempts at producing connections, however minimal, between local events and people–diminish to the point of disappearance. However, the elimination of human integrity in *Far Away*, does not equate with a politics of nihilism. Instead the play is effective in the way that Klaić considers dystopian art to be–as a last refuge for the utopian impulse. The play's vision is utterly insufferable, and as such implicates the necessity of social re-connection, a re-connection that can defend against the political amnesia so central to the world of *Far Away*.

CHAPTER THREE

CHURCHILL'S HISTORY PLAYS:
LIGHT SHINING IN BUCKINGHAMSHIRE AND *VINEGAR TOM*

All men have stood for freedom; and now the common enemy has gone
you are all like men in a mist, seeking for freedom, and know not where it
is: and those of the richer sort of you that see it are afraid to own it. For
freedom is the man that will turn the world upside down, therefore no
wonder he hath enemies.
(*LS*, 219)

Look in the mirror tonight.
Would they have hanged you then?
Ask how they're stopping you now.
Where have the witches gone?
(*VT*, 176)

The History Play

The history play tends to have it both ways. It defers to the authority of
history at the same time as employing artifice and creativity. Herbert
Lindenberger considers the term "historical drama" as incorporating a
tension between fact and fiction, "the first word qualifying the fictiveness
of the second, the second questioning the reality of the first."[1] Historical
drama invites the expectations of authenticity and verisimilitude that the
representation (or re-enactment) of the past implies. However,
contemporary reinvention of historical characters and events inevitably
invites questioning over the "historical truth" of the representation. In
addition, the multiplicity of signification created in the dramatic

---

[1] Herbert Lindenberger, *Historical Drama: The Relation of Literature and Reality*
(Chicago: University of Chicago Press, 1975), x. For a discussion of the
relationship between history, fiction, and truth, see Norman Mailer, *Armies of the
Night: History as a Novel, the Novel as History* (Harmondsworth: Penguin, 1970).

reproduction of the past within a contemporary moment contributes to the problematising of history in the history play.[2] This is in addition to the fact that the partiality of historical narrative tends to become more clearly identifiable in the self-conscious, self-reflexive performance of history on stage. The philosophy of history, historiography, and the politics of historicism thus become subtexts of the history play.

Of course, the history play is not exclusively associated with the expression of Left politics but was reinvigorated with prolific effect in the 1960s and 1970s by socialist dramatists.[3] Brechtian distancing, the challenge to bourgeois versions of history, the recuperation of hidden histories, and the demonstration of how change occurs were all preoccupations of Left playwrights. Richard Palmer divides the "new history" engaged with by modern dramatists into psychohistory, oppositional history, Marxist history, social history, local history, feminist history, deconstructionist history, and postmodern history.

The difficulties in the further categorisation of history plays into subsections soon become evident. Not only do some history plays, particularly Churchill's, engage with several historical approaches (social, Marxist, oppositional, feminist) but they also, at times, move in and out of historical space. *Vinegar Tom* reproduces real historical events and figures (such as the reproduction of a typical witch hunt scenario and the inclusion of the historical figures, witch hunters and Reverends, Heinrich Kramer and James Sprenger), events and figures that are interrupted by fictional contemporary songs by actors in contemporary dress. This dialogue between the representation of historical research and contemporary commentary on it becomes a key feature of the overall signification of the drama.[4] Therefore in order to understand more fully the significance of the

---

[2] This also recalls Walter Benjamin's idea of seizing "hold of a memory as it flashes up at a moment of danger." "Theses on the Philosophy of History," *Illuminations*, trans. Harry Zohn (London: Fontana Press, 1992), 245-55, 247.

[3] Some examples include: Trevor Griffiths, *Occupations* (London: Faber, 1980) about the Italian factory occupations in the 1920s with Gramsci as one of the main characters; Steve Gooch, *Will Wat, If Not, Wat Will?* (London: Pluto Press, 1975) about the peasant uprising in 1381; John McGrath, *The Cheviot, The Stag and The Black, Black Oil* (London: Methuen, 1981), a historical agit-prop covering two hundred years of Highland and Northern Scottish history from the Highland Clearances to North Sea Oil exploitation in the 1970s; Pam Gems, *Queen Christina* (London: Methuen, 1986) about the Swedish seventeenth-century ruler, intellectual, and cross-dresser; David Hare, *Fanshen* (London: Faber, 1986) about village life in revolutionary China.

[4] For discussions of the development of "historiographic metafiction" in novels of the same period, see Linda Hutcheon, *Narcissistic Narrative: The Metafictional*

negotiation between the choice of material presented and the way it is presented, it is helpful to consider briefly some of the assumptions that inform a discussion of historical drama.

The Politics of Historiography

The editors of *Visions of History*, who were part of MAHRO: the Radical Historians Organisation (an offspring of the New Left), state:

> We live in a society whose past is given to us in images that assert the inevitability of the way things are. In more or less subtle ways, politicians and the media invoke history to show that the contemporary distribution of wealth and power is at once freely chosen and preordained. By the same token, past efforts to contest prevailing social and political arrangements disappear from dominant versions of our history–when they are not simply labelled as foreign or dismissed as utopian. Yet there is a tradition of radical history writing that has worked to overcome this kind of historical amnesia. It has sought to rescue from oblivion the experiences and visions of past movements against social and political domination, and to analyse historically the structures and dynamics of domination today.[5]

This articulation of history as a political counter-action to a liberal historical consensus, a reconstitution of hidden historical narratives, and a deconstruction of the past as a static body of knowledge bracketed off from, and independently informing, the present, appropriately describes the perspectives of both the New Left and socialist playwrights regarding the significance of historical intervention.

Historian, John Tosh, describes history as "collective memory, the storehouse of experience through which people develop a sense of their social identity and their future prospects."[6] The interaction between representations of the past and the struggle over articulating the present, forms the basis of Left historical engagement, particularly visible in the 1970s. For socialists, the writing of history from outside of universities–

Paradox (London: Methuen, 1984); Patricia Waugh, *Metafiction: The Theory and Practice of Self-conscious Fiction* (London: Methuen, 1984).

[5] Henry Abelove et. al., eds. *Visions of History* (Manchester: Manchester UP, 1976), ix. The book comprises interviews with E. P. Thompson, Eric Hobsbawm, Sheila Rowbotham, Linda Gordon, Natalie Zemon Davis, William Appleman Williams, Staughton Lynd, David Montgomery, Herbert Gutman, Vincent Harding, John Womack, C. L. R. James, and Moshe Lewin.

[6] John Tosh, *The Pursuit of History: Aims, Methods and New Directions in the Study of Modern History* (London: Longman, 1991), 1.

the traditional centres of history production–is an important contribution to the notion of "people's history" and to the idea of the role of "experience" in writing history. Marxist historian, Raphael Samuel, notes in the Foreword to *People's History and Socialist Theory* how much of this type of history is produced "in WEA [Workers' Educational Association] groups ... in community arts projects, in women's studies groups and in the work of independent worker-historians."[7] Hence, the self-conscious synthesis of knowledge production, experience, and political activity results in a lively interaction between theory and practice. In the conclusion of his seminal book on the 1640s English Civil War and revolution, *The World Turned Upside Down*, Christopher Hill notes "the radicals assumed that acting was more important than speaking." He genially cautions, as well as concedes, "it is a thought worth pondering by those who read books about the seventeenth-century radicals, no less than by those who write them."[8] Although there were useful contributions to a praxis based upon the dynamics of an arduous historiography and a living political practice, there was simultaneous frustration at what Linda Gordon describes as "an inevitable tension between activists and scholars."[9]

Edward Thompson's emphasis on experience, perhaps at the expense of theory discussed in more detail in Chapter 1, was illustrative of another but related tension within Left history. His hugely influential book, *The Making of the English Working Class*, positioned the construction of the working class within a framework that focused on ways in which this class experiences itself through the cultural practices of work, politics, community, leisure activities, and religion.[10] Sociologist Gregor McLennan accused Thompson of depending on "historical methodology" at the expense of "general theoretical issues."[11] Tosh cites Thompson's neglect of "detailed discussion of the transition from one mode of production to another"; because of this he "fails to acknowledge the rootedness of class in economic relations," which leads to his inflation of "the role of collective agency"; therefore, since he is "lax in his theory" he is accused

---

[7] Raphael Samuel, Foreword to *People's History and Socialist Theory* (London: Routledge & Kegan Paul, 1981), xi-xiii, xi.

[8] Christopher Hill, *The World Turned Upside Down: Radical Ideas during the English Revolution* (London: Penguin, 1972), 386.

[9] Linda Gordon, Interview by Carol Lasser, in *Visions of History*, eds. Abelove et al., 73-96, 6.

[10] Edward Thompson, *The Making of the English Working Class* (London: Gollancz, 1963).

[11] Gregor McLennan, *Marxism and the Methodologies of History* (London: Verso, 1981), 127.

of becoming "trapped within the subjective experience of his protagonists."[12] However, as discussed in Chapter 1, Thompson did not ignore or reject theory; he attempted to balance theory and experience against the grain of what he saw as a destructive strain of French poststructuralism, a strain that tended to undermine subjectivity, agency, historicism, and experience. Nonetheless, in focusing so much on a critical rejection of Althusserianism, the under-theorising of experience remained a problem in Thompson's work.

In relation to the impact of 1968, Marxist-feminist historian Sheila Rowbotham states, "the stress was on learning through doing and on the need for experience to be the source of theory," and "it was assumed that your politics were communicated not only through what you said but in what you did and how you did it."[13] Feminism contributed with particular force to the idea of the necessity of politicising all aspects of cultural practice, as opposed to privileging a narrow concentration on work-based issues. This progression beyond the focus of political programmes and constitutions in order to explore opportunities for the politicisation of all areas of social life and cultural practice also meant a move away from (or a development of) firmly held orthodox Marxist principles to an exploratory form of political practice. A certain vulnerability went with this direction, as Rowbotham illustrates, "we could never find adequate words to meet the aggressive question from men in left groups in the early days: 'well what is it that you want?' The dispute is about an idiom of politics."[14]

While Marxist history challenged the traditional historical focus on events and individuals, it was feminist historiography that developed this further in highlighting not only the exclusion or suppression of the female subject in history but also the limitations and modes of censure that characterised the "idiom of politics," an idiom that in turn structured the framework of historical production. The multi-faceted and complex subject of consciousness is one such neglected area. When addressed by socialist historians, women's subjectivity and consciousness tended to be subsumed within masculine parameters. The frequently assumed equation of the interests of middle-class women with middle-class men, and respectively, the trivialising of conflict between working-class women and

---

[12] Tosh, *The Pursuit of History*, 173.
[13] Sheila Rowbotham, "The Women's Movement and Organising for Socialism," in *Beyond the Fragments: Feminism and the Making of Socialism*, eds. Sheila Rowbotham, Lynne Segal, and Hilary Wainwright, (London: Merlin Press, 1979), 21-155, 31.
[14] Rowbotham, "The Women's Movement and Organising for Socialism," 70.

working-class men was an example of this tendency. Sexual politics, the subject of desire, and the analysis of lived personal relationships were similarly constructed as softer, feminised facets of the historical superstructure.

These issues can be seen to be played out with intensity in *Light Shining* and *Vinegar Tom*. Both plays were written and performed in 1976, the year that saw the start of the retreat from the political optimism that had characterised the preceding few years, particularly from 1968. Rowbotham comments in relation to the WLM, "the idea of separation as a political solution became stronger from about '76." She locates the causes of this in the fact that "an unresolved conflict emerged between creating a movement of liberated women and a movement for the liberation of all women."[15] The Left as a whole became more defensive in the context of recession and the resurgence of high levels of racist and fascist activity, and the emerging sense of lost opportunity began to destabilise and fragment Left thinking and political practice.

Light Shining in Buckinghamshire

As mentioned in the previous chapter, the title of the play is taken from a pamphlet written by a group of radical Levellers from Buckinghamshire, who promoted the idea of the abolition of property: "all men being alike privileged by birth, so all men were to enjoy the creatures alike without property one more than the other."[16] But as historians Frances Dow and Brian Manning affirm, the Leveller leadership dissociated the Leveller movement from the views of this pamphlet and distanced themselves from the Diggers.[17] Churchill's (and Joint Stock's) choice of the name of this pamphlet for their play sets up the political tenor of the drama. The play's title is premised upon a dissenting wing of an oppositional movement, which thus suggests that this is not a nostalgic and uncritical celebration of the forerunners of the modern Labour, socialist, and counter-cultural movement. *Light Shining* is certainly an accolade to the seventeenth-century revolutionaries, but it avoids functioning purely as Left-wing heritage by posing critical questions that bring the discourses of the 1640s

---

[15] Rowbotham, Interview by Dina Copelman, in *Visions of History*, eds. Abelove et al., 49-69, 58.

[16] Quoted in Hill, *The World Turned Upside Down*, 117.

[17] See Frances Dow, *Radicalism in the English Revolution 1640-1660* (Oxford: Blackwell, 1985), 79; Brian Manning, *1649: The Crisis of the English Revolution* (London: Bookmarks, 1992), 130.

revolutionaries and contemporaneous 1970s socialist and counter-cultural activists into dialogue.[18]

Light Shining includes numerous fragments of historical material. In A Note on the Production, Churchill states,

> the characters Claxton and Cobbe are loosely based on Laurence Clarkson, or Claxton, and Abiezer Coppe, or Cobbe, two Ranters whose writings have survived; the others are fictional, except for the Putney debates, which is a much-condensed transcript of three days of debate among Army officers and soldiers' delegates which took place in 1647.[19]

Churchill also includes a list of documentary material that consists of,

> *Fear, and the pit* ... Isaiah 24, xvii-xx, *A Fiery Flying Roll* Abiezer Coppe 1649, *All Seems Beautiful* ... *Song of Myself* Walt Whitman, *The Putney Debates* 1647, *The True Levellers Standard Advanced* Gerrard Winstanley, 1649; *The English Soldier's Standard to Repair to* 1649, *The Moderate*, a Leveller newspaper, 1649 and *The sleep of the labouring man* ... Ecclesiastes 5.[20]

She additionally reveals that in the preparatory work for writing the play, "there was a new direction for insatiable reading." She says, "it leaps at me from a dense notebook, Hill of course, Morton on the Ranters, and pages and pages of quotations from the time."[21] This transparency of historical engagement and illustration of methodologies intimates the play's concern with the relationship between historiography and the construction of historical narrative.

The first Act opens with all of the actors singing from *Isaiah 24* "The Lord's Devastation of the Earth." This establishes the millenarian context for the play with lines such as, "the earth is utterly broken down, the earth is clean dissolved, the earth is moved exceedingly" (191), lines that image the present as the time for cataclysmic change. The biblical register additionally provides an instructive preamble to Cobbe's prayer, a prayer dense with meaning as he vacillates swiftly between confession, admissions of guilt and the probing of religious principles. He expresses a

---

[18] The Levellers Day march in Burford, held annually in May, displays, perhaps, a nostalgic idealisation of past revolutionary struggle at the expense of a contemporary revolutionary politics.

[19] Churchill, A Note on the Production, in *Light Shining in Buckinghamshire*, 184.

[20] Churchill, Introduction to *Light Shining in Buckinghamshire*, 189.

[21] Churchill, "Caryl Churchill," in *The Joint Stock Book: The Making of a Theatre Collective*, ed. Rob Ritchie (London: Methuen, 1987), 118-21,119.

sense of moral culpability at his "lust when the girl gave meat last night," (191) but questions the disparity of moral judgement between that apportioned to the "rich men of Antichrist on horses," who swear, and the beggar who swears "when they whipped him through the street" (191). Hill's research discovers that the historical Coppe "agreed that adultery, fornication and uncleanness were sins, but emphasised that those that cry out against adultery or uncleanness in others were greatly guilty of heart-adultery." Furthermore, Hill reveals that the sins Coppe emphasised were "pride, covetousness, hypocrisy, oppression, tyranny, unmercifulness, despising the poor."[22] The character Cobbe in the first Act of *Light Shining* is at an early stage of his political movement towards Ranterism. He begins to question the vested interests intrinsic in the construction of sins, but does not yet display the confidence of understanding that is expressed later in "Cobbe's Vision," a vision that appears to be emblematic of his full conversion to the materialist and spiritualist radicalism of the Ranters.

The following scene entitled "The Vicar talks to his servant (Claxton)" traces several key features in the configuration of power and interest. Claxton, like Cobbe, becomes a Ranter, and the interconnecting sites of the political, economic and religious dramatised in this scene also provide a materialist context for Cobbe's burgeoning critique contained in the previous scene. Cobbe's growing articulacy, including his manipulation and subversion of theological and philosophical discourses provide a strong contrast to Claxton's laconic responses to the Vicar, who controls their "conversation," as is evident in the scene's title. The Vicar's management of the exchange controls not only what, how much, and when, things are said, but also the way in which the exchange is interpreted. Even with Claxton's explicit clarification of his baby's worsening illness, the Vicar repeatedly interprets this differently. His ludicrous offer of an orange for the sick baby similarly confirms his power to determine his own sense of generosity and kindness. The conflict over the determination of meaning through language as well as through non-linguistic means is a conflict that intensifies throughout the play.

The Vicar's religious hypocrisy and abuse of power is shown to be connected to his economic prosperity, and this is in turn linked to his support for the Royalist cause. Political actions are reduced by him to the practice of sins, the Parliamentary cause identified as deriving "from their lusts, from greed and envy and pride, which are from the devil" (192). After having his servant pour him a glass of wine, he exclaims,

---

[22] Hill, *The World Turned Upside Down*, 212.

if God meant us to have heaven on earth, why did he throw us out of paradise? They must be brought before the magistrates and forced to come next Sunday. ... This is a godly estate and they will be evicted if they don't submit. (193)

As his control of the moral and political discourse wanes, the Vicar threatens to evict his disobedient tenants. The irony is further compounded by his consumption of wine and oranges, while at the same time saying, "we all have to suffer in this life" (193).

Eviction and homelessness connect with the following scene, "Margaret Brotherton is tried." She is vagrant, not a particularly uncommon situation during this period. Behind the ordered veneer of the English countryside, Hill identifies the "seething mobility of forest squatters, itinerant craftsmen and building labourers, unemployed men and women seeking work," as well as "strolling players, minstrels and jugglers, pedlars and quack doctors, gipsies, vagabonds, tramps," who tended to go to London and the big cities or other locations where labour was required.[23] Anne Llewellyn Barstow discusses the specificity of women's experiences of poverty and homelessness, explaining that the beginnings of capitalism saw the break-up of smallholdings because of the new economic reality that required larger groups of cheap wage labour. However, "women, who had supported themselves (and often their families) from their gardens and dairies, lost their main source of income, and they could not compete with men for paid jobs." Because of this, many women who were previously financially independent were forced into poverty during the years 1550 to 1700. The changing economic landscape in Western Europe resulted in a significant increase in female beggars, "who so discomfited their better-off neighbours that the neighbours accused them of witchcraft in order to get rid of them."[24] As well as alluding to Brotherton's vulnerability to witchcraft accusations and thus directly connecting Light Shining to Vinegar Tom, this context additionally provides a historical framework within which the experiences peculiar to poor women during this period can be more clearly understood.

Like Claxton's exchange with the Vicar, Brotherton's with the Justices of the Peace is also characterised by disempowerment and abuse. This is particularly highlighted by her muted responses; the stage directions read, "she is barely audible" (193). But this intensifies the focus of the audience's attention on her since spectators have to strain to hear her quiet

---

[23] Hill, The World Turned Upside Down, 48-49.
[24] Anne Llewellyn Barstow, Witchcraze: A New History of the European Witch Hunts (London: Pandora, 1994), 103-4.

replies, which in turn are offset by the blustering, lengthy exchanges by
the other two. She does, however, respond to the question of whether she
is guilty of begging, "I don't know what you mean" (193). She refuses the
terms of their justice, emphasising the artificiality (and political partiality)
of the criminalising of begging. Brotherton's history of moving from place
to place frustrates the Justices' attempts at processing the trial as they
struggle to categorise her. Poverty is considered an immoral reflection on
the character of the poor; the first Justice says, "and we don't give money.
So you can't drink it ... they hear there's free bread and cheese, free fuel"
(194). Her lack of response is given more emphasis (in the form of a silent
pause) when asked why she is not married. Again the terms of this
question construct her as a passive object of patriarchal authority and the
question is therefore appropriately answered by silence, a silence that
indicates both refusal of comprehension and complicity. The symbolic
violence of this mode of questioning culminates in what the Justices
consider the lenient sentence of being "stripped to the waist and beaten"
(194).

The contiguity of religious and political thinking during this period is
clearly pronounced in the scene "Star recruits," which takes place at a
prayer meeting. Star's propaganda for the Parliamentary cause is
expressed through a millenarian discourse, "Christ watch over this meeting
and grant that your kingdom will come, amen" (194). Millenarian
utopianism and political egalitarianism are the ideological incentives to
fight; eight pence a day and a musket are the material motivations.
Briggs's friend is not yet politicised and he asks, seemingly naively, on
which side the army will fight. Briggs's answer–that Star is with
Parliament–is in turn intuitively problematised by his friend's rejoinder,
"he's a gentleman, inne, Mr Star?" (196). This episode forewarns of the
post-revolutionary consolidation of power on the part of Star's class. It
also recognises the value of political insights and knowledges deriving
from the everyday experiences of ordinary people. Briggs's friend may not
have known for which side Star was recruiting, but this ignorance is also
grounded in a class-conscious intelligence that tends to blur *all*
gentlemen's political interests.

The palpable sense that "something's going on" (196), as Briggs's
friend puts it, continues into the next scene, "Brotherton meets the man."
In the context of poverty, homelessness, and cold weather, the unnamed
man says, "if only I knew when Christ was coming" (198). Heaven on
earth is warmth, shelter, and food for the cold and hungry vagrants and
dependence upon Christ coming shows the urgency of the need for change
for the poor: "if only the money would last till the world ends then it

would be all right" (198). Anxiety and desperation increase as they struggle to stay alive: "it doesn't matter not eating if you can drink. Doesn't matter not drinking if you can sleep. But you can't sleep in this wind" (197). This disturbing image of poverty and homelessness resonates with the earlier scene where the Justices of the Peace mock Brotherton's vagrant condition with accusations of lies, greed, and immorality. Hence, this statutory discourse on poverty is objectified as a self-serving ideology, one that bears no relation to the material reality of those subjected to poverty.

The next scene "Briggs joins up" maintains the development of the food motif in the play by counterpoising the malnutrition of Brotherton and the man with Star, the army officer, who is eating meat. Star introduces the nationalist argument of the myth of the Norman Yoke, which claims that Anglo-Saxon freedom and democracy were lost because of the Norman Conquest.[25] Star declares,

> you're a Saxon. I'm a Saxon. Our fathers were conquered six hundred years ago by William the Norman. ... When you join this army you are fighting a foreign enemy. ... Parliament is Saxon. The Army is Saxon. Jesus Christ is Saxon. The Royalists are Normans and the Normans are Antichrist. (199)

Like the Vicar in the earlier scene, Star narrows the field of political signification into polarisations of good and evil, Saxon and Norman, Parliamentarian and Royalist. This is effective propaganda, easily organised into incentives but it is also good preparation for the war in Ireland, and leaves a hierarchy of class and gender division intact.

Indeed, class distinction is upheld and maintained in the army. Added to Star's initial complaint to Briggs for not removing his hat ("as a sign you're as good as me?" [198]), Star says, "you haven't got a horse, I know, so I can't put you in the horse, though there's more thinking men there with hats on and writing their grievances down on paper. But you'll find plenty to talk about in the foot" (199). The preservation of class divisions in the army indicates the Parliamentary leadership's desire to sustain a class hierarchy post-revolution. The leadership's tight management of behaviour within the organisation ("it's an army of godliness. There's no swearing" [199]) is symptomatic of their intention to control the revolutionary movement as a whole in order to gain and maintain post-revolution ascendancy. This act of censure against swearing

---

[25] See G. E. Aylmer, *The Levellers in the English Revolution* (London: Thames and Hudson, 1975), 98.

gains more significance later in the play when the audience witnesses the Ranters' use of swearing as an exercise in radical political practice.

The absence of pre-revolutionary class parity within the Parliamentary camp is repeated in relation to gender hierarchy in "Hoskins interrupts the Preacher." Noticeably prominent in the religious sects, women were clearly attracted to the policy of spiritual equality between the sexes. Keith Thomas notes that the emphasis on a direct relationship with God and individual regeneration were accorded to both men and women and that "once admitted to the sect women had an equal share in church government."[26] Thomas states:

> a woman preached weekly at the General Baptist Church in Bell Alley in Coleman Street, but we also know that there were women preachers outside London, in Lincolnshire, Ely, and Hertfordshire, and as far afield as Yorkshire and Somerset.[27]

However, this prompted significant male resistance; as Thomas says, "even among the Baptists, men showed a marked reluctance to relinquish this sovereignty."[28] The tension between the growing articulation and self-assertion of women, particularly women preachers on the one hand and patriarchal anxiety on the other provides an illuminating political framework for this scene.

The preacher attempts to define and control the discursive parameters within which the politics of revolution can be discussed, and locates the authority of this control in God. Hoskins challenges the preacher's advocacy of predestination by claiming that everyone is saved. This challenge is a refutation of the spiritual inequality that divides and pacifies the congregation. Hoskins' intervention transforms the passive spectator role of listening to and receiving a sermon into the participatory task of entering into dialogue, which in turn democratises the event. This scene closely analogises the contrasting positions within the revolutionary movement; the Preacher attempts to control the revolutionary forces with a view to revolutionising society for one class only while Hoskins promotes self-empowerment and self-organisation for all. The Preacher represents himself as open and accommodating ("it has got about that I allow answers to my sermons" [202]) thereby creating the illusion of democratic debate,

---

[26] Keith Thomas, "Women and the Civil War Sects," *Past and Present* 13 (April 1958): 42-62, 44.
[27] Thomas, "Women and the Civil War Sects," 47.
[28] Thomas, "Women and the Civil War Sects," 47.

but as he only "allows answers to [his] sermon if they are sober and godly" (202), he clearly controls the terms of discussion.

Hoskins' reference to the prophet Joel in response to the Preacher's quotation of Saint Paul ("I suffer not a woman to teach, not to usurp authority over the man, but to be in silence" [201]) was a common practice amongst women preachers, according to Thomas. The democratisation of access to God is promoted in the quotation from Joel, as reiterated in Hoskins' citation of "your sons and your daughters shall prophecy" (201). This in turn serves to undermine the legitimacy of the hierarchical family as well as the structure of society as a whole. Thomas states,

> we do not find an exact parallel in the history of the family, for, then as now, no religious body would recognise it as more than a secular social unit. But we must not underestimate the importance of sectarian claims to limit the father's authority in the sphere of conscience, for it was precisely the supposedly divine origin of his position and his role as household priest which had mattered; in the family, as in the commonwealth, it was religion that had kept the subject in obedience.[29]

Hoskins challenges the Preacher's modes of doctrinal regulation as she disputes the images of fear he depends upon to pacify the congregation, "he's chosen me. He's chosen everyone" and "there is no pit, there is no snare" (201). The Preacher's retort of "get her out" to Hoskins' repeated questioning–with the stage direction *"two of the congregation throw Hoskins out"* (202)–is resonant of the Justices' of the Peace earlier violation of Brotherton. Unwilling to relinquish control or to permit the boundaries of debate to be widened, the Preacher calls upon misogynist refrains to bear witness to his authority, "woman, you are certainly damned" (202).

The brutality of Hoskins' treatment is dramatised further in "Claxton brings Hoskins home." The sight of her physically battered on stage, as Claxton's wife bathes her bruised head, provides the audience with an ongoing reminder of the violent chastisement of unruly women. Claxton's wife is given no more of a name than "wife." Although partly motivated by compassion, she echoes the trial of Brotherton in her repeated questions of Hoskins' marital, habitation, and familial statuses. Indeed, the Preacher would be proud of Claxton's wife's internalisation of his dictums,

> but women can't preach. We bear children in pain, that's why. And they die. For our sin, Eve's sin. That's why we have pain. We're not clean. We

---

[29] Thomas, "Women and the Civil War Sects," 54.

have to obey. The man, whatever he's like. If he beat us that's why. We
have blood, we're shameful, our bodies are worse than a man's. All bodies
are evil but ours is worst. That's why we can't speak. (204)

Hoskins attempts to make visible the real causes of children dying, "they
die because how we live. My brothers did. Died of hunger more than
fever. My mother kept boiling up the same bones" (204-5). While
Claxton's wife expresses her sense of disturbance at Hoskins' and
Claxton's subversive dialogue ("no, don't start. Don't speak. I can't"
[205]), she is simultaneously alert to the threat of physical admonishment
from the church, "I'm not going there if they beat women" (203).

The attempt to make visible the relations of oppression is also present
in Claxton's imaginative political analogies. These begin to theorise the
prophesy in Revelations of the disappearance of the sea, an event that
could be interpreted as a future without exploitation because the brutality,
profiteering, scavenging, and greed that characterise marine life correlate
with the drowning subjection of the lower classes in society. It is
significant too because, although arising from an ambiguity in the Bible, it
introduces a secular political discourse based upon the natural world and
its material, rather than spiritual, environment. Claxton begins to regain
control over the means of signification, "now I think this is why. I can
explain this. I see into it." While not a mature theory, his speculative
insights nevertheless depict the poor quality of life of the deprived and
oppressed, "we can't live in it. We drown. I'm a drowned man" (205).
Moreover this metaphor of corruption, exploitation, and suffocation
signals the necessity for complete change, for a total social revolution.

A further metaphor for revolution is included in the next scene,
"Cobbe's Vision." One of the actors announces and reads from Abiezer
Coppe's pamphlet, *A Fiery Flying Roll*, the vision from which is an image
of rebirth,

I was utterly plagued and sunk into nothing, into the bowels of the still
Eternity (my mother's womb) out of which I came naked, and whereto I
returned again naked. And lying a while there, rapt up in silence, at length
(the body's outward form being all this while awake) I heard with my
outward ear (to my apprehension) a most terrible thunderclap, and after
that a second. And upon the second, which was exceeding terrible, I saw a
great body of light like the light of the sun, and red as fire, in the form (as
it were) of a drum, whereupon with exceeding trembling and amazement
on the flesh, and with joy unspeakable in the spirit, I clapped my hands,
and cried out, Amen, Halelujah, Halelujah, Amen. (206)

This mystical revelation carries with it the trinity of Cobbe's/Coppe's, Christ's, and humanity's rebirth. The separation between the historical Coppe and Churchill's Cobbe becomes momentarily blurred as the historical Coppe's pamphlet is quoted from directly, the quotations of which form part of the story of the fictional Cobbe. Past and present, and fact and fiction are thus brought together in a dynamic performance of possibility.

The richly elaborate language and lofty imagery contained in Coppe's text contrasts with Claxton's more materially grounded metaphor. The former is clearly written rather than spoken language and is suggestive of the burgeoning of different means of communication, including writing, which formed an important part of the political practice of religious radicals. However, according to Morton the historical Coppe was "no doubt, unbalanced, and by extravagance of both of his conduct and language deprived himself of the chance of a hearing"; although, at the same time, Morton identifies "a genuine nobility in much of his writing, not least in the passages where he states his belief in the need for common ownership."[30] Morton also notes that the vision representing Coppe's conversion to Ranterism described in *A Fiery Flying Roll*, which culminates in a voice saying "go to London, to London, that great city, and tell them I am coming" (206), is followed a few months later with "an appeal to the London poor, in a series of sermons in the streets in which the rich were denounced."[31]

The interweaving of radical religious and secular materialist representations continues in "Two women look in a mirror." This scene is a dramatisation of class consciousness, class empowerment, and re-appropriation of commodities, and is a scene where women protagonists are the central agents. This scene provides an additional image of female potentiality to add to the assertive and challenging vagrant preacher and the diffident wife already represented. The spirit of revolution remerges in this scene; the first woman remarks "nothing happened to me. You can take things" (207). Codes of self-discipline, essential to the maintenance of the social order, become exposed as artificial and illusory. Revolutionary alternatives begin to become tangible possibilities.

The final scene before the Putney Debates, "Briggs recalls a battle," builds on earlier menacing forewarnings of betrayal of the plebeian classes by the leaders of the Parliamentary cause. Briggs says "when I hit this boy across the face with my musket I was suddenly frightened as he went

---

[30] A. L. Morton, *The World of the Ranters* (London: Lawrence & Wishart, 1970), 89.
[31] Morton, *The World of the Ranters*, 100.

under that he was on my own side" (208). Briggs's identification with "this boy," a boy no doubt of Brigg's class, is a moment where previously clear boundaries between the two sides are blurred. It signals a transitory confusion over their fundamental differences, and alludes to the similar subordination, and thus comparable interests of lower-class soldiers on both sides. Briggs's revolutionary optimism, however, determines the way he makes sense of this:

> but after I was wounded, lying with my head downhill, watching men take bodies off the field, I didn't know which was our side and which was them, but then I saw it didn't matter because what we were fighting was not each other but Antichrist and even the soldiers on the other side would be made free and be glad when they saw the paradise we'd won. (208)

Star's earlier recruitment speech recurs in Briggs's attempt to make sense of the event. Briggs's sense of trust in the Parliamentary leadership is depended upon now to explain away the unpleasant ambiguities he has in his own mind with regards to fighting men of his own class.

The troublesome forewarning of Briggs's observations is confirmed in the Putney Debates, a scene that serves as the political axis of the play. This scene is where the terms of revolutionary outcome are decided and it also draws on the audience's knowledge of the period. It is a reproduction of an edited version of a contemporary transcript of the 1647 Army Council discussions with known figures such as Oliver Cromwell and Henry Ireton, figures who, unlike the Levellers, do not need to expand their introductions to the audience beyond their names. The fact that these two figures, who have famously dominated this historical period, appear in *Light Shining* only as functionaries of certain interests, works to normalise ordinary women and men as central, albeit subjected, agents in history. It also serves to highlight the fact that the ordinary characters are not party to the political outcome of the revolution within which they have struggled.

The crux of the debate is over who comprises the "people of England" as referenced in the Levellers' "An Agreement of the People." One of the Leveller leaders, Rainborough argues, "all inhabitants that have not lost their birthright should have an equal vote in elections," whereas Ireton's position is, "no person hath a right to an interest in the disposing of the affairs of this kingdom that hath not a permanent interest in this kingdom" (212). This clearly exposes the division between Cromwell and the leaders of the New Model Army on the one side, who fought for the liberation to trade more freely, accumulate capital and property more easily, use labour without restraint and oversee the expansion of the productive forces, and the Diggers, Ranters, and sections of the Levellers on the other side, who struggled for total liberation (including economic liberation) for all. Ironically, the revolutionary leaders appeal to continuity of tradition, and of adhering to commitments, as an argument against sweeping change. Ireton declares, "when I hear men speak of laying aside all commitments I tremble at the boundless and endless consequences of it" (211). The leadership wish to consolidate their political and economic positions quickly, and to swiftly repair the seams of rupture, relying on conservative discourses so soon after their promotion of new and radical ones.

Wildman states,

> the gentleman here said five parts of the nation are now excluded and would then have a voice in elections. At present one part makes hewers of wood and drawers of water of the other five, so the greater part of the nation is enslaved. I do not hear any justification given but that it is the present law of the kingdom. (215)

Sexby adds that many of the soldiers who fought for the Parliamentary cause have no property and thus have effectively been turned into mercenaries. But although the Levellers argue here for political democracy, their defence of property ("that there's property, the law of God says it, else why hath God made that law, Thou shalt not steal?" [213]) distinguishes them from the Diggers, who consider themselves the "True Levellers" due to their belief in literalising economic and social levelling.

Ireton compares a man without property to a "foreigner," "if this man do think himself unsatisfied to be subject to this law, he may go into another kingdom" (215). The majority of the population are thus assumed to be tacitly in support of a social system over which they have no control, since if this were not the case, they have the freedom to execute their wills and move. In using this analogy, Ireton additionally characterises "Englishness" as more pertinently alluding to those who own property, since those who do not are comparable with "foreigners." In response to Ireton's explanation that soldiers fought against a society ruled by one individual in favour of one ruled by the representatives of those with property, Wildman announces, "I have not heard anything that doth satisfy me" (217). The scene is closed by Cromwell who responds to the impasse by moving the problem from the main forum of debate to that of a committee meeting.

Morton states that the Levellers soon realised the Grandees' plan of reneging on their pledge to put the "Agreement" into action in favour of the much diluted "Officers' Agreement." On 20 January 1649 both the third "Agreement" was published and the King's trial commenced, but by the time it was clear that the "Agreement" was not being enacted, the King had been executed. Hence, "with a purged House of Commons the Council of State was firmly in control and the Grandees felt strong enough to do without Leveller support."[32] This allowed for the actions on 28 March 1649 to take place; Prince, Overton, Walwyn, and Lilburne were arrested and brought to the tower.

The opening scene in Act 2, "Diggers," where one of the actors reports the actions of twenty or thirty people living at St. George's Hill in Surrey–actions that include sowing parsnips, carrots and beans, and where Winstanley makes an announcement from "The True Levellers' Standard Advanced" (1649)–provides a counterpoint to the Putney Debates. The scene acts as a demonstration of a political and economic alternative to the outcome of the Putney Debates and further displays the continuation of different modes of political resistance. As mentioned, the Diggers called themselves the "true Levellers" because of their commitment to absolute levelling, a commitment expressed notably in terms of the equality of property called for in the pamphlet, "More Light Shining in Buckinghamshire." There was some confusion, however, over the distinction between Levellers and Diggers, which illustrates that, as Hill states, "unofficial 'Leveller' thought and action went a good deal further than the constitutional leaders, and raised the property issue in ways that the latter found embarrassing."[33]

The Diggers' formation of a community based on common ownership of land, production, and produce, contrasts with the Ranters' focus on theory, ideology, and personal liberty, and is different again to the Leveller leadership's prominence in the army and in constitutional negotiations. The Diggers appealed to the expanding poor, who were migrating to the wastes and commons, to impoverished wage labourers, and to those with little or no land. Manning states,

the Diggers visualised that initially their new society of collective production and common ownership would be established by the poor on the commons and wastes, and that they would not interfere with the possessions of the lords of manors and their tenants but leave them free to continue under the existing system of private property, until under moral and economic pressure they would voluntarily surrender their properties and join the Digger communities.[34]

---

[32] Morton, *The World of the Ranters*, 211.
[33] Hill, *The World Turned Upside Down*, 118.
[34] Manning, *1649*, 116.

Unlike the Ranters, however, the Diggers did not rely on the coming of Christ to implement a liberated society; they believed that God "required human action and worked through human agents."[35] Hence, the Diggers represented a fusion of radical theology and political rationalism that is described by Hill as "a kind of materialist pantheism."[36]

The second half of the scene consists of actors describing the destruction of the community, "we were fetched by above a hundred people who took away our spades ... and taken to prison at Walton" (220). As in the cases of Brotherton's vagrancy and Hoskins' preaching, the Diggers are met with brutal aggression for their activities, "one of us had his head sore wounded, and a boy beaten. Some of us were beaten by the gentlemen, the sheriff looking on" (220). The authorities are clearly threatened by these self-organisational and collectivist activities, activities that circumvent official structures, and activities that additionally implicate the artificiality of differentiated rights to land, property, the means to produce and the yields of production. In this sense, then, these practices refute the tacit consent that Ireton abstractedly summons in defence of his argument for a limited franchise. However, this refutation does not result in the Diggers moving abroad but rather in building alternative communities in England, actions that are not included in Ireton's delineation of the choices available for those who do not consent.

An escalating sense of irreversible political illumination unleashed by the revolution pervades the next few scenes. "Claxton explains" describes his unstoppable drive forward, "wherever I go I leave men behind surprised I no longer agree with them. But I can't stop" (220). "Briggs writes a letter" sees Briggs adhering firmly to his role as agitator and struggling to reinvigorate the militancy in the army against increasing negative pressure from the Officers. Furthermore, he recognises the injustice of war against Ireland; he says to Star, "if I was Irish I'd be your enemy. And I am" (223). Even the butcher recognises injustice in "A butcher talks to his customers"; his fury develops into a surreal attack on the grotesqueness of the rich,

> you're very generous and Christian to each other. There's never a night you don't have dinner. ... You look less like a man needing dinner than anyone I've ever seen. What do you need it for? No, tell me. To stuff yourself, that's what for. To make fat. And shit. When it could put a little good flesh on children's bones. It could be the food of life. If it goes into you, it's stink and death. So you can't have it. (227-28)

---

[35] Manning, *1649*, 119.
[36] Hill, *The World Turned Upside Down*, 142.

A richly poetic challenge to the gross inequality of consumption, this scene also contributes to the existing array of food symbolism. It contains added force by its location in the scene directly after "A woman leaves her baby," a scene where a woman in poverty has to abandon her baby as malnutrition prevents her from providing milk.

However, this development of new political knowledge is located alongside a performance of betrayal and class consolidation. Added to the scenes of post-revolution poverty and hunger, "The Vicar welcomes the new landlord" satirically exposes the resemblances between old squires and new parliament landlords. Star strives to reject the old language and nomenclatures, "Parliament is selling the confiscated land to parliament men. That does not make me the squire. Just as the country is better run by parliament than by the King, so estates will be better managed by parliament men than by royalists" (224). Star's allegiance to the Officers as opposed to the Levellers has been rewarded and he assumes the privileges of a squire in parliamentary clothing. His thinly-veiled perfidy is made to appear as altruistic efficiency as he effectively implies his intention to evict tenants, an intention that is presented as an unselfish act:

> when I say enclose the commons, I don't mean in the old sense, as the old squire did. I mean to grow corn. To make efficient use of the land. To bring down the price of corn. I'm sure the tenants will understand when I explain it to them. (225)

Star's decision not to write off or reduce rent arrears, even though the tenants have maintained soldiers in their cottages, is explained by him to be "in their own interests" (225) since extra money is needed to buy corn. An emerging ideology of progression, efficiency, and benevolence begins to form the veneer that masks exploitation and self-interest.

The final scene before "The meeting" is "Lockyer's funeral," where one of the actors describes the funeral of the Leveller leader, Robert Lockyer. Amidst the mood of tragedy and defeat, a glimmer of hope for the future lies in the "many thousand citizens" in attendance compared to the fact that "King Charles had not had half so many mourners" (228). But melancholy turns into pathos in "The Meeting" as the characters, sitting in a tavern, appeal increasingly to millenarian fantasy in the context of the crushing of their political expectations. Briggs, the lone voice of secularism, expresses an acute sense of defeat: "that man [the beggar of Cobbe's story] will die without his birthright. I've done all I can and it's not enough" [236]). The others, in contrast, repress their political hopes in favour of an uncritical deference to an escapist mysticism. Claxton declares that Christ "will come in everyone become perfect so the landlords all repent stealing the land"; Hoskins claims, "he's coming in clouds of glory," and Cobbe, as a rejoinder to Briggs's scepticism, asks, "do you think God would do all this for nothing?" (234). Their relocation of hope from the sphere of human activity to the realm of divine intervention is a tragic reaction to a shattering defeat and betrayal. Briggs recognises that the mawkish self-denial that informs this mode of expression endangers the revolutionary legacy, "Christ, don't waste those seven years we fought" (238).

However, in this scene there is also an emphasis on the Ranters' counter-cultural practices. Cobbe, for instance, produces a stream of profanities,

> Damn. Damn. Damn. Damn. Damn. There's angels swear, angels with flowing hair, you'd think they were men, I've seen them. They say damn the churches, the bloody black clergy with their fat guts, damn their white hands. Damn the hellfire Presbyterian hypocrites that call a thief a sinner, rot them in hell's jails. They say Christ's wounds, wounds, wounds, wounds. Stick your fingers in. Christ's arsehole. He had an arsehole. Christ shits on you rich. Christ shits. Shitting pissing spewing puking fucking Jesus Christ. (230)

According to Hill, the historical "Coppe was alleged on one occasion to have sworn for an hour on end in the pulpit."[37] Cobbe's repeated swearing gathers momentum and the language and rhythm become energetic and dynamic. As well as contravening codes of decency, Cobbe also humanises Christ, objectifying him in all his human physicality, and projecting him as a revolutionary champion of the oppressed. This refusal of civil decorum, class hierarchy, and religious orthodoxy was perceived as subversive, as underlined by the Blasphemy Act, an act that was introduced in August 1650 and that was specifically aimed at the Ranters' social practices.[38] Hill states,

> it denounced anyone who maintained himself or herself to be God, or equal with God; or that acts of adultery, drunkenness, swearing, theft, etc. were not in themselves shameful, wicked and sinful, or that there is no such thing as sin 'but as a man or woman judgeth thereof.' The penalty was six

---

[37] Hill, *The World Turned Upside Down*, 202.

[38] "Lower-class use of oaths was a proclamation of their equality with the greatest, just as Puritan opposition to vain swearing was a criticism of aristocratic and plebeian irreligion." Hill, *The World Turned Upside Down*, 202.

months imprisonment for the first offence, banishment for the second, the death of a felon if the offender refused to depart or returned.[39]

Hoskins continues to probe the ideological apparatus of social control, "I steal all I can. Rich steal from us. Everything they got's stolen. What's it mean 'Thou shalt not steal'? Not steal stolen goods?" (231). Hence, she highlights the class interests behind the notion of "theft," and thus politicises her practice of it.

Peter Marshall describes the Ranters as "the most anarchistic individuals to emerge in the English Revolution." He writes, "as antinomians, they sought total emancipation from all laws and rules and advocated free love." This meant that they "attacked private property and called for its abolition, and rejected all forms of government, whether ecclesiastical or civil." Their desire was that "humanity would be returned to its original state where there would be no private property, class distinctions or human authority."[40] Morton describes the Ranters as a predominantly urban movement and situates their emergence during "a time of political defeat of the radical, plebeian element in the revolution, and indeed, as a consequence of that defeat."[41] It seems that the positive emphases of Marshall's account of the Ranters as a radical group with revolutionary principles and a belief in, and practice of, personal liberty, are represented sympathetically in *Light Shining*, but the implications of the pathos explicit in Morton's following comments are visibly present too,

> what the Levellers had failed to do with considerable mass support, organising ability, and an attractive programme based on a well considered political theory in a time of exceptional political fluidity was far beyond the powers of groups of confused mystical anarchists, at a time of political retreat, whose programme really amounted to little more than awaiting the day when 'God the Great Leveller' would come upon the rich and mighty.[42]

The Ranters' challenge to conservative codes of social behaviour, which included swearing, pantheism, drunkenness and the expression of sexual freedom is shown to be limited, particularly in the context of the lack of organisational structure, the want of theoretical coherence, and the over dependence on a millenarian discourse.

---

[39] Hill, *The World Turned Upside Down*, 208.
[40] Peter Marshall, *Demanding the Impossible: A History of Anarchism* (London: Fontana Press, 1993), 102.
[41] Morton, *The World of the Ranters*, 111.
[42] Morton, *The World of the Ranters*, 111.

The final scene of the play, "After," is a brief, post-restoration performance of revolutionary defeat and the dissipation of hope. Hoskins thinks "Jesus Christ did come and nobody noticed" (240). She recognises that it was a missed opportunity but is confused over why and how it was missed. Cobbe mentions his blasphemy trial where he "threw apples and pears around the council chamber," adding, "that seemed a good answer" (240). This is his final act of refusal to collude in a discourse that assumes a set of hierarchies, and doctrines he believes to be essentially exploitative and immoral. Answering the charges against him would be to legitimise the trial, whereas throwing apples and pears around the courtroom is both an attempt to construct himself as mad as well as signalling the madness of the charges. Brotherton reports that she stole two loaves of bread for which another woman was caught. Her remark of "bastards won't catch me" (240) vacillates between defiance and defensiveness. The politics of individual acts of theft might be theoretically just, but seem to be ineffective, as well as immoral, if resulting in the arrest of an innocent person.

Claxton speaks the last lines of the play:

> there's an end of outward preaching now. An end of perfection. There may be a time. I went to the Barbados. I sometimes hear from the world that I have forsaken. I see it fraught with tidings of the same clamour, strife and contention that abounded when I left it. I give it the hearing and that's all. My great desire is to see and say nothing. (241)

These lines come from the Ranter, Joseph Salmon's recantation, *Heights in Depths and Depths in Heights*, which was written in 1650 as a condition of his release from prison. Hill states,

> he had a Hobbist vision of 'the whole world consuming in the fire of envy one against another,' from which quietism was the only escape. 'I am at rest in the silent deeps of eternity, sunk in the abyss of silence, and (having shot this perilous gulf) am safely arrived into the bosom of love, the land of rest ... My great desire (and that wherein I most delight) is to see and say nothing.' He emigrated to Barbados, where in 1682 he (or someone of the same name, described as a shoemaker) was in trouble for trying to organise an Anabaptist congregation.[43]

The ending of the play is sombrely ambivalent. Censorship and repression thwart the production of self-expression and communication, and Claxton

---

[43] Hill, *The World Turned Upside Down*, 219 (quotation within from Joseph Salmon, *Heights in Depths and Depths in Heights* [London, 1651], 28).

retreats to Barbados. But although the majority of the audience is not likely to know that Claxton's lines come from Salmon, who appeared to have attempted to rekindle a political spark in the form of organising an Anabaptist congregation, they do hear the line, "there may be a time," a line that gestures forwards, driven by an aspirational impulse, albeit provisionally, and with deference to some future moment.

The fact that *Light Shining* does not close in a swathe of utter gloom is an important gesture towards the production of a constructive dialogue between past and present. Historical reconstruction is performed in complete simultaneity with moments that strongly signify the contemporary. Churchill self-consciously collides past and present narratives,

> the revolutionary hopes of the late sixties and early seventies were near enough that we could still share them, but we could relate too to the disillusion of the restoration and the idea of a revolution that hadn't happened.[44]

She additionally provides specific examples of the actors' observation of contemporary social deprivation as a source for, and a parallel with, that of the past. Churchill explains, "we tried acting out parables; 'vagrants'—the actors went out and observed tramps in the street and brought back what they had seen."[45] The construction of the historical is thus performed in negotiation with interpretations of the contemporary, and historical material opened up in terms of its continuing impact on the present.

In fact, the explicit practice of making reference to past and present simultaneously is visible in most of the vignettes that form *Light Shining*. The squatters and tenants' disputes, the discourses on poverty, the Ranters' promotion of free sexuality, and Briggs's description of war all resounded vociferously with contemporaneous preoccupations. "Margaret Brotherton is tried" contains a mode of questioning that evoked the growing racist discourse on immigration, and echoed Enoch Powell's 1968 "Rivers of Blood" speech.[46] The first Justice of the Peace demands, "tell us about your third cousin's wife's brother who has work for you. No? Or have you been told you get something for nothing here?" (194). The increasing confidence in articulation and political activism by women connected directly with the growth of the WLM.

---

[44] Churchill, "Caryl Churchill," in *The Joint Stock Book*, 119.

[45] Churchill, "Caryl Churchill," in *The Joint Stock Book*, 119.

[46] Enoch Powell made his "River Tiber foaming with much blood" speech in Birmingham on 21 April 1968. See Rodney Castleden, ed., *British History: A Chronological Dictionary of Dates* (London: Parragon, 1994), 269.

The early pay and conditions rhetoric represented in "Star recruits" ("the pay is eightpence a day. Better than labouring. And it's every day. Not day labour. Not just the days you fight" [196]) once more reverberates with echoes of trade union negotiations, industrial disputes, and work conflicts of the day. The Putney Debates is a performance that emphasises the power intrinsic in the structural framework of negotiations. It alludes to a common model of "debate" and "negotiation" wherein unwritten rules and the assumption of a shared understanding of "common sense" are depended upon to reinforce the power of the dominant party. The terms of debate are not up for debate. The modern Labour Party and Trade Unions are characterised by this model both internally (between the leadership and the grass roots, and between differing factions) and externally (the former with establishment forces, and the latter with employers and the Labour Party). The limitations of "negotiating" with a more powerful group, as demonstrated in the Putney Debates, corresponded with modern debates within the Left over the relationship between reformist and revolutionary political approaches, discussed in Chapter 1.

Light Shining dramatises readings of historical documentation and engages with historical representation. It contributes directly to socialist history production as well as addressing some of the silences in that field. Female characters, such as Hoskins and Brotherton, are situated centrally in the drama and are played as equal in historical importance to Briggs, Cobbe, and Claxton. The most potent image of the potentiality of class solidarity is figured as female in "Two women look in a mirror." The history staged is produced out of a combination of different processes and practices. Usurping the conventional bourgeois privileging of heroes and battles, Churchill represents war and revolution as a broad experience that occurs as much off the battlefield and away from Kings and Generals. The historical vision is at the same time, however, inextricably intertwined with the concerns of the 1970s, and specifically with the challenging questions faced by the Labour, socialist, and counter-cultural movements.

Vinegar Tom

Vinegar Tom does not stage a specific witch hunt and does not take place at a precisely identifiable time or a particularly recognisable location; rather it is set "in and around a small village over a period of a few weeks in the seventeenth century."[47] It does, however, include historical sources, most prominently, edited passages from *The Malleus Maleficarum*, and its

---

[47] Churchill, Introduction to *Vinegar Tom*, 132.

authors Heinrich Kramer and James Sprenger, appearing as Edwardian
music hall gents in the original production.[48] Churchill additionally
acknowledges Barbara Ehrenreich and Deirdre English's feminist classic,
Witches, Midwives and Nurses as having "a strong influence on the
play."[49] She also read about the Essex witch trials in Alan Macfarlane's
Witchcraft in Tudor and Stuart England, where she was struck by "how
petty and everyday the witches' offences were."[50] More generally, the
events that initiate the witch hunt in *Vinegar Tom*, as well as the
subsequent examples of "evidence" of witchcraft, are typical of those cited
in histories of witch hunts.

Analysing *Vinegar Tom* alongside *Light Shining* provides a richer
context for both plays and reveals their peculiarly interconnecting natures.
Attempts to discredit the Ranters involved characterising them as demonic.
Morton states,

> in December and January 1650-1 appeared a whole swarm of anti-Ranter
> pamphlets, many anonymous, crudely printed, mostly apparently from the
> same press, and for the most part of the most scurrilous witchhunting
> character. Not only are they full of allegations of obscene orgies and
> suggestions that the Ranters were Royalist agents or concealed Jesuits, but
> such greater absurdities as that the Devil in person attended their
> meetings.[51]

Vinegar Tom extends the persecution and political witch hunting of
radicals in *Light Shining* to a broader and less discriminating projection of
evil onto women, particularly old, poor, unconventional, and sexually
assertive women. It becomes clear, for example, that Hoskins and
Brotherton of *Light Shining* could have been victims of a witch hunt.
Vinegar Tom is in part an admonition to the effacement of women's
political subjectivity in liberal and socialist historiography.

Unlike the sense of "event" given rise to by the revolution, the witch
hunts are sporadic and relentless, covering three centuries, and spread
across Europe. Also unlike the revolution, the witch hunts have none of

---

[48] Henrich Kramer and James Sprenger, *The Malleus Maleficarum: The Hammer
of the Witches*, ed. Montague Summers (New York: Dover, 1971; first published in
1487).
[49] Barbara Ehrenreich and Deidre English, *Witches, Midwives and Nurses: A
History of Women Healers* (London: Writers and Readers Publishing Cooperative,
1976); Churchill, Introduction to *Vinegar Tom*, 129.
[50] Churchill, Introduction to *Vinegar Tom*, 130; Alan Macfarlane, *Witchcraft in
Tudor and Stuart England* (London: Routledge & Kegan Paul, 1970).
[51] Morton, *The World of the Ranters*, 104.

the sense of heroism and progression that both the Whig narrative of the ascendancy of Parliament and the socialist narrative of the revolutionary struggles of the radical sects evoke. The Europe-wide witch hunts are instead the histories of the state-sanctioned massacre and public execution of tens of thousands or possibly millions of (mostly) women.[52] Ehrenreich and English state, "women made up some 85 percent of those executed–old women, young women and children"; according to Anne Llewellyn Barstow, "on average 80 percent of those accused and 85 percent of those killed were female"; James Sharpe claims that "over 90 percent of those accused between 1560 and 1675 of malefic witchcraft in Essex ... were women."[53] Furthermore, Barstow states that most of the men accused of witchcraft "were related to women already convicted of sorcery–husbands, and sons, or grandsons–and thus were not perceived as *originators* of witchcraft."[54] Hence, witchcraft was thought of as something peculiarly female.

Considering the widespread identification of witchcraft and the large number of witch hunts in England, particularly at the time of the increase in accusations during the period of 1560 to 1650, it is surprising how few histories have been produced in this field from within academic institutions. In Hill's *The World Turned Upside Down*, there are five brief references to witchcraft, an example of which is, in providing a context for the significance of rationalist drive in the radical sects, Hill states, "magic and superstition still played a big part in popular thought, as was shown in the brief outburst of witch persecution in Suffolk in 1645."[55] Although the object of Hill's book is not the witch hunts but rather radical religious/political activity in revolutionary England, it nevertheless seems that a practice so prominently and disturbingly intertwined with the politics and social order of the seventeenth century should be given more attention than the brief and rather trivialising commentary dedicated to it. Feminist theologian Mary Daly states,

---

[52] Ehrenreich and English make reference to the fact that many writers have estimated the number of witches killed to have been in the millions. *Witches, Midwives and Nurses*, 24. Barstow estimates the figure to be around 100,000. *Witchcraze*, 21. James Sharpe claims that probably fewer than 50,000 were killed. *Instruments of Darkness: Witchcraft in England 1550-1750* (London: Penguin, 1996), 5.

[53] Ehrenrecih and English, *Witches, Midwives and Nurses*, 24; Barstow, *Witchcraze*, 24; Sharpe, *Instruments of Darkness*, 188-89.

[54] Barstow, *Witchcraze*, 24-25.

[55] Hill, *The World Turned Upside Down*, 364.

it is the custom of historians of the early modern period to omit discussion
of the witchcraze. Usually the omission is almost, but not quite, absolute.
This is more effective than complete nonmentioning of the subject, for it
gives the impression that witch-hunting has been "covered"–which, of
course it has.[56]

Thus Churchill can be seen as extending the idea of staging the plebeian
radical history (usually silenced in Whig narratives) in *Light Shining*, to
representing the particularity and significance of women's persecution and
resistance in history, usually ignored, or at best underestimated, in (male)
socialist narratives.

Churchill provides the following context for *Vinegar Tom*,

I rapidly left aside the interesting theory that witchcraft had existed as a
survival of suppressed pre-Christian religions and went instead for the
theory that witchcraft existed in the minds of its persecutors, that "witches"
were a scapegoat in times of stress like Jews and blacks. I discovered for
the first time the extent of Christian teaching against women and saw the
connections between medieval attitudes to witches and continuing attitudes
to women in general. The women accused of witchcraft were often those
on the edges of society, old, poor, single, sexually unconventional; the old
herbal medical tradition of the cunning woman was suppressed by the
rising professionalism of the male doctor.[57]

Churchill constructs a dialogue between past and present in analysing the
oppression of women. She additionally provides transparency in the
production of her historical intervention, a transparency evidenced through
her display of a choice of a specific theoretical framework for her
historical drama–as opposed to providing the illusion of facts speaking for
themselves.

The play opens with Alice and an unnamed Man at a roadside.
Resonant of *Waiting for Godot*, the absent Godot of Beckett's play is
replaced by the (generic) Man, whose insistence on determining the
meaning of his and Alice's sexual and verbal exchange is also symbolic of
the lack of female ownership and control of the means of signification in
the play. The first few lines of dialogue reveal the Man's desire for Alice
to confirm his fantastical projection of himself as the devil, "am I the
devil? ... They always say, a man in black met me in the night, took me in
the thicket and made me commit uncleanness unspeakable" (135). Her

---

[56] Mary Daly, *Gyn/Ecology: The Metaethics of Radical Reminism* (London:
Women's Press, 1979), 206.
[57] Churchill, Introduction to *Vinegar Tom*, 129-30.

refusal to collude with him ("I've seen men in black that's no devils unless clergy and gentlemen are devils" [135]), initiates a conflict over the power to determine meaning and to constitute the terms of debate. The infamous no-win situation of witch-ducking, made reference to by Ellen towards the end of the play ("I could ask to be swum ... No, why should I ask to be half drowned?" [170]), and which is symbolised in the song "If you float," is the deathly logic of having no access to the means of establishing meaning, and thus subject to the mercy of a justice consisting of an impenetrable misogynistic discourse.

The Man's reference to the Ranters in *Light Shining* ("there's some in London say there's no sin" [136]) provides another clear reciprocity between the two plays. *Vinegar Tom* provides a history that is adjacent to, overlapping with, and informing the revolutionary narrative of *Light Shining*, and thus offers a more complex historical vision and an alternative contribution to the explanations for revolutionary defeat. The solidarity and sexual parity that was gestured towards in *Light Shining* excites Alice ("I'd like to go to London and hear them" [136]) though she would settle for performing the role of "a wife with a husband her master" (136), but the Man is more interested in continuing his fantasy, "will you kiss my arse like the devil makes his witches?" (136). Daly notes the relationship between male sexual fantasy and the alleged sexual practices of witches, as outlined in *Malleus Maleficarum*, asserting that witches often became the depository of male sexual fantasies. The misogyny of such fantasies is signalled clearly in the Man's response to Alice's question of whether he enjoyed watching a witch burn in Scotland, "I may have done" (137).

The next scene establishes Jack and Margery's class identity, an identity that becomes a crucial factor in their initiation of the witchcraft accusations. They are looking forward to economic expansion; Jack says, "the river meadow is the one to get," and Margery replies, "I thought the long field up the hill" (138). The connection between their desire to increase their property and the possibility of Joan and Alice's eviction is made explicit. Jack comments, "I've been wondering if we'll see them turned out" (138); Margery replies, "I don't know why she's let stay. If we all lived like her it wouldn't be the fine estate it is" (139). Macfarlane states,

it seems that population growth and changes in land-ownership created a group of poorer villagers whose ties to their slightly wealthier neighbours became more tenuous. People increasingly had to decide whether to invest their wealth in maintaining the old at a decent standard of living or in improvements which would keep them abreast of their yeoman neighbours.[58]

Jack and Margery's position in the economic structure is illustrated further when Betty arrives, the father of whom is the landowner who inspects the estate. Margery's deference to Betty ("I love to see her. She was always so soft on your lap, not like ours all hard edges" [139]) is equal in intensity to her contempt for Joan and Alice, as she says of the latter, "she's just what I'd expect of a girl brought up by Joan Noakes" (139).

Unlike Jack and Margery, Alice and Joan are self-reflective in relation to their problems. Instead of positioning themselves at the moral centre, they recognise their inscription in an identity of unworthiness. Joan asks "what would I do going out? ... Where would I go? Who wants an old woman?" and Alice complains, "oh mum, I'm sick of myself" (141). While the language of communication between Jack and Margery is characterised predominantly by production relations, Joan and Alice draw on a more personal and affectionate idiom, an idiom that displays a private confidence and trust in each other. Joan's dissatisfaction with the limitations placed upon her by her age and gender, and Alice's sense of frustration induced by the restricted subject positions available to her, are reflected in the song "Nobody Sings." The song locates the construction of female identity in the limiting sphere of the visual and aesthetic, rendering the female subject invisible: "they were blinded by my beauty, now they're blinded by my age" (142). There is also an allusion to the collusion of women in this practice: "I looked at all the women when I passed them in the street. Nobody sings about it but it happens all the time" (141). The song laments the seeming hopelessness of producing meaning outside of a patriarchal framework, as well as implicating women in this process because of their apparent complicity in patriarchal signification.

The following scene further establishes the context for the witchcraft accusation. Joan asks Margery to lend her some yeast, making reference to ancient codes of charity and generosity, "a little small crumb of yeast and God will bless you for kindness to your poor old neighbour," to which Margery replies, "you're not so badly off, Joan Noakes. You're not on the parish"; Joan retorts, "if I was I'd be fed. I should be on relief, then I'd not trouble you. There's some on relief, better off than me. I get nothing" (144). Macfarlane states,

> during the period between 1560 and about 1650 the informal institutions which had dealt with the old and poor, Church relief, the manorial

---

[58] Macfarlane, *Witchcraft in Tudor and Stuart England*, 205.

organisation, and neighbourly and kinship ties were strained. This was the period of witchcraft accusations. People still felt enjoined to help and support each other, while also feeling the necessity to invest their capital in buying land and providing for their children. The very poor were not the problem. They could be whipped and sent on their way, or hired as labourers. It was the slightly less affluent neighbours or kin who only demanded a little help who became an increasing source of anxiety. To refuse them was to break a whole web of long-held values.[59]

Sharpe explains that in a worsening economic context "the old woman seeking alms was transformed from a proper object of charity to a threat to the stability of the village." He adds, "a second strand of thinking would argue that such women were anomalies in the patriarchal order and thus fit targets for the type of hostility which might lead to their being accused of witchcraft."[60] Margery says to Joan, "dirty old woman you are, smelling of drink, come in here day after day begging, and stealing too, I shouldn't wonder" (144), an accusation that seems to demonstrate the play's incorporation of both these explanations into its dramatisation of a credible witchcraft allegation. Margery's reference to Joan's lack of economic independence is coupled with an investment in a discourse that constructs old and poor single women as repellent and disgusting.

Scene 5, again, recalls *Light Shining*. Susan's recital of the evil nature of woman as the cause for pain in childbirth echoes Claxton's wife's conversation with Hoskins,

> they do say the pain is what's sent to woman for her sins. I complained last time after churching, and he said I must think on Eve who brought the sin into the world that got me pregnant. I must think on how woman tempts man, and how she pays God with her pain having the baby. So if we try to get round the pain, we're going against God. (146)

In fact Alice and Susan provide an overlap in characterisation with Hoskins and Claxton's wife. Alice's repeated attempts to escape her subject position, her questioning engagement with her social context, and her efforts to participate in sexual activity as an active subject rather than passive object are all evocative of Hoskins. There is an implicit suggestion through the intertextuality of *Light Shining* and *Vinegar Tom,* that given the opportunity, Alice would become a Ranter. Similarly, Susan is rigidly constricted within the ideological boundaries of marriage and the politics of gender and class relations determined by church dicta, which in turn are

---

[59] Macfarlane, *Witchcraft in Tudor and Stuart England*, 205-6.
[60] Sharpe, *Instruments of Darkness*, 172.

a reminder of Claxton's wife's ideological entrapment and her comparable sense of subjectivity. Susan's mention of the fact that her husband does not like her to swear (145) provides added texture to the Ranters' conscious practice of swearing as a tactic of non-compliance and resistance. Hence, Susan's fleeting reference to this is an example of *Vinegar Tom's* politicisation of private historical space.

In scene 6 Betty is tied to a chair about to be bled by the doctor. Churchill explains in relation to writing *Light Shining* that "there was a scene I could never get right despite rewrites and improvisations, a girl tied up to be bled by a doctor, from Hoskins' early life, which ended up, cut very short, in *Vinegar Tom*."[61] Further illustrating the inter-theatrical nature of the play, this scene additionally contributes to the idea of an impenetrable discourse that dominates and controls the women in the village,

> why am I tied? Tied to be bled. Why am I bled? Because I was screaming. Why was I screaming? Because I'm bad. Why was I bad? Because I was happy. Why was I happy? Because I ran out by myself and got away from them and–Why was I screaming? Because I'm bad. Why am I bad? Because I'm tied. Why am I tied? Because I was happy. Why was I happy? Because I was screaming. (149)

The quasi-Socratic mode of questioning and answering displays, ironically, the full corruption and perversion of the deployment of "logic." The circularity of Betty's speech transforms the content into a mantra wherein internal cohesion and correspondence to the external world cease to matter.

Ehrenreich and English critique the alleged scientific rationalism of the newly professional doctor, which was supposedly in contrast to magic deployed by women healers, "it was witches who developed an extensive understanding of bones and muscles, herbs and drugs, while physicians were still deriving their prognoses from astrology and alchemists who were trying to turn lead into gold."[62] In this scene, the doctor's response is ironic in its appeal to classical Greek mythology for early modern medical authority,

> hysteria is a woman's weakness. Hysteron, Greek, the womb. Excessive blood causes an imbalance in the humours. The noxious gases that form inwardly every month rise to the brain and cause behaviour quite contrary

---

[61] Churchill, "Caryl Churchill," in *The Joint Stock Book*, 120.
[62] Ehrenreich and English, *Witches, Midwives and Nurses*, 33.

to the patient's real feelings. After bleeding you must be purged. Tonight you shall be blistered. You will soon be well enough to be married. (149)

The conflation of femininity and sickness arises in the song that brackets this scene, "Oh Doctor." According to the doctor "woman" equates biologically with weakness and illness, whereas the song locates a woman's difficulty in feeling psychologically and physically healthy ("what's wrong with me the way I am? I know I'm sad I may be sick. I may be bad" [150]), in the social signification of what it means to be female. Malady, melancholy, sickness, and disempowerment characterise the health of female subjectivity.

Scene 7 is where Jack and Margery begin to transform Joan into a witch. They desperately seek a cause for the illness of their calves; Jack says, "would God send all this to a good man? Would he? It's my sins those calves shaking and stinking and swelling up their bellies in there"; Margery replies, "unless it's not God … If we're bewitched, Jack, that explains all" (152). Macfarlane explains, "once a person sought to relate an injury to personal motivation there were three alternatives from which to choose," which were, "blame himself, his neighbours, or God."[63] Jack and Margery select the second option, and reinforce their sense of moral worth in the process: "the devil can't bear to see us so good" (153). Margery's earlier refusal of yeast to Joan, and Joan's consequent cursing of her, supplies the preliminary "evidence" of witchcraft: "devil take your man and your cows, she said that, and your butter. She cursed the calves see and she's made them shake. She struck me on the head and in the stomach" (153). Macfarlane states,

> a witchcraft accusation was a mechanism whereby a person who broke with communal values, and who was expecting retaliation for this, could reverse the guilt. Instead of accepting ensuing suffering as deserved punishment, he could project the blame on to the person who had ostensibly been upholding such values. Thus the woman who went round making demands on neighbours in Essex, and who used traditional sanctions, such as cursing, to enforce them, was the witch.[64]

Hence, the witchcraft accusation in *Vinegar Tom* explicitly reflects the typical historical scenario as outlined by Macfarlane. Daly's historical research suggests "the targets of attack in the witchcraze were not women defined by assimilation into the patriarchal family," but instead were often

---

[63] Macfarlane, *Witchcraft in Tudor and Stuart England*, 194.
[64] Macfarlane, *Witchcraft in Tudor and Stuart England*, 204.

"women who had rejected marriage (spinsters) and women who had survived it (widows)."[65] Joan thus additionally corresponds to the social profile of a witch, as described by Daly, in terms of her cultural indigestibility.

The visit of Alice and Susan to Ellen's cottage establishes the latter as an empowering counterpoint to the repressive practices of the male doctor. Ehrenreich and English state,

> the witch-healer's methods were as great a threat (to the Catholic Church, if not the Protestant) as her results, for the witch was an empiricist: she relied on her senses rather than on faith or doctrine, she believed in trial and error, cause and effect. Her attitude was not religiously passive, but actively inquiring. She trusted her ability to find ways to deal with disease, pregnancy and childbirth–whether through medications or charms. In short, her magic was the science of her time.

In contrast to the doctor's dependence on the bible and classical Greek medical theory, Ellen's reference points are healing and herbs. Her offer to train Alice ("there's all kinds of wisdom. Bit by bit I'd teach you" [155]) demonstrates the popular practice of self-education and the passing on of knowledge in a non-competitive, non-institutionalised manner: "for centuries women were doctors without degrees, barred from books and lectures, learning from each other, and passing on experience from neighbour to neighbour and mother to daughter."[66] Ellen represents a powerful mode of self-expression and autonomy, and provides a possibility for articulation and self-organisation not wholly subjected to, or absorbed by, dominant forms of thinking and practice. She symbolises the possibility of alternative ways of approaching life as a woman, responding to Alice's preoccupation with the unnamed Man in the following way, "clever girl like you could think of other things" (155).

Ellen also has a visit from Jack and Margery in scene 10. Margery explains to Ellen, "we want to be certain" (157) that Joan is a witch. Their identification of Joan's cat, Vinegar Tom, and a rat, as her familiars and imps, draws on a specifically English phenomenon in witchcraft accusations. Thomas describes "the peculiarly English notion that the witch was likely to possess a familiar or imp or devil, who would take the shape of an animal, usually a cat or a dog, but possibly a toad, a rat, or

---

[65] Daly, *Gyn/Ecology*, 184.
[66] Ehrenreich and English, *Witches, Midwives and Nurses*, 18.

even a wasp or butterfly."[67] Another English idiosyncrasy in witchcraft accusations was the idea that the witch had a mark on her body that was insensible to pain; hence, Packer's pricking of Joan, Susan, and Alice in scenes 14 and 15. Thomas explains, "the witch's mark was sometimes thought of as a teat from which the familiar could suck the witch's blood as a form of nourishment."[68] Hence, Goody's remark to Packer in relation to the "evidence" of Alice's guilt in scene 18, "no need to shave the other for she has three bigs in her privates almost an inch long like great teats where the devil sucks her" (173).

This intrusive and voyeuristic practice is symptomatic of the monkish sexualising of the witch. While Thomas claims, "in England the more blatant sexual aspects of witchcraft were a very uncommon feature of the trials,"[69] and Macfarlane concludes, "analysis of the types of offences attributed to witches in Essex showed no sexual content,"[70] Churchill's project is clearly more in line with Barstow's findings, "the emphasis [was] on female sexuality in the trial records and procedures,"[71] and is directly coterminous with the research of Ehrenreich and English, "witches are accused of every conceivable sexual crime against men. Quite simply, they are 'accused' of female sexuality."[72] Jack's return to Ellen's cottage to seek advice over the disappearance of his virility ("it's gone. I can't do anything with it" [158]), identifying Alice as the cause, is an example of *Vinegar Tom's* incorporation of the idea of the patriarchal construction of the witch as a dangerous sexual predator. Jack continues, "I've heard how witches sometimes get a whole boxful and they move and stir by themselves like living creatures" (158).

The song "If Everybody Worked as Hard as Me" is a sharp satire on the relationship between the protestant work ethic, patriotism, marriage, and love. The conventionally private sphere of human emotion–love–assumed to be universal, natural, and trans-historical is shown to be politically charged, "nobody loves a scold, nobody loves a slut, nobody loves you when you're old, unless you're someone's gran. Nobody loves you unless you keep your mouth shut. Nobody loves you if you don't support your man" (160). Love is alluded to as being unavailable to subjects of particular identities or individuals who do not follow

---

[67] Keith Thomas, *Religion and the Decline of Magic* (London: Penguin, 1971), 530.
[68] Thomas, *Religion and the Decline of Magic*, 530.
[69] Thomas, *Religion and the Decline of Magic*, 679.
[70] Macfarlane, *Witchcraft in Tudor and Stuart England*, 161.
[71] Barstow, *Witchcraze*, 10.
[72] Ehrenreich and English, *Witches, Nurses and Midwives*, 26.

established codes of conduct. The politics of the private spaces of love, marriage, and children, are made public and are situated in equal political equation to, and in an inextricable relationship with, the public spaces of work and the national interests of the country. In this way the song is a Marxist-feminist meta-dramatic commentary that critiques the seemingly natural, but power-laden, theoretical frameworks of liberal, and to a lesser degree, (masculinist) socialist knowledge production.

Scene 14 occurs in the public space of the village square. The bell ringer announces, "if anyone has any complaint against any woman for a witch, let them go to the townhall and lay their complaint" (164). Village residents are encouraged to inform on fellow community members and in this way they can project their problems onto nuisance neighbours and in the process purge themselves. The sight of Joan, a vulnerable old woman with her skirts pulled up, being held by Goody with witch hunter, Packer, pricking her legs, is a key image of humiliation and disempowerment in the play. In a visual motif it brings together the various strands of misogynist projection of the woman, dehumanised for being old, female, poor, single and a "scold"; Goody calls her a "stinking old strumpet" (165). Alice is the next victim, and according to Barstow, "mother-daughter pairs were especially suspect, and many were burned or hanged together."[73] A powerful moment signalling the success of witch hunts as a mode of social control is Susan's betrayal of Alice, "I know something of her" (166). The positive dramatisation of solidarity in *Light Shining* is replaced here with fear, division, and disunity, and the result is ritualised executions. The fact that Packer subsequently accuses Susan of witchcraft illustrates the play's refusal to endorse betrayal as an activity that necessarily brings with it self-advancement. Instead this moment is politically instructive in that it presents the lack of unity as a genuine obstacle to emancipation as well as having potentially fatal consequences.

Goody's description of the pay and conditions of witch hunting secularises the practice and makes explicit its economic relations. She says of Packer,

> he's well worth the twenty shillings a time, and I get the same, which is very good of him to insist on and well worth it though some folk complain and say, 'what, the price of a cow, just to have a witch hanged?' But I say to them think of the expense a witch is to you in the damage she does to property, such as a cow killed one or two pounds, a horse maybe four pounds, besides all the pigs and sheep at a few shillings a time, and chickens at sixpence all adds up. For two pounds and our expenses at the

---

[73] Barstow, *Witchcraze*, 142.

inn, you have all that saving, besides knowing you're free of the threat of sudden illness and death. (168)

Paying Packer and Goody to hang witches is described in terms of investing in an insurance scheme or a protection racket. An early anaesthetising sales discourse provides a surreal and grotesque image of the price of (female) human life. She continues, "better than staying home a widow. I'd end up like the old women you see, soft in the head and full of spite with their muttering and spells" (168). It is clear that Goody has made a choice to become a witch hunter rather than leave herself vulnerable to a witchcraft accusation. Her mention of the "old women you see" could be a description of Joan, thus suggesting an ironic identification between the two women.

The issue of women's complicity in their own, and other women's, subjugation is openly dramatised in *Vinegar Tom*. A collective sense of commonality of women's experiences is seen to be problematic. Betty's class privilege exempts her not only from labour but from a witchcraft accusation and Margery's pursuit of economic expansion and social climbing locates her interests as at odds with Joan and Alice, whose welfare depends upon a more communal mode of living. Alice's single status, but active sexuality, is perceived as posing a threat to married women in the village. Hence, other forms of identity, such as class, age, and marital status are represented as complicating factors in the depiction of female subjectivity. Nevertheless, there is a tangible sense of unity in the performance of an oppressed gendered subjectivity of all the female characters, and in this way, the absence of a strategic practice of solidarity is staged as a barrier to liberation.

Vinegar Tom refuses to idealise femininity in its representation of female collusion in the witch hunts but it is unambiguous in its location of power in a system that is based upon class and gender hierarchies. Margery and Goody, the two female characters who act most aggressively against the interests of women, are represented as doing so in the context of their economic interests, a repressed dissatisfaction with marriage, and the stark "choice" between witch or witch hunter. The performance of Kramer and Sprenger, reciting lines from *The Malleus Maleficarum*, leaves the spectator in no doubt as to the contribution of misogyny in establishing culpability for the deaths of so many women:

KRAMER: Why is a greater number of witches found in the fragile feminine sex than in men?
SPRENGER: Why is a greater number of witches found in the fragile feminine sex than in men?

KRAMER: 'All wickedness is but little to the wickedness of a woman.'
Ecclesiastes.
SPRENGER: Here are three reasons, first because
KRAMER: woman is more credulous and since the aim of the devil is to
corrupt faith he attacks them. Second because
SPRENGER: women are more impressionable. Third because
KRAMER: women have slippery tongues and cannot conceal from other
women what by their evil art they know. (176-77)

The tension between the highly contrived and humorous delivery and the
quoted historical material provides a vivid sense of the sinister that goes
someway to articulating the disturbing nature of the justification for the
witch hunts.

Indeed much of what Kramer and Sprenger say in the play is almost
direct, although edited, quotation from *The Malleus Maleficarum*. In this
publication they state,

> what else is woman but a foe to friendship, an inescapable punishment, a
> necessary evil, a natural temptation, a desirable calamity, a domestic
> danger, a delectable detriment, an evil of nature, painted with fair colours!
> ... When a woman thinks alone, she thinks evil.[74]

There are paragraphs in plenty detailing the natural deficiencies and evil
natures of women, and Churchill's edited selection is just a tiny sample.
The concluding lines spoken by Kramer and Sprenger consist of Kramer
explaining, "it is no wonder there are more women than men found
infected with the heresy of witchcraft"; Sprenger replies, "and blessed be
the Most High, which has so far preserved the male sex from so great a
crime" (178). This, in conjunction with the song "Evil Women," the song
that closes the play, illustrates Churchill's historical and political
insistence on placing gender oppression as indisputably central to
historicising the witch hunts.

Unlike *Light Shining*, the historical space of *Vinegar Tom* is
punctuated by songs that are sung by actors in contemporary dress, and out
of character. In this way, the historical material is broken up and shot
through with moments of contemporary commentary that tend to mediate
between past and present constructions of women. The jaunty rhythms of
the contemporary songs offer an alternative to the rhyming couplets of
Kramer and Sprenger but are in a similarly oblique genre that is capable of
containing the dense and intense mixture of horror, anger, and sadness.
The songs can be seen to explode with full dramatic gesture into the

---

[74] Kramer and Sprenger, *The Malleus Maleficarum*, 43.

historical gaps and silences that characterise mainstream historical narrative. They are expressive of the frustration of the double bind to which the events themselves and their continued lack of attention in historical writing give rise. Although the songs clearly serve to confront the spectator with the play's contemporaneous relevance, they also work as meta-dramatic critiques of historiography and the makings of a history play. The songs encourage the audience to recognise neutrality in the writing of history as an illusion, thereby politicising the experience of watching the play. Hence, the spectator is persuaded to take a position on the play's political interventions rather than reside in a space of indecision or impartiality.

Like *Light Shining*, *Vinegar Tom* works more generally as an engagement with the present as well as the past. In the context of political activity by the WLM, the play was peculiarly topical in the mid-1970s. The play's concern with subjectivity and consciousness, sexuality and women's health, contraception, abortion and marriage are all issues at the forefront of concerns of the WLM and women in general. Alice's exchange with Susan reflects a modern desire for new kinds of identities and relationships:

> ALICE: I want a man I can have when I want, not if I'm lucky to meet
> some villain one night.
> SUSAN: You always say you don't want to be married.
> ALICE: I don't want to be married. Look at you. Who'd want to be you?
> (147)

Furthermore, the effects of class difference between the women in the village echoes an area of increasing importance within the WLM, and which became a major cause of debate and disagreement.

Vinegar Tom stages a history that is often trivialised—or even ignored—in mainstream histories and underestimated in socialist historiography. It can be read as a less acknowledged, but adjacent, history to the 1640s English revolutionary narrative, although it contains none of its pride and inspiration. The economic reasons provided for explaining the witch hunts—changing economic relations where mostly old, poor women who depended upon an older, more communal, social and financial system became a burden—problematises the sense of progression bestowed on the then revolutionary forces of capital. The angry tenor of *Vinegar Tom* reflects the continued sidelining of the witch hunts for more than four centuries and its confrontation of the full horror of this practice is also an insistence on rethinking the way this period is articulated.

CHAPTER FOUR

CLASS AND GENDER: *TOP GIRLS* AND *FEN*

What good's first woman if it's her? I suppose you'd have liked Hitler if he was a woman. Ms Hitler. Got a lot done, Hitlerina. Great adventures.
(*TG*, 138)

I've seen women working in my fields with icicles on their faces. I admire that.
(*Fen*, 171)

Introduction

This chapter explores the interaction of gender and class identities in Churchill's *Top Girls* and *Fen* within the context of Marxist-feminist debate. It is divided thematically into three sections, which provide coverage of the main points of discussion concerning the interaction between class and gender subjectivities both inside and outside the plays. The first section looks at the ambiguities surrounding the politics of motherhood. The second examines women's practices and identities as workers, working both inside and outside of the domestic sphere. The third section considers the treatment of gendered identity in traditional analyses of social class and examines the implications of engaging with women as a unified class.

The previous chapter traced a growing insistence in Churchill's work of placing gender oppression at the centre of a socialist vision. *Light Shining* and *Vinegar Tom* in particular, are greatly influenced by the upsurge in activity by the WLM and can be seen to encapsulate a sense of advancing struggle, pushing forward in demands and campaigns. *Top Girls* and *Fen* continue this political trajectory but with differences. In the case of *Top Girls*, a close scrutiny is paid to the impact of class division on the oppression of women, and the implications of this for a feminist politics. As part of this perspective, the politics of contemporaneous feminism is implicitly interrogated. Just as *Vinegar Tom* can be seen as an adjacent historical narrative to *Light Shining*, *Fen* acts out the rural, working-class scenes, which provide the context for the lives of Marlene's family and community in *Top Girls*, a context from which Marlene herself escapes. *Fen* invokes a vision of agricultural, female, working-class culture, which in turn makes comment on the lack of opportunity in both feminist and socialist politics for these women to make sense of, and challenge, their own oppression.

As discussed in the introduction to Chapter 1, Churchill has clearly stated her identification with both socialism and feminism. She asserts that "socialism and feminism aren't synonymous, but I feel strongly about both, and wouldn't be interested in a form of one that didn't include the other."[1] Both *Top Girls* and *Fen* explore the problem of the relationship between class and gender oppression and insist on the importance of confronting both in a politics of emancipation. The political and academic context for these plays coincided with the proliferation of debate concerning the relationship between the origins, forms, and manifestations of the different, although inter-related, oppressions of class and gender, and strategies for liberation from them. From the early 1970s to the early-mid-1980s, there was an abundance of publications that addressed this issue, which arose primarily out of a (Marxist-feminist) concern within the WLM to situate feminist politics within an anti-capitalist framework on the one hand, and on the other, the struggle of feminists within the wider Labour movement to argue for the gender neglect of traditional Marxism to be addressed.[2] However, in 1978 the first *m/f* was published, which included Rosalind Coward's move away from radical- and Marxist-feminism towards discourse theory and a concentration on representation.[3] This was symptomatic of the retreat from grand narratives, Marxist theory, and class-based politics, as discussed in the first chapter. By 1985 the

---

[1] Caryl Churchill, Interview, in *Interviews with Contemporary Women Playwrights*, eds. Kathleen Betsko and Rachel Koenig (New York: Beech Tree Books, 1987), 75-84, 78.
[2] See for example, Juliet Mitchell, *Woman's Estate* (Middlesex: Penguin, 1971); Rayna R. Reiter, ed., *Toward an Anthropology of Women* (London: Monthly Review Press, 1975); Batya Weinbaum, *The Curious Courtship of Women's Liberation and Socialism* (Boston: South End Press, 1978); Zillah Eisenstein, ed., *Capitalist Patriarchy and the Case for Socialist Feminism* (London: Monthly Review Press, 1979); Michèle Barrett, *Women's Oppression Today: Problems in Marxist Feminist Analysis* (London: Verso, 1980); Lydia Sargent, ed., *The Unhappy Marriage of Marxism and Feminism: A Debate of Class and Patriarchy* (London: Pluto Press, 1981); Alison M. Jaggar, *Feminist Politics and Human Nature* (Sussex: The Harvester Press, 1983).
[3] Rosalind Coward, "Sexual Liberation and the Family," *m/f* 1 (1978): 7-24.

search for compatibility between Marxist and feminist frameworks was virtually abandoned with the discourses of poststructuralism and postmodernism superseding this impasse. The de-prioritisation (and arguably the disappearance) of the category of class, as well as of Marxist and socialist discourses more generally, is well illustrated in Donna Landry and Gerald Maclean's assertion in *Materialist Feminisms* that "socialism must be re-invented from within feminism and other new social movements, such as those that contest racism and heterosexism."[4] Terms such as Marxist or socialist-feminism tended to be replaced at this time by the rather more indistinct category, "materialist feminism."

Women and Motherhood

Varda Burstyn discusses the limitations of the available terminology with which to analyse women's oppression,

> if terms like state and class denote inequality, conflict and organised domination with respect to the relations of economic stratification, terms like sex or gender carry no such denotative or even connotative meanings in relation to men-as-a-group and women-as-a-group.[5]

Burstyn's comments are clearly reflective of early 1980s politicised discourses; nevertheless, she is right to identity terms such as "sex" and "gender" as concealing the power dynamics that characterise the social relations that make up these categories. The terms "mother" and "motherhood" are equally, or more, problematic. Popularly signifying the most natural, universal, and trans-historical role, the terms efface the social, political, and economic relations that constitute them. They are, additionally, terms that implicate all women; those who do not become mothers–women who transgress–are recuperated as "barren," or constructed variously as unmaternal, unfulfilled, selfish, unfeminine, and deviant. Consequently, the ideologies of motherhood become inescapably defining characteristics of the identity of all women. Motherhood signifies as self-evidently recognisable and understandable, and is imbued with a capacity for explaining the development of other identities and relationships. Feminists are also confronted with the inadvertent but

---

[4] Donna Landry and Gerald Maclean, *Materialist Feminisms* (Oxford: Blackwell, 1993), 1.
[5] Varda Burstyn, "Masculine Dominance and the State," *The Socialist Register* (1983): 45-89, 49.

inevitable reauthorisation of the ideologies of motherhood each time the identity is discussed, debated, or even named.[6]

Motherhood as a key manifestation of the social relations of reproduction is neglected by Marxist schools, particularly when compared with its counterpart of production in Frederick Engels's famous work. However, *The Origin of the Family* contains passages where reproduction is instilled with at least equal social importance,

> according to the materialistic conception, the determining factor in history is in the last resort, the production and reproduction of immediate life. But this itself is of a twofold character. On the one hand, the production of the means of subsistence, of food, clothing and shelter and the tools requisite therefore; on the other, the production of human beings themselves, the propagation of the species.[7]

Nonetheless, the Marxist tradition has tended to de-prioritise the politics of reproduction, which seems partly to do with Engels's subsequent subsumption of the mode of reproduction under the mode of production (a subsumption that occurs with the advent of private property); to some extent a result of a tendency within traditional Marxist thinking towards biological explanations for women's oppressed identity; and in some

---

[6] Reading gender as a socially constructed category (as distinct from the biological category of sex) can reinforce the distinction between men and women as naturally different and to some extent as biologically determined groups. Christine Delphy makes the following insightful points, "for most people, including many feminists, anatomical sex (and its physical implications) creates, or at least permits, the domination of one group by another. We believe, however, that it is *oppression which creates gender*; that logically the hierarchy of the division of labour is prior to the technical division of labour and created the latter: i.e. created the sexual roles, which we call gender. *Gender in its turn created anatomical sex*, in the sense that the hierarchical division of humanity into two transforms an anatomical difference (which is in itself devoid of social implications) into a relevant distinction for social practice. Social practice, and social practice alone, transforms a physical fact (which itself is devoid of meaning, like all physical facts) into a category of thought." "Patriarchy, feminism and their intellectuals," in *Close to Home: A Materialist Analysis of Women's Oppression* (London: Hutchinson, 1984), 138-53, 144.

[7] Frederick Engels, Preface to the First Edition, *The Origin of the Family, Private Property and the State (*Moscow: Foreign Languages Publishing House, 1954; first published in 1884), 8.

measure a consequence of the masculinist dominance within Marxism as a movement and body of work.[8]

The neglect of motherhood within Marxist thinking is accompanied by a lack of attention to the socialisation of children. Wally Secombe writes,

> Freud's pioneering emphasis on the centrality of the first six years of life for the formation of the adult personality has never been seriously refuted. Marxists, however, in harbouring a healthy distrust for psychological explanation of social phenomena have over-compensated by largely ignoring the importance of child socialisation in reproducing bourgeois social relations. As Sartre has suggested, one would almost suppose from reading many Marxists that a person's consciousness suddenly appears when they take their first job.[9]

In addition to its scepticism towards "psychological explanations of social phenomena," Marxism has also tended towards complicity with liberal humanist divisions of private and public worlds and has not focused enough on the activities that occur in the mode of reproduction and the domestic sphere.

In the 1970s and early 1980s feminists and Marxist-feminists subject the hitherto neglected area of motherhood and domestic work to thorough investigation, including the analysis of its economic value; its position, relationship, and interaction with the economic base and superstructure; and its cultural and ideological significances. "Materialist radical feminists," such as Christine Delphy, discern two modes of production: the industrial and familial; the first gives rise to capitalist exploitation and the second to patriarchal exploitation. The husband's appropriation of the wife's domestic labour within marriage is the first facet of women's

---

[8] Terrell Carver discusses some of the assumptions that Engels depends upon for his account, such as the idea that men are sexual predators and women the passive recipients. "Engels' Feminism," *History of Political Thought* 4.3 (Winter 1985): 479-89; Mitchell states, "the biological function of maternity is a universal, atemporal fact, and as such has seemed to escape the categories of Marxist historical analysis. From it follows–apparently–the stability and omnipresence of the family, if in very different forms. Once this is accepted, women's social subordination–however emphasised as an honourable, but different role … –can be seen to follow inevitably as an *insurmountable* bio-historical fact. The causal chain then goes: Maternity, Family, Absence from Production and Public Life, Sexual Inequality." "Women: The Longest Revolution," *New Left Review* 40 (November/December 1966): 11-37, 20.

[9] Wally Secombe, "The Housewife and Her Labour under Capitalism," *New Left Review* 83 (January-February 1974): 3-24, 15.

oppression, according to Delphy; the second is male control of reproduction.[10] In her groundbreaking book, *The Dialectic of Sex*, Shulamith Firestone, another radical feminist working within a materialist framework, uses Marxist categories and methodologies to establish sex conflict (as opposed to class conflict) as the motor of human history and as the primary oppression. She locates women's biological, reproductive nature as the cause for their entrapment and oppression by men.[11] Marxist-feminists such as Zillah Eisenstein, Juliet Mitchell, Linda Gordon, Heidi Hartman, and Lydia Sargent examine the economic relationship between the domestic sphere (the reproduction of children, who are also future workers and the reproduction of labour power in the provision of domestic work for husbands) and capital, as well as addressing the power relations between men and women.

In addition to analyses of the economic relations of the domestic sphere, such as Maxine Molyneux's article, "Beyond the Domestic Labour Debate," which concludes, "it is the work of child-care which constitutes the most entrapping material relation for women and which at the same time is of the most benefit to the capitalist state," other Marxist-feminists attempt to connect economic relations with the psychological and social impact of motherhood.[12] Mitchell applies the Marxist theory of alienation to motherhood, claiming that "reproduction is a sad mimicry of production." She makes an analogy between the worker's alienation from his product (due to the exploitation and division of labour) and the mother's alienation from her child, whom the mother perceives is a product of her own creation. Mitchell states,

> no human being can create another human being. A person's biological origin is an abstraction. The child as an autonomous person inevitably threatens the activity which claims to create it continually merely as a *possession* of the parent. Possessions are felt as extensions of the self. The child as a possession is supremely this. Anything the child does is therefore a threat to the mother herself who has renounced her autonomy through this misconception of her reproductive role.[13]

---

[10] Delphy, "The Main Enemy," in *Close to Home*, 57-77.

[11] Shulamith Firestone, *The Dialectic of Sex: The Case for Feminist Revolution* (London: Jonathan Cape, 1970).

[12] Maxine Molyneux, "Beyond the Domestic Labour Debate," *New Left Review* 116 (July-August 1979): 3-27, 25.

[13] Mitchell, "Women: The Longest Revolution," 22. Mitchell appears to be drawing on Simone de Beauvoir, who writes, "a mother can have *her* reasons for wanting a child, but she cannot give to *this* independent person, who is to exist tomorrow, his own reasons, his justification, for existence; she engenders him as a

In this formulation, motherhood involves painful contradiction. The reification and sentimentalising of motherhood as the most natural and desirable identity for women masks the unpaid labour, unreciprocated devotion, the strong sense of self-sacrifice, and the alienation to which women as mothers are subject in the context of a capitalist and patriarchal system.

In *Top Girls* and *Fen*, as is the case in many of Churchill plays, mothers and motherhood are placed centre stage. However, motherhood is not the focus of the play, but is rather represented as a pervasive component of women's identities and women's worlds. Churchill assumes the normality of a female populated space.[14] In this way the political focus develops the achievements of *Vinegar Tom*; Churchill no longer represents the struggle for women to articulate themselves but rather assumes a shared agreement in public discourse of the acceptability of female subjects as active agents. Nevertheless, some critical responses to *Top Girls* have privileged motherhood as a major locus of meaning in the play. Churchill picks up on this,

> a lot of people have latched on to Marlene leaving her child, which interestingly was something that came very late. Originally the idea was just that Marlene was 'writing off' her niece, Angie, because she'd never make it, I didn't yet have the plot idea that Angie was actually Marlene's own child. Of course women are pressurised to make choices between working and having children in a way that men aren't, so it *is* relevant, but it isn't the main point of it.[15]

The temptation to read the ethical demands of motherhood as providing an explanatory framework within which to make sense of *Top Girls* seems to stem from the wider social significance with which motherhood is marked. In this sense, motherhood becomes an unavoidable hermeneutic category in the play.

Fen is made up of a variety of representations of motherhood; indeed, several generations of mothers provide the familial context for Val and her children. But as in *Top Girls*, motherhood is not the primary focus of

---

product of her generalised body, not of her individualised existence." *The Second Sex* (London: Vintage, 1997; first published in 1949), 514.

[14] Texts constructing a canon of female writers and contributing to a woman-centred criticism, undoubtedly pave the way for Churchill's work in the 1980s. See Elaine Showalter, *A Literature of their Own: British Women Novelists from Brontë to Lessing* (London: Princeton University Press, 1977).

[15] Churchill, Interview, in *Interviews with Contemporary Women Playwrights*, eds. Betsko and Koenig, 77-78.

exploration. It is instead represented as part of the specifically female set of social relations that keep women caught within a cycle of poverty and a paradoxical matrix of affection, love, and happiness, combined with pain, frustration, and misery. Val's predicament, which forms the crux of the story, is one that bluntly establishes Marlene's belief in "choice" as illusory, as Val fails to achieve fulfilment and happiness either inside or outside of the sphere of motherhood. The desperation of Val's response to the absence of meaningful choices available to her connects with the intolerability of the vision that closes *Top Girls*.

The differing images of motherhood in *Fen* combine to express the extent to which women are constituted by discourses on motherhood; "I'd never have left you, Val" (160) says May to her daughter in her continuation of the tradition of self-sacrifice in motherhood. Angela abuses her stepdaughter, Becky, in a sadomasochistic expression of cruel rejection and intimate connection. In a scene that begins antagonistically but closes in mutual laughter, Angela says to her, "Becky, why do you like me? I don't want you to like me" (184). Margaret, who becomes an alcoholic because of the death of her young daughter, is saved by God who sends her a sign. The son of her friend, Mavis, asks for more jam; the letters M for her own name, Margaret, and J for Jesus confirm to Margaret that she has been religiously called, the pathos of which is reinforced by her friend, Alice, and the Baptist women's meeting, who endorse the legitimacy of the "sign." While minding one of her baby grandchildren, Shirley, a fifty-year-old grandmother with a sixteen-year-old granddaughter, says to Val, "you expect too much Val. Till Susan was fifteen I never went out" (169).

Paradox and contradiction characterise the dinner party guests' interaction with their own relationships to motherhood in the first Act of *Top Girls*. Pope Joan denudes pregnancy and childbirth; after interpreting labour pains as a stomach upset, she finally realises what is happening, "the baby just slid out on to the road" (71). The libertarian sense of pleasure at demythologising the clichéd naturalness of childbirth, accompanied by jokes and laughter from the others ("the cardinals won't have known where to put themselves" [71]) produces a sustained moment of anarchic delight shared by actors and audience alike. But the consequence of committing such a cardinal sin ("women, children and lunatics can't be Pope" [69]) is brutal punishment; Joan concludes her story, "they took me by the feet and dragged me out of town and stoned me to death" (71). Clearly, Joan is executed because she usurps the male role of Pope and in doing so subverts the law of the father, but in denaturalising pregnancy and childbirth, and indeed in her exposure of the fragility of the sex/gender construction, Joan must also be censured. The silence in the theatre that usually follows the disturbing end to Joan's speech seems to be reflective of the inadequacy of available responses to such misogynist violence.

An uncompromising adjudication of motherly conduct in public discourse is replaced in this Act with a more ethically nuanced construction of motherhood. The shock at Patient Griselda's acceptance of the removal of her children competes with the mitigating circumstances of her required, albeit "chosen," obedience to her husband. Nijo's connection with this experience ("No, I understand. Of course you had to, he was your life") contrasts with Marlene's ("Walter was bonkers") and Gret's ("bastard" [77]), which, although critical of Griselda's obedience, clearly place the blame on Walter. Isabella's diplomatic response ("I can see you were doing what you thought was your duty. But didn't it make you ill?" [77]) attempts to probe further while still focusing on Griselda's well-being. Clearly, some of the women reveal immense complicity with sexist systems, such as Griselda's conscious acceptance of obeying her husband and Nijo's willing participation in the Emperor's patriarchal order. Nonetheless, attempts to understand, and connect with, the emotional labyrinth of motherhood–as opposed to adjudicating motherly conduct–is the pervasive characteristic of the interactions between these women.

In both plays women who do not have children are in varying degrees signified in terms of their negation of motherhood. Isabella in *Top Girls* displays a conventionally masculine desire for travel and adventures, and is herself aware of the way that this affects her gendered identity, "I always travelled as a lady and I repudiated strongly any suggestion in the press that I was other than feminine" (62). Her repeated references to her sister, Hennie, as her "own pet" (65), whom she leaves at home, are susceptible to the suggestion of a displaced maternal structure of feeling that acts as a substitute for "real" motherhood. The interviewees in the employment agency, Jeanine and Louise, figure to some extent in terms of their relationship to motherhood and marriage. Jeanine's employment options are considered in the context of Marlene's assumption that she will have children in the future, whereas Louise "pass[es] as a man at work" (106), a fact that seems to complement her implied single and childless status, "I've lived for that company, I've given my life really you could say because I haven't had a great deal of social life, I've worked in the evenings" (105-6). The power of motherhood to shape identity encourages an audience to view work as Louise's surrogate family.

The "tough bird[s]" (102), Win and Nell, also signify in opposition to motherhood and domesticity. Nell refuses "to play house, not even in

Ascot" (102) and her rejection of maternity seems to connect with her conventionally masculinist preoccupation with the hard sell, "I can sell anything, I've sold in three continents, and I'm jolly as they come but I'm not very nice" (115). Win appears less able to pursue the seemingly unproblematic individualism that characterises the employment agency, as illustrated in her bout of psychological ill-health on returning from America, "I came home, went bonkers for a bit, thought I was five different people" (119). Her attempt to live outside of the circuit of domesticity and motherhood is not straightforwardly successful. The struggle to perform a positive sense of autonomy outside of maternal discourses is a key dimension of the characterisation of both of these women.

In *Fen*, Angela embodies characteristics of the archetypal wicked stepmother. The ideology of motherhood, constructed in part from the seamless linkage between biology, nature, and social behaviour, consigns the stepmother to the margins of this identity. It constantly reiterates her biological fraudulence as she attempts to perform an authentic motherly role, while simultaneously judging her on her ability to do so. The stepmother is thus caught in an oscillation between the reminder of her illegitimacy as a mother and the coercion to perform a motherly role to her partner's child. The deep resonance of the significance of fairytale characters, such as the wicked stepmother in Cinderella, who is among the first figurative social roles imparted to children, places the stepmother in the category of deviant women, and who in turn can be included amongst the targets of attack in *Vinegar Tom*. In fact a faint reverberation of the witch hunts is tangible in Becky's rejoinder to Angela's abusive behaviour, "I'll tell someone. You'll be put in prison, you'll be burnt" (154). Angela forces Becky to drink hot water, burning her in the process, which alludes to the practice in British prisons of scalding prisoners with cups of hot water, but it simultaneously recalls Mary Daly's discussion of the breaking of the mother/daughter bond, where the latter is encouraged to inform on the former in witch hunt trials, and watch her hang or burn.

Angela's failure to fulfil the (unattainable) expectations of step-motherhood is illustrated in the following exchange with Becky:

BECKY: Can I sit down now, Angela?
ANGELA: No, because you asked. Drink it standing up. And you didn't call me mum.
BECKY: You're not, that's why.
ANGELA: Wouldn't want to be the mother of a filthy little cow like you. Pity you didn't die with her. (153)

The responsibility Angela has for the care of Becky is not rewarded with the respect, however partial and illusory, paid to biological mothers. The degree of authority that biological mothers are granted in the domestic sphere is missing in Angela's role as a stepmother and this brings with it an acute sense of disempowerment, a disempowerment that precipitates abuse of the teenage girl.

Nell, in *Fen*, is a more positive, dynamic, and progressive character, particularly in terms of her partial success at sustaining an autonomous identity outside of the social relations of motherhood. The forty-year-old agricultural worker, unlike "top girls" Marlene, Nell, and Win, identifies with the collective as opposed to the individual, and her concern for fellow workers and the wider community, contrasts with the privileging of motherhood and the family that characterises May and Shirley. *Fen's* Nell suffers, however, through experiencing the isolation that attends the contravention of deep-rooted behavioural expectations of women. Her femininity is also questioned as the children, Becky, Deb, and Shona discuss whether she is a man, deciding instead that she must be a "morphrodite" (155). *Vinegar Tom* momentarily resurfaces when Shona asks, "is she a witch?" (155). The significance of Nell's non-participation in the expected relations of marriage and motherhood is suddenly brought into sharp relief, as the audience witnesses the girls turning on her with the garden hoe, "kill you with the hoe. You're horrible" (156).

The ideological reification of motherhood provides an important context within which *Top Girls'* Marlene and *Fen's* Val figure. Both Marlene and Val attempt to escape, what Alison Jaggar describes as, "the pervasive and suffocating ideology of the family," which "sentimentalises mother love as the highest, because the most self-sacrificing, form of love."[16] However, both fail in varying degrees to negotiate this challenge successfully. Val's failure is total, resulting in her death. Unable to live apart from her children or her lover she kills herself with Frank's help. She finds it impossible to reconfigure her identity outside of the restricted confines of motherhood and marriage and thus feels fixed in a limiting role, "it's like thick nothing. I can't get on. Makes my arms and legs heavy" (172). Her desire to form relationships outside of the family unit threatens to undermine this unit and she is censured by her community for attempting to do so. The Baptist Alice, who is a disappointing successor to the religious radicals in *Light Shining*, says, "I know she's wicked but she's still my friend," and Angela says, "she's the one acting funny. Leave her own kiddies. If I had my own kiddies I wouldn't leave them" (164).

---

[16] Jaggar, *Feminist Politics and Human Nature*, 153.

Private ownership of children, where parents, and often the mother in particular, bear exclusive responsibility for the child's care and upbringing is the specific context within which the fraudulence of Angela's motherhood is maintained and Val's actions deemed deplorable.[17]

Marlene clearly fares better than Val and achieves success as a businesswoman. However, she is only able to attain this success by transferring her responsibilities as a mother to her sister, and neglecting both her sister and her daughter/niece. Her visit to them after six years evokes the performance of the absent father, who hands out presents to compensate for his lack of responsibility. It is noticeable, too, how Marlene suppresses this part of her life, presumably and partly in order to be able to avoid the castigation that Val experiences in *Fen*. In response to Isabella's question of whether she has a sister, Marlene answers "yes *in fact*" [my italics] (56), and later in Scene 3, Nell asks Win about Marlene's family, "what's she got, brother, sister? She never talks about her family" (120). Marlene's self-representation is one that excludes familial bonds and this extends to a more general repression of the personal sphere. While the audience hears of Win's weekend away with her married lover and Nell's flings, Marlene's dinner party celebration is a fantasy and we are left with the impression that she spent the weekend alone. The erasure of motherhood from her identity seems to be accompanied by a more general evasion of the personal.

Val and Marlene's challenges to the ideologies of motherhood arise from different political impulses. Val cannot comply with the insistence on the exclusive nature of love and the demand for self-sacrifice. Her emotional aspirations extend beyond this to include others in a non-competitive form. However, her desire for affection and love for others outside of the family unit is shown to be problematic,

VAL: Can't you give me a hug without Jesus?
ALICE: Of course not, we love better in Jesus.
VAL: I'd rather take valium. (176)

In contrast to her mother, Val attempts to break the mother/daughter cycle of self-sacrifice and martyrdom, saying to her daughter, "Shona, when you grow up I hope you're happy" (185). Her inability "to get used to how

---

[17] This issue is pursued in Churchill's *Owners* (1972), where Alec's belief in Zen philosophy prompts him to challenge the privatised, individualistic values of capitalist society and results in him attempting to save someone else's baby from a fire and dying in the process. See Churchill, *Owners*, in *Caryl Churchill Plays: 1* (London: Methuen, 1985), 1-67.

things are" (179), and her subsequent suicide capture the sense of tragedy that is a consequence of the self-negating expectations of female behaviour.

Marlene's departure from her family is partly connected to her Thatcherite values; "I believe in the individual" (138), she announces as an explanation for her political allegiances. It is also associated with her perception of what her life would have been like if she had stayed in the Fens, "what was I going to do? Marry a dairyman who'd come home pissed? Don't you fucking this fucking that fucking bitch fucking tell me what to fucking do fucking" (133).[18] She considers working-class culture to be sexist and suffocating ("beer guts and football vomit and saucy tits and brothers and sisters" [139]), and she therefore invests in a right-wing discourse of "adventures" (137), "monetarism" (138) and the "free world" (140). Her rejection of motherhood is ironically to gain fulfilment from the pursuit of a political ideology that is buttressed by the most conservative ideas concerning motherhood, gender relations, and the family. Moreover, Marlene's response to Joyce's charge that she would not have been able to attain this success had she kept her daughter, Angie, only highlights further the impossibility of such an achievement for a working-class, single mother,

> I know a managing director who's got two children, she breast feeds in the board room, she pays a hundred pounds a week on domestic help alone and she can afford that because she's an extremely high-powered lady earning a great deal of money. (134)

Only a "high-powered lady earning a great deal of money" could combine motherhood and professional employment in this way; as Joyce correctly points out to Marlene, "so what's that got to do with you at the age of seventeen?" (134).

The political signification of *Top Girls* can be interpreted as finely balanced between an excoriation of a right-wing feminism that privileges the individual woman's quest for success, leaving class relations and capitalist values intact, and an inadvertent endorsement of a conventional moral code concerning the duties of motherhood, as symbolised in Mrs Kidd's description of Marlene as "one of these ballbreakers" (113), who leaves her own child in order to pursue a career. For the play not to fall into the latter, the unacceptability of the absence of meaningful choices available to both Marlene and Joyce must be perceptible to the audience.

---

[18] There is a reverberation here of the conversation between Ellen and Betty in *Vinegar Tom*. See Chapter 2, page 62.

Churchill states, "I quite deliberately left a hole in the play rather than giving people a model of what they could be like. I meant the thing that is absent to be present in the play."[19] The individual performance and its context clearly affect its reception, and the potency of motherhood as a regulating code will compete against the radical strands in the play, so that some performances will, no doubt, reinstate rather than critique contemporary discourses on motherhood.[20] However, if performed with recognition of the play's socialist-feminist commitment, *Top Girls*, like *Fen*, can successfully denaturalise the ideologies of motherhood.

Women as Workers

Women's identities as workers in employment–in the productive mode– are mediated by their gender. While women have become increasingly independent through their participation in the labour market, many are arguably more subjugated through the double exploitation of their labour both inside and outside of the home. As Zillah Eisenstein states, "ideology adjusts to this by defining women as working mothers."[21] The reification of motherhood becomes a distorting lens through which women's

---

[19] Churchill, Interview by Laurie Stone, in "Making Room at the Top," *The Village Voice* XXVIII.9 (1 March 1983): 80-81, 81.

[20] Churchill describes a performance in Greece, "where fewer women go out to work, the attitude from some men seeing it was, apparently, that the women in the play who'd gone out to work weren't very nice, weren't happy, and they abandoned their children. They felt the play was obviously saying women *shouldn't* go out to work–they took it to mean what they were wanting to say about women themselves, which is depressing." Interview, in *Interviews with Contemporary Women Playwrights*, eds. Betsko and Koenig, 77-78. However, British reviews similarly misinterpret *Top Girls* by evading the socialist perspective or misunderstanding the gender politics. Robert Cushman writes, "it manages to be an amazingly full polygonal presentation of a feminist predicament: career-women behaving like career-men." *The Observer* (5 September 1982). Julie Burchill similarly (mis)reads *Top Girls* as a play proposing that "women shouldn't wear suits, apply red lipstick, carry briefcases or apply for well-paid jobs, because that, apparently, is acting like a 'man.'" "A Woman's Work is Never Done," *The Guardian Weekend* (16 February 2002). Churchill responds, "*Top Girls* doesn't say, as Julie Burchill thinks (February 16), that women shouldn't succeed at work because that's 'acting like a man.' It starts off feminist (hurray for women's success) and ends up socialist (boo to capitalist success). I'm appalled by the views she tries to attribute to me." Letter. *The Guardian Weekend* (23 February 2002).

[21] Eisenstein, "Developing a Theory of Capitalist Patriarchy and Socialist Feminism," in *Capitalist Patriarchy*, 5-40, 29.

identities as workers are constituted. This affects the types of employment that women commonly undertake–such as teachers, carers, cleaners, nurses, and clerical workers–which are often reflections and extensions of their roles as wives and mothers. Where women do undertake work in manufacturing, as Nancy Chodorow states, "it is generally in the production of nondurable goods like clothing and food, not in 'masculine' machine industries like steel and automobiles."[22] Hence, unlike the class-interested motivations attributed to working- and middle-class men vis-à-vis pay and conditions and career prospects respectively, women are less likely to be perceived as autonomous workers with similar interests. Instead, work is often considered to be inessential to women either economically because of the assumption that they supplement the male wage or ideologically because work is not thought to contribute towards women's self-worth or dignity. Women's productivity and creativity have traditionally been perceived to be confined to their natural capacity for childbirth, and this has often been at the expense of other spheres of cultural practice and economic activity.

The area of work few women manage to escape–domestic labour–has been another source of discussion and debate within Marxist-feminism. Heidi Hartman restates the argument that women are the recipients of low wages; this economic fact induces them to marry, and that once married they are expected to become primarily responsible for the domestic sphere of work, which means that "men benefit ... from both higher wages and the domestic division of labour." Women's childcare and domestic responsibilities in the private sphere contribute further to their disadvantaged position within the labour market. The divisions of labour both inside and outside of the home strengthen a gendered hierarchy, which Hartman considers to be "the present outcome of the continuing interaction of two interlocking systems, capitalism and patriarchy."[23] The interaction between women's position in the workforce and in the family thus produces a powerful economic and ideological entrenchment of their subordination both inside and outside of the home.

There are several methods of valuing domestic labour within capitalist society and the detail of these is not of concern here, but as Eisenstein says, "it is unpaid work that is sexually assigned."[24] The private space of

---

[22] Nancy Chodorow, "Mothering, Male Dominance, and Capitalism," in *Capitalist Patriarchy*, ed. Eisenstein, 83-106, 91.

[23] Heidi Hartman, "Capitalism, Patriarchy, and Job Segregation by Sex," in *Capitalist Patriarchy*, ed. Eisenstein, 206-47, 208.

[24] Eisenstein, "Capitalist Patriarchy and Female Work," in *Capitalist Patriarchy*, 169-172, 170.

the home–the setting for the sentimental discourses of love, intimacy, and shared family interest–helps to disguise the social and economic relations of domestic labour. Secombe compares the exploitation of the "housewife" with the male wageworker and notes that the latter is able to express discontent over his alienation. In contrast, this is not an option for the "housewife," since she is not remunerated for her labour and thus "must account for her work in non-economic terms." Furthermore, she is expected to undertake this work unselfishly, as part of her self-sacrificial role and as a "labour of love." Secombe observes that "a housewife who admits that she hates her work is not a 'good mother'" and "often, therefore, her alienation from her work must be repressed from consciousness, lest she implode with guilt and feelings of personal inadequacy."[25] Although his account is a little theatrical, Secombe usefully highlights the way that ideology works to conceal the labour involved in domestic responsibilities, and the anxiety that arises from its concealment.

Both plays are concerned with women's working practices, and women's identities as workers. *Top Girls* stages a range of different types of work performed by women, and is, of course, centred on Marlene's promotion to Managing Director of an employment agency. The women at the dinner party signify to a large degree through their occupations, and the audience encounters several clients interviewed at the employment agency for different types of work. Joyce and Angie are also identified in terms of their relationship to the labour market. In *Fen,* the majority of the action comprises women working, often performing strenuous labour in harsh conditions.[26] This is accompanied by scenes of domestic labour, stories of women's working practices in the past, and the village girls' current job expectations. The harsh labour of the Fen women is counterbalanced with the appearance of the Japanese businessman and a symbol of international capital, Mr Takai, the local landowner, Mr Tewson, and a City financier Miss Cade. Churchill thus dramatises an economic community of different representations of capital and labour. A noticeable omission, though, is the (male) industrial proletarian who is the usual protagonist of Marxist economic theory. Churchill thus directs our political attention towards female rural workers in *Fen* and female clerical workers in *Top Girls,* figures who have been neglected by traditional

---

[25] Secombe, "The Housewife and Her Labour under Capitalism," *New Left Review* 83 (January-February 1974): 3-24, 20.
[26] According to Geraldine Cousin, "Churchill's original title for the play was *Strong Girls Always Hoeing,* from a Government Agricultural Report of 1842: 'Strong girls who are always hoeing can do the work better than men and they cost only 1/6 instead of 2/-.'" *Churchill* (London: Methuen, 1989), 47.

Marxist approaches as well as by the wider Labour and trades union movement.

A wider parody of the value attached to employment and professionalism in late capitalist society is implicit in the dinner party scene in *Top Girls*. Marlene chooses to celebrate with women whose "work" consists of being an international traveller, a royal courtesan/Buddhist nun, the leader of a revolution in a Breughel painting, a Pope, and the obedient wife of a Marquis and protagonist of a Chaucer tale. In so doing, Marlene places her own professional achievement alongside those of the others. Her comment, "well it's not Pope but it is managing director," (67) seems only to alert the audience to the emptiness of the achievement, which is reinforced in Isabella's response, "I'm sure it's just the beginning of something extraordinary" (67). The absence of extraordinariness involved in the management of a business that makes profits from selling workers to other companies lingers somewhat satirically over the celebrations. Of course, it is highly unusual for women to attain top management positions,[27] but it is the lack of profundity and moral substance in this particular achievement that frames the audience's response to Marlene's "success." A simultaneous expression of dissatisfaction at monetary accumulation and a competitive business sensibility haunts the celebrations.

Fen dramatises the sort of work that Marlene might have been performing if she had not escaped to London. Escape does indeed seem the only alternative to an insular and somewhat static mode of production that has been in place for generations, as illustrated in Frank's mimicking of Mr Tewson, "I remember when your dad worked for my dad" (151). In fact a sense of unchanging drudgery is initiated in the first action of the play; the stage directions read, *as the audience comes in, a boy from the last century, barefoot and in rags, is alone in a field, in a fog, scaring crows*" (147). As well as accentuating the lack of progressive change in conditions for rural workers, this also disrupts the boundary of the opening of the play, prompting the audience, as they arrive, to consider the significance of this ghostly figure of poverty.[28] The delivery of the

---

[27] Bill Naismith reports that The Policy Studies Institute found that in 1979 under 2% of high earners were women. Commentary, *Top Girls* (London: Methuen, 1991), xxi-liii, xxxii.

[28] This is one of the first actions we see Jude Fawley performing in a novel first published in 1896 that also represents the frustrated hopes and tragic oppression of the rural working-class: "the boy stood under the rick … and every few seconds used his clacker or rattle briskly. At each clack the rooks left off pecking, and rose and went away on their leisurely wings, burnished like tassets of mail, afterwards

opening lines by Mr Takai, symbol of international capital, reflects the super-exploitation of the Fen workers, and continues the deconstruction of a capitalist narrative of progress.[29]

Most of the action of *Fen* is centred on female manual labour. Potato picking, onion packing, and stone picking, sometimes undertaken in bad weather, are the backdrops to several scenes. However, as the stage directions indicate in Scene 10, *"they keep working hard throughout the scene"* (163); hard work is the substance of the performance as well as its context. The women's vulnerability as low-paid workers with no security is underlined at several moments. Mrs Hassett's response to Val's request to leave work early ("you think twice before you ask me for work again because I'll think twice an' all" [148]), and her threat to all of the workers ("if I catch you with them moonlighting gangs out of town you don't work for me again" [149]) are two such examples. Thinly disguised threats of instant redundancy are accompanied by Tewson's glorification of the extensive possibilities for female exploitation, "better workers than men. I've seen women working in my fields with icicles on their faces. I admire that" (171). Connecting moral worth with women's tendency towards hard work is responded to as a compliment by Shirley ("better than men all right") whereas Nell translates this as women's susceptibility to greater exploitation, and retorts accordingly, "bloody fools, that's all" (171).

Domestic labour replaces wage labour as the motor of action in Scene 11. Inserted between two agricultural labouring scenes, this scene is also positioned at the centre of the play, a position that mirrors the location of domesticity in many women's lives. The stage directions read,

> *Shirley working in the house. She goes from one job to another, ironing, mending, preparing dinner, minding a baby. Val is there, not doing anything. Shirley never stops throughout the scene.* (167)

Directly after watching her pack onions, the audience sees Shirley performing several domestic chores simultaneously. Val's inactivity produces a complex contrast that invites the audience to read the gendered inscription of domestic work. Having left her children and moved in with her lover, Val's retreat from her motherly role leads to her *"not doing*

---

wheeling back and regarding him wearily, and descending to feed at a more respectful distance." Thomas Hardy, *Jude the Obscure* (London: Penguin, 1996; first published in 1895), 11.

[29] However, this representation draws on racist stereotypes ("I think it is too foggy to take pictures" [147]), which in turn delimits its subversive function. A (white) North American businessman might have been a better choice.

anything." This rare escape from the drudgery of employment and the demands of domestic work should bring with it an opportunity for Val to rest but she is fretful and guilty ("I can't remember what they look like" [168]), and she begins to iron after finding that she feels too emotional to hold the baby. Val's subject position, a position constructed through narratives of work, domesticity, and family responsibilities, does not allow for her to be "not doing anything."

Representations of female labour in *Top Girls* are predominantly concentrated around the employment agency. In contrast to the women in *Fen*, who are involved in production, the employment agency is closer to consumption in its activity of buying and selling workers. The veneer of a feminist space where "tough birds" dominate is acutely ironic because the employment agency perpetuates insecure temporary work for women, which tends to undermine general working conditions and is often casualised. It is a trade union's nemesis in its representation of the individual worker as opposed to the collective, and in its neglect of the rights and conditions that have been fought for over several generations. The employment agency also contributes to a double exploitation of the worker: the worker not only has to subject herself to her employer, but is also answerable to the agency.

This is apparent in the first scene of Act 2. In Marlene's interview, she subtly disempowers Jeanine. After Jeanine tells her that she is a secretary, Marlene asks, "secretary or typist?" (84). Marlene's embrace of a narrow idea of efficiency means that Jeanine is harried into making choices within a tightly restricted margin. Marlene additionally is complicit in sexist employment practice shown by her response to Jeanine's assertion that she is saving to get married, "does that mean you don't want a long-term job, Jeanine? … Because where do the prospects come in? No kids for a bit?" (85). Marlene recognises that employers discriminate, which is why she advises Jeanine to keep this quiet, but she simultaneously displays an arrogance and sense of superiority, preventing her from identifying with her interviewee. This display of superiority also indicates her disrespect for women who do not, or cannot, "choose" to "make it." The gendered inscription of secretarial employment, which frequently consists of service, often to a male employer, is reinforced by Marlene, who continues to subject Jeanine to a process of subtle intellectual derision and social undermining.

Similarly, Marlene does not see the repetition of a sexist paradigm that accompanies the "success" of the rich businesswoman. The admiration she has for the "high-powered lady" who "pays a hundred pounds a week on domestic help alone" (134) eclipses Marlene's ability to appreciate the low-paid, female, domestic "help," without whose exploited labour, "success" would not be possible. Unable or unwilling to place the individual's success in a broader context of social and economic relations, Marlene fails to appreciate the irony of the connection with her own circumstances. Her sister, Joyce, provides the unpaid domestic labour that frees Marlene to pursue her career, and the former survives by doing "four different cleaning jobs" (136), again low-paid domestic work. Marlene's response to women's oppression is to invest in an ideology of a narrowly defined, profit-centred, and competitive idea of individualism. These reference points prompt her misguided attempt to "compliment" Joyce ("you've got what it takes" [141]) in her desire to reconnect with her sister after their furious row in the last Act.

No character "makes it" in *Fen*. In fact the sheer endurance of the women workers and the continuity of exploited female labour are emphasised through the play's connections of past, present, and future images of female working practices. The female ghost working barefoot in the fields in Scene 9 connects regressively to past generations of women workers. An alternative "choice" for women is represented by Shirley, who tells Val that she "went into service" (168) for a year at the age of fifteen. One of Churchill's sources for the play, Mary Chamberlain's collection of biographical stories of women's lives in the Fens, includes several older women, interviewed in the mid-1970s, who had been domestic servants.[30] The present continues to offer agricultural work, fieldwork, light industry, and domestic labour, all of which remain the dominant "opportunities" open to working-class Fen women.

The future for female workers in *Fen* looks bleak. Becky, Deb, and Shona sing the "Girls' Song," which expresses the occupational expectations and desires of the girls in the village. None of them cite agricultural labouring or factory work as among their prospective jobs, but the jobs they list are all feminised spheres of work. Hairdressing is mentioned five times, nursing four, teaching once and cooking once. In addition to the fact that this song of hope is narrow, limiting, and characterised by the feminised qualities of caring, service, and domestic activities, there is also a strong suggestion in the play–through the emphasis on generational continuity–that most of the girls will end up following their mothers' working practices. "I don't think I'll leave the village when I grow up" (157-58) is recited in different forms four times, and "I want to have children and get married" (157), three. Getting

---

[30] Mary Chamberlain, *Fenwomen: A Portrait of Women in an English Village* (London: Routledge & Kegan Paul, 1983).

married, having children, and doing housework intersperses the references to different feminised occupations, and provides a circularity within which the girls are trapped.

The girls in *Top Girls*, Angie and Kit, are also identified in terms of their anticipated relationship to the labour market and their own attitudes to marriage and their futures. Angie does not perform well in Marlene's calculation of success ("she's a bit thick. She's a bit funny"), a calculation that qualifies her only as "a packer in Tesco" (120), and we hear from Joyce that Angie has "been in the remedial class the last two years" (131). She does not meet conventional measures of intelligence, but she simultaneously shows independence and creativity in her surreptitious arrangement of the sisters' reunion, and in making her own way to Marlene's workplace in London. She also demonstrates astuteness when she highlights Marlene's dislocation from her family, as she says in response to Marlene's query of where Frank is, "didn't you know that? You don't know much" (128). However, it seems clear that her rebellious spirit of not wanting to marry, challenging her mother, and attempting to be an active agent in her own familial circle, along with her somewhat visionary quality ("I think I'm my aunt's child. I think my mother's really my aunt" [95]) will not be rewarded by good employment opportunities. Rather than becoming "a teacher or a nursery nurse" (126), occupations that Marlene, somewhat patronisingly suggests to her, she is more likely to fulfil Joyce's predictions, "I expect her children will say what a wasted life she had" (140).

Kit, on the other hand, is conventionally clever. She is doing well at school, wants to be a "nuclear physicist" (97) and is "good at English" (96). Her sensitivity to global issues (fear of nuclear war) and her solidarity with Angie ("I love Angie" [97]) position her as a more hopeful working-class female figure in the play. Lacking the signs of Marlene's self-characterisation ("I'm not clever, just pushy" [126]), Kit offers something of a challenge to the celebration of business success, profit, and the individual by continuing her engagement with, and concern for, the wider social and political environment. The possibility of a progressive negotiation in the future of class and gender solidarity in the figure of Kit, and the breaking out of a restrictive life of a working-class woman in the Fens does not present itself as a clearly identifiable performance, but at the same time, it is an audible (albeit muted) and visible (although marginalised) presence in the play.

The work performed by women in *Top Girls*, while "glossier" than the work in *Fen*, is rather lacking in substance. Reflecting the topical celebration of enterprise and monetarism, the jobs represented are mostly

focussed around advertising, marketing, and sales. But the seemingly
exciting connotations of these fields are soon dispelled as we hear that
Jeanine is put forward for marketing lampshades (86), Louise is offered
the chance to apply for middle management in a cosmetics company since
it is an area that is "easier for a woman" (106), and Shona's story of
burning up the M1 in a Porsche selling electrical goods turns out to be a
fantasy (117). Hence, the claim that there is a sudden emergence of
successful career women in the labour market is intimated to be somewhat
illusory or at least shown to be tempered by restrictions of female labour
to feminised spheres of work, spheres that are often lacklustre and
soulless.

The work women carry out in *Fen*, while more productive in an
immediate sense, is hugely exploited, without trades union representation,
performed in harsh conditions, very low-paid and is exhausting manual
labour. This work, unlike that in *Top Girls*, is not branded with the
evocative label of a "career," but is seen by the women who perform it as
no more than economic activity that is necessary for survival. In this sense,
both plays convey the respective harshness and hollowness of women's
work in an economy that is constituted by competition and profit.
Furthermore, both plays deconstruct the politics of "choice" that dominate
Thatcherite discourses of the early 1980s; the employment choices for
women in *Top Girls* are shown as narrow and restrictive, and the
employment choices for female workers in *Fen* are exposed as effectively
non-existent.

Women and Class

The relationship between women as an oppressed gendered group and the
category of social class is framed by theoretical ruminations on the origins
of women's oppression and the formation of social classes.[31] Without
participating in this complex debate (which includes such questions as
whether gender oppression arose out of the emergence of social classes or
whether it predated it; whether the evidence of matrilineal descent equates
with some form of matriarchy or whether it is not in itself evidence of
power) it is worth noting the confusion that has surrounded this debate,
and recognising that the "origins" question remains problematic in the

---

[31] The most significant contribution to this is Engels, *The Origin of the Family*. For
an appraisal of biological, socio-biological, cultural, symbolic, psychoanalytical,
historical and materialist theories on the origins of gender and class, see Stephanie
Coontz and Peta Henderson, eds., *Women's Work, Men's Property: The Origins of
Gender and Class* (London: Verso, 1986).

theorising of gender and class. The propensity to prioritise either social class or gender has tended to produce a gender-neglecting class analysis on the one hand or a class-impotent feminism on the other. Marxist-feminism has attempted to address this, although with limited success. Part of the problem has been confusion over defining women's relationship to the economic base and analysing their place in the totality. The richness of analytical material that exists in the Marxist tradition has been both enabling and disabling for the analysis of gender: enabling, because the tools of historical materialism provide a theoretical framework for examining oppression, but disabling because historical materialism has tended towards assuming the historical subject and the agent of change as male. Additionally, because of the privileging by Marxists of class conflict as the exclusive central antagonism in historical development at the expense of other social antagonisms, there has been a reluctance to confront male privilege that arises out of women's subordination; women's oppression is viewed instead as a gain for capital and not a condition that benefits men.

There have been a number of challenges to the male-centred theorisation of social class.[32] Erik Olin Wright argues that families should not be treated as unitary class blocks, refuting in particular the notion that a married woman's class position should be derived from her husband's.[33] He points out that while families may pool incomes, that income may not be distributed equally. In addition, it is not necessarily the case that families rather than individuals are organised into class struggle. Wright cites scenarios where "a woman engaged in union struggles of various sorts could have a husband who is a manager or a petty bourgeois generally opposed to unions."[34] The potential, then, for class conflict to exist within families as well as between families is an important recognition in the development of a gender-sensitive class analysis. Elizabeth Fox-Genovese discusses women's marginal position in class analyses as partly attributable to the structures of the capitalist social formation, structures that invariably assume human subjectivity to be

---

[32] See Joan Acker, "Women and Social Stratification: A Case of Intellectual Sexism," *American Journal of Sociology* 78 (1973): 936-45; Delphy, "Women in Stratification Studies," in *Close to Home*, 28-39; Pamela Abott and Roger Sapsford, *Women and Social Class* (London: Tavistock Publications, 1987); Erik Olin Wright, "Women in the Class Structure," *Politics & Society* 17 .1 (1989): 35-66.

[33] For an exposition of the position Wright argues against, see John Goldthorpe, "Women and Class Analysis," *Sociology* 17 (1983): 465-88.

[34] Wright, "Women in the Class Structure," 40.

male. She argues that the "preferred distinctions between production and reproduction, subsistence and market, public and private"–distinctions in which both capitalist and socialist discourses engage–serve to marginalise women.[35] Hence, the representatives of both capital and labour have tended to treat women as appendices to, or dependents upon, a male agent, thereby denying women economic and political subjectivity, and more generally, a full sense of social autonomy. These issues are compounded by what Chris Middleton describes as a "persistent reluctance" by Marxists "to apply economic concepts to relations of production that have become embedded in intimate and perhaps affectionate personal relationships."[36] The everyday experience of oppression, an oppression intertwined with women's personal relationships, is all but dismissed by orthodox Marxists as a structural effect of class division, and an ideological product of capitalist culture.

Radical feminists, such as Kate Millett, recognise this weakness and make gendered subordination the starting point for analysing women and social class. Millett views the prioritising of women's oppression, or the "birthright priority whereby males rule females," as "sturdier," "more rigorous," "more uniform," and "more enduring" than other oppressions.[37] Her analysis of women's class interests is contingent upon women's lack of economic, social, and political autonomy,

> perhaps, in the final analysis, it is possible to argue that women tend to transcend the usual class stratifications in patriarchy, for whatever the class of her birth and education, the female has fewer permanent class associations than does the male. Economic dependency renders her affiliations with any class a tangential, vicarious, and temporary matter.[38]

However, the constitution of women as a class in itself is equally problematic. It tends to mask the very real material disparities and power differentials that exist between women. This analysis does not seem to be able to account effectively for those women who participate in the

[35] Elizabeth Fox-Genovese, "Placing Women's History in History," *New Left Review* 133 (May-June 1982): 5-29, 26.
[36] Chris Middleton, "Patriarchal Exploitation and the Rise of English Capitalism," in *Gender, Class and Work*, eds. Eva Gamarnikow et. al. (London: Heinemann, 1983), 11-27, 19.
[37] Kate Millett, *Sexual Politics* (London: Rupert Hart-Davis, 1971), 25.
[38] Millett, *Sexual Politics*, 38. The echo of Engels in the phrase "in the final analysis" is an interesting irony; Millett and other radical feminists, such as Firestone, often use Marxist categories but replace class with gender as the central and original antagonism.

activities of capital accumulation, the exploitation of labour, or colonial practices. The radical feminist treatment of marriage as a patriarchal institution prevents analysis of the variety of forms of marriage that have emerged at different historical moments. In response to Delphy's identification of marriage as a patriarchal institution, Michèle Barrett and Mary McIntosh argue,

> unlike marxist feminists, she does not see it as necessary to understand how the state's policies on marriage, which establish and strengthen men's control over women, are affected by class domination and class struggle.[39]

The theorisation of women as a class, while useful in its analysis of the common oppression suffered by women as women, eclipses the differences between women, pays inadequate attention to women's oppression in different historical, economic, and cultural contexts, and displaces capitalism as the focus of political challenge.

A "solution" to the problems of the relationship between class and gender identities is not attempted here; rather, bringing together the most useful elements of both contributes towards an approach that recognises the limitations of subsuming one under the other, and acknowledges the inextricable connections between class and gender conflicts. Both *Top Girls* and *Fen* reproduce the intersection of class and gender oppression. *Top Girls* plays out the vulnerability of a class-insensitive feminism, while simultaneously implicating a class politics that ignores a feminist agenda. *Fen* performs a palpable sense of the lived dynamic of the two oppressions, foregrounding the lives of working-class women as both the setting and protagonists of the drama.

Although Churchill describes the first Act of *Top Girls* as celebrating women's success and starting off as feminist,[40] the dinner party scene stages a complex set of social relations that includes a critique of this too. As well as supporting a feminist space, this Act simultaneously points to the limitations of this in a socio-political context where women are divided by class, race, ethnicity, and ideology. The most frequently mentioned example of this is the waitress, who serves the diners throughout the Act without saying a word.[41] Marlene seems totally self-assured in her

---

[39] Michèle Barrett and Mary McIntosh, "Christine Delphy: Towards a Materialist Feminism?" *Feminist Review* 1 (1979), 95-106, 99.

[40] See note 20.

[41] In the BBC/Open University video production directed by Max Stafford-Clark in 1991, the waitress shares a drink with the diners at the end of the act, thereby reducing the class difference signified by her earlier silent service.

exchange with the waitress, showing no signs of connection or even rudimentary expressions of respect–please and thank you, "I'd like a bottle of Frascati straight away if you've got one really cold" (55). The vignette connects ironically with the last Act of the play, where it is revealed that Joyce also provides service for middle-class women by performing four cleaning jobs in the village, "I hate the fucking cows I work for and their dirty dishes with blanquette of fucking veau" (140).

Several of the women in the first Act of *Top Girls* display fluency in reactionary discourses. Isabella declares, "there are some barbaric practices in the east," adding the caveat, "among the lower classes" (60), when questioned by Nijo. She says further on, "I was nearly murdered in China by a howling mob" and "some people tried to sell girl babies to Europeans for cameras or stew!" (69). She describes how, when she came back to England, she "talked and talked explaining how the East was corrupt and vicious" (72). Hence, in contrast to Millett and Delphy's radical feminist refutation of the authenticity and agency of the bourgeois woman, Isabella clearly asserts her will and plays an active role in Empire building, albeit a role that is plainly shaped by her gendered identity.

Both Nijo and Griselda express themselves in accordance with patriarchal configurations of femininity. Although Nijo displays extraordinary resourcefulness by travelling on foot through Japan, this is positioned rather uneasily alongside the active complicity she reveals in relation to her subjection to the ultimate patriarch, the Emperor, "what I enjoyed most was being the Emperor's favourite and wearing thin silk" (58). She illustrates the narrow, restrictive, and oppressive range of codes that signify femininity; her comment, "the first half of my life was all sin and the second all repentance" (59) reproduces the virgin/whore paradigm. Although connecting with the upper classes (indicated by her response, "I wouldn't know" [60] to Isabella's claim that the lower classes in the East perform barbaric acts), she has no independent wealth nor an autonomous class position, "how else could I have left the court if I wasn't a nun? When father died I had only His Majesty. So when I fell out of favour I had nothing" (61). Nijo's patriarchal context is vividly conveyed; without the Emperor or her father to serve, the absence of male authority was not freedom but "nothing." Her only option was to dedicate "what was left" of herself "to nothing" (61), to become a Buddhist nun, again a subservient role within a theological patriarchy. Nijo illustrates well Millett's insistence on the transience of women's class identities; however, it should be noted that Nijo is a pre-capitalist figure, who lives in a feudalist, as opposed to a capitalist, patriarchy.

Griselda is the logical extreme of patriarchal determination. As the obedient wife who always complies with her husband's wishes, she is the product of male "creativity" (Boccaccio, Petrarch, and Chaucer) and thus an almost perfect reflection of the patriarchal imagination. Almost perfect, because even she has a moment of resistance, "I do think–I do wonder–it would have been nicer if Walter hadn't had to" (81). All of the diners, except for Nijo ("no, I understand ... he was your life" [77]), find it impossible to connect with Griselda's defence of her husband, a husband who tests her loyalty by taking away her children, sending her away, and pretending to marry someone else. On the one hand, Griselda and Nijo act as foils to the fairytales that romanticise marriage with stories of chivalrous princes, and on the other, they undermine the idea that an all-female space will automatically give rise to a feminist politics. Although both Griselda and Nijo can be interpreted as products of their patriarchal contexts, there are nevertheless many uncomfortable residues of these patriarchal motifs in the contemporary sections of the play, as illustrated in Mrs Kidd's exchange with Marlene; of her husband, Howard, she says, "I put him first every inch of the way" (112).

Fen is unrestrained in its dramatisation of the divisions between women on the basis of social class. Mrs Hassett, the gangmaster, is portrayed as thoroughly ruthless in her role as an employer. She manages the agricultural labourers for Tewson, the farmer, and is materially rewarded for it, which is recognised by the others; "you've got two colour tellies to spoil" (148) says Nell in response to Hassett warning the workers not to claim unemployment benefit or to moonlight since it will "spoil it for all of us" (149). The stage directions introduce Hassett to the scene as standing "*at the bottom of the field watching them*" (148), as they pick potatoes. She repeatedly asserts her economic power by threatening to dismiss them and reiterating the insecurity of their jobs; "I don't owe you nothing for today ... not if you want another chance" (149) she says to Val, who leaves work early. Hassett says to Wilson, who finishes first, "the idea's to get the work done properly not win the Derby. Want to come again?" (149). Her intimidating and coercive behaviour is reiterated in her swipe at Nell, "think you'd get a better deal by yourself? Think you'd get a job at all?" (150) Her final remarks ("I'm off now, ladies and gent. Can't stand about in this wind. I should get a move on, you've plenty to do" [150]) place her firmly in the tradition of the callous, selfish, exploitative boss, whose interests are located firmly in the accumulation of capital at the expense of the interests of the workers. Significantly, Hassett does not socialise with the other women, who play darts in the pub together in Scene 18.

Miss Cade, a financier from the City, is represented as little more than an economic functionary. An illustration of "moguls," "tycoons," and "barons" (161), as Tewson characterises her, Cade is a figure that will reappear in different guises in Churchill's *Serious Money* in 1987. Although Tewson shows some hostility towards Cade and the City, their interests are not so dissimilar:

> TEWSON: My family hold this land in trust for the nation. ... When I say nation. You don't want to go too far in the public responsibility direction. You raise the spectre of nationalisation.
> CADE: No danger of that. Think of us as yourself. (162)

Market fixated, awash with figures, and characterised by sales speak ("the farmers who have sold to us are happy, Mr Tewson" [161]), Cade's values are an anathema to the rural, working-class women in *Fen*. Their economic interests are clearly at odds, and the scope for unity along gender lines seems somewhat extraneous in these material circumstances.

With the exception of Mrs Finch, the Minister's wife, the other women in *Fen* signify largely through their working-class identities. They identify as working class primarily through their economic activity; the audience watches them work for much of the action. In addition, there are several traditional references to class struggle, such as Ivy's reminiscences of her husband's trade union activism ("[Jack] walked through the night to the union meeting" [177]). Furthermore, Nell's frequent deployment of a revolutionary discourse ("best hope if they all top themselves. Start with the queen and work down and I'll tell them when to stop" [172]) provides many of the customary reference points for the representation of a working-class community.

However, *Fen* successfully expands the framework within which class identity and class politics are made meaningful. Building on the foundations of conventional class signification, Churchill pushes women to the forefront of the drama, and thus to the centre of a socialist discourse. In addition to the sense of drudgery that dominates these women's lives, the audience also witnesses an alternative mode of communication between the Fen women, one that is playful, symbolic, and visionary but simultaneously tragic. For instance, Nell's gripping story of her grandfather discovering a man still alive in a coffin at a couple's house contributes to a sense of cultural richness that is kept alive in the village. In contrast though, the harsh grind and sense of geopolitical insularity that gives rise to a creative imagination also produces sadomasochistic practices, such as the mutilation of cattle as described in Shirley's story of her ancestors, discussed more fully in Chapter 2. This other mode of cultural expression–a mode of solidarity expressed through shared memories and narratives, but also a mode that seems resistant to class and gender definitions–is a key medium through which the women maintain a sense of themselves in the context of oppression and alienation.

Top Girls overlaps with *Fen* in its representation of the rural working-class lives of Joyce and Angie. Joyce's four cleaning jobs, however, situate her in an isolated working environment with no fellow workers with whom to share stories and solidarity. There are no identifiable possibilities through which she can make her voice and actions heard, and thus no perceivable hope for her, or, most probably, either for Angie, other than the remote possibility that a future Labour government might instigate change. While there is always the chance of a re-emergence of trade union militancy amongst the workers in *Fen*, particularly with Nell's continual use of a socialist idiom, there seems to be no such possibility in Joyce's life. The lack of realisation of her class agency is mostly due to the privatised, casual, and isolated labour she undertakes, but it is also due to her gendered identity, particularly as it affects her domestic role, and her subsequent invisibility within Marxist terms because of it.

Marlene is not prepared to remain long in this difficult environment, "I knew when I was thirteen, out of their house, out of them, never let that happen to me, never let him, make my own way, out" (139). However, ironically, Marlene's political identification with neoliberalism serves only to align her with a system that keeps her family and community in poverty, and perpetuates division. Joyce mentions their father ("that bastard" as Marlene calls him), asking, "what sort of life did he have? Working in the fields like an animal" (138). Marlene's vivid sense of the utter intolerability of domestic violence and domestic drudgery eclipses her capacity to acknowledge her father's class oppression, and the resulting poverty that both her parents endured:

> MARLENE: She was hungry because he drank the money. / He used to hit her.
> JOYCE: It's not all down to him. / Their lives were rubbish. They
> MARLENE: She didn't hit him.
> JOYCE: were treated like rubbish. He's dead and she'll die soon and what sort of life / did they have? (139)

Their father's violence is not, to Marlene's repugnance, given the appropriate attention, either by Joyce or by the socialist movement more generally. It is this that leads to her swift dismissal of working-class identification.

Although the exchange between Marlene and Joyce becomes
momentarily melodramatic, it nevertheless corresponds to genuine
economic and political differences between them,

MARLENE: Them, them. / Us and them?
JOYCE: And you're one of them.
MARLENE: And you're us, wonderful us, and Angie's us / and Mum and
Dad's us.
JOYCE: Yes, that's right, and you're them. (140)

This is a clear illustration of class division within families and it is also an
example of women expressing strong class identities and allegiances.
Marlene's competitive drive is motivated by her Hobbesian belief that one
exploits or is exploited. She identifies her success in business as
constituting her autonomy ("I'm original" [140]) and as the only
alternative to an oppressive life in poverty in the Fens. Nevertheless,
Marlene's "achievement" has occurred as a result of her neglect and
mistreatment of others, as well as her isolation from the social sphere;
hence, this "achievement" seems to fall short of personal fulfilment in any
humanly meaningful sense.

In its population of the stage with many different female characters,
Top Girls reflects back to women a sense of their own autonomy, but it
also problematises this, particularly through the figure of Marlene. It
demonstrates the limitations of a feminist practice neglectful of anti-
capitalist concerns. Marlene's striving for individualism is seen as deeply
flawed both morally, in terms of its adherence to a selfish and exploitative
philosophy, but equally in terms of its mistaken identification of autonomy
as something that depends upon the subordination of others. In its
assumption of feminism in its politics and dramatic structure, *Top Girls*
shows every sensitivity to the needs and desires of Marlene, who cannot
accept the restrictive and narrow life that a working-class woman in a rural
environment is expected to lead. However, the play crucially rejects a
class-neglectful politics that encourages such an economic and political
complicity with capitalist systems as exemplified by Marlene. *Top Girls*
dramatises the complexity of this impasse, encouraging audiences to
continue to engage with the unresolved relationship between class and
gender oppressions.

Fen is similarly concerned with the relationship between these
oppressions and additionally preoccupied with the economic, social, and
political framework within which hidden communities of working-class
women live. Inspired by Chamberlain's History Workshop Series,
Fenwomen, and in a similar continuum to *Light Shining* and *Vinegar Tom*,

Fen creates a dramatic record of the social and oral histories of women in an isolated Fen village. Furthermore the play rehabilitates the activity of productive labour as a legitimate and compelling subject for representation on stage. Equally though, *Fen* includes a vivid sense of the imaginary that seems both to arise from, but also compete against, the harsh material conditions that form the substance of the drama. As part of the play's achievement in inscribing this agricultural working-class community both dramatically and historically, *Fen* successfully widens the parameters of socialist and feminist representation.

CHAPTER FIVE

THE TRIUMPH OF CAPITALISM?
SERIOUS MONEY AND *MAD FOREST*

Sure this is a dangerous system and it could crash any minute and I
sometimes wake up in bed
And think is Armageddon Aids, nuclear war or a crash, and how will I end
up dead?
(*SM*, 306)

I got to the square and people are shouting against Ceauşescu, shouting
'Today in Timişoara, tomorrow in all the country.' I look at their lips to
believe they say it. I see a friend and at first I don't know him, his face has
changed, and when he looks at me I know my face has changed also.
(*MF*, 124)

Introduction

This chapter explores ways in which two plays written and performed in
the closing years of the 1980s and the start of the 1990s–*Serious Money*
(1987) and *Mad Forest* (1990)–take up and respond to a perceived crisis of
the Left and a supposed newfound hegemony of the success of capitalist
economics and liberal democracy as the best and only workable socio-
economic systems.[1] The plays and the worlds they dramatise may seem
rather unconnected: a murder and corporate takeover in the City of
London, a setting populated by a mix of the old bourgeoisie and new
yuppies, both of whom make big money–compared with a staging of
before and after the Romanian revolution seen predominantly from the
perspectives of one middle- and one working-class family. The revolution
in Romania and the demise of communism in Eastern Europe more
generally form part of a sequence of events that is reconstituted in

---

[1] For a version of this discussion focused solely on *Mad Forest*, see Siân
Adiseshiah, "Revolution and the End of History: Caryl Churchill's *Mad Forest*,"
Modern Drama 52.3 (Fall 2009): 283-99.

neoliberal discourse as evidence that proclaims the failure of the communist project and the endurance and ultimate success of free-market economics and liberal democracy. *Mad Forest* and *Serious Money* powerfully intervene in events that typify the economic and political milieu characteristic of the closure of the decade, a closure that is often considered to bear out Francis Fukuyama's earlier claims that the triumph of capitalist democracy signalled the end of history.

Situating *Mad Forest*

Mad Forest dramatises the burgeoning frustration and growing articulacy of a population repressed under a totalitarian dictatorship, and suffering economic hardship, political censorship, and cultural stagnation. The revolution in *Mad Forest*, like other Eastern European revolutions, is a crystallisation of yearning for the collapse of the repressive regime, an end to economic hardship, and the eradication of an autocratic administration. However, the play is enriched by the dramatisation of revolution in an Eastern European country that is least typical in relation to these events.[2] George Galloway and Bob Wylie talk about it as "the most extraordinary end, through the most extraordinary revolution, of the most extraordinary dictatorship in all of Eastern Europe."[3] Unlike other Eastern European states, where administrations in the main peacefully conceded change in response to an overwhelming demand, Romania was the site of bloody revolution with mass demonstrations, the shooting of protesters, and the taking up of arms by civilians against a resistant state;[4] hence, the

---

[2] I say least typical because of Nicolae Ceauşescu's hostility to Moscow and Romania's idiosyncratic Stalinist regime. I am using "Stalinism" in the same way that Alex Callinicos does: "by 'Stalinism' I mean, not one person's rule or even a body of beliefs, but the whole system of social power that crystallised in the USSR in the 1930s, was exported to Eastern Europe in the second half of the 1940s, and survived till the late 1980s when it began to collapse, a system characterised by the hierarchically organised control of all aspects of social life, political, economic, and cultural, by a narrow oligarchy seated at the apex of the party and state apparatuses, the *nomenklatura,*" *The Revenge of History* (Oxford: Polity Press, 1991), 15.

[3] George Galloway and Bob Wylie, *Downfall* (London: Futura, 1991), 4.

[4] While Moscow did not sanction the suppression of democracy movements and indeed entered into negotiations with pro-democracy campaigners who had previously been imprisoned, as Timothy Garton Ash remarks, "Romania was the exception that proves the rule. It is no accident that it was precisely in the state for so long the most *in*dependent of Moscow that the resistance of the security arm of

importance of the second part of the play, which forms its structural centre–the revolution–comprising quasi docudrama-style testimony spoken by a diverse range of unnamed characters, who do not appear in any other part of the play. Unlike other regimes, which responded to the escalating demands for change, and would not risk the unpredictable outcome of mass uprisings, Ceauşescu clung firmly to power, condemned the actions of other Eastern European states, and in so doing, precipitated the uprising.

The revolution in December 1989, the election that followed in May, and the events that took place over the proceeding few weeks and months are a site of intense contestation. Galloway and Wylie write,

> some of the great events of Romanian history have become tangled in a web of claim and counter-claim, myth and reality. Timisoara 1989 is no exception. Controversy still reigns about these events. How many people died, and exactly who killed them, are at the heart of the debate.[5]

The spread of mass protest from Timisoara to Bucharest on 21 December was accompanied by the political manoeuvring of some of the bureaucracy, but the extent of this is unknown. Historian, Martyn Rady claims,

> the rapidity with which the new government of the National Salvation Front was formed, strongly suggests that close discussions between members of the party 'old guard,' the army and the *securitate* may already have been underway by the time of Ceauşescu's flight.[6]

The brief but well-documented revelation on Romanian and world television that some of the crowd in the Ceauşescu-organised support rally on 21 December were heckling and booing Ceauşescu, and the shock that many television spectators experienced on observing the famously startled look on his face and the waving of his arms before the recording was prematurely cut, contributed to the sense of theatricality surrounding these remarkable events. This was intensified by the melodramatic exit of Nicolae and Elena Ceauşescu by helicopter from the roof of the Central Committee Building, the second helicopter's dropping leaflets warning the

---

the powers-that-were was most fierce, bloody and prolonged." *We the People* (Cambridge: Granta in association with Penguin, 1990), 141.
[5] Galloway and Wylie, *Downfall,* 110.
[6] Martyn Rady, *Romania in Turmoil: A Contemporary History* (London: IB Tauris, 1992), 102.

Romanian people of the immediate danger to their country's autonomy and integrity, and the videotaped trial and execution of the Ceauşescus.

Post-revolutionary Romania saw the National Salvation Front (NSF) gain a huge majority in the election (Ion Iliescu gained 85.07% as the NSF candidate for the Presidency, and the NSF gained 66.3% in the Chamber of Deputies), many of whom were members of the old bureaucracy, although several of the leaders had been dissident members.[7] Explaining the election results from the right, Harry Barnes Jr. (United States Ambassador to Romania 1974-77) insisted, "there is a strong Romanian cultural tradition that the way to survive is to get out of the way of harm."[8] In contrast, British Marxists suggested that the NSF was the party least in favour of rapid change to a free-market capitalist system, a system that, in turn, would inevitably lead to mass unemployment and economic hardship. Alan Woods, former leading theoretician of the Militant tendency states,

> first, the workers (and peasants) identify the Front with the revolution. They see attacks on Iliescu as attacks on the revolution itself, and this they are not prepared to tolerate. Secondly, unlike Poland and other countries in Eastern Europe, the masses have made substantial gains since the revolution. Life is still hard, with widespread shortages and queues, but compared to the Ceauşescu period, things are immeasurably better.[9]

Ceauşescu's regime was unique in paying off its national debt, and thus the NSF had a significant financial margin with which to appease poverty and hardship.

However, British Marxists also differed in their readings of the opposition to the NSF. Chris Harman, a leading figure in the Socialist Workers Party described the infamous events of 13-15 June, where miners arrived to help defeat violent opposition to the NSF, as, "not a workers' protest of any sort but a pogrom organised by structures of the state." Acting on the orders of the state, according to Harman, the miners were also targeting vulnerable groups, such as gypsies, "in the days that followed the pogrom the *Guardian* reported that some miners were unhappy at their role as Iliescu's storm troopers and were calling for a

---

[7] Rady, *Romania in Turmoil*, 171.
[8] Harry Barnes Jr., Introduction to *Romania After Tyranny*, ed. Daniel N. Nelson (Oxford: Westview, 1992), 1-7, 3.
[9] Alan Woods, "Romania: A Difficult Road to Restoration," *Militant International Review* 44 (Summer 1990): 32-40, 37.

strike."[10] Contrastingly, Woods responded to the same events by saying, "some of the human consequences of this can be regretted, but not the central fact that an attempt at capitalist counter-revolution was defeated by the movement of the workers themselves."[11] Galloway and Wylie seemed to concur with Woods's analysis that the protesters were threatening the revolution, and that in general, whereas ordinary workers and peasants supported the NSF, "the intellectuals, the middle-class, were the heart of the opposition."[12]

Consequently, the material with which *Mad Forest* engages is fraught with contention, accusations on all sides, claims, and counter-claims. Not only was there speculation that a *coup d'état* characterised the NSF's control of the revolution, but also that an attempted counter-*coup d'état* was put down by miners in June 1990. What seems clear amid this confusion, however, is that the brief revolutionary period–the window of opportunity when ordinary Romanians were self-empowered–was quickly lost when power was once again deferred.

Situating *Serious Money*

Serious Money rejoices, albeit ironically, in the most concentrated and abstract form of capitalism–the buying and selling of money, stocks, shares, debt, and futures. It re-enacts a satirical celebration of the accumulation of wealth, exploitation, and of profit making for its own sake. The projection of a world that assumes, endorses, and exults in a neoliberal capitalist order as the most desirable as well as the most natural socio-political environment seems to precipitate the collapse of the Soviet Bloc and in this case, the revolution in Romania. The social, political, and economic world of *Serious Money* is the grotesque epitome of the capitalist landscape, towards which the "shock therapists" of Eastern Europe wished swiftly to head. In contrast to the openness and fluidity that characterise the ideological perspective of *Mad Forest*, *Serious Money* is a straightforward satire on the logic of capital in the play's unambiguous representation of a closed world of greedy, exploitative, and dehumanised characters. On one level, the play highlights the irony of the word "free" in free-market, and shows democracy to be a sham when underpinned by free-market economics. Unlike the confusion surrounding the Romanian

---

[10] Chris Harman, "Why They Can't Deliver," *Socialist Worker Review* 133 (July/August 1990): 11.
[11] Woods, "Romania," 37.
[12] Galloway and Wylie, *Downfall*, 209-10.

revolution, the City of London is represented as knowable and fixed in its political and economic signification. Indeed, as discussed in Chapter 2, some members of the audience, who worked in the City, enjoyed watching themselves parodied on stage, seeming not to contest the viewpoint of the play. In this sense, it is less the content and processes of financial capitalism that are in dispute in *Serious Money*, but rather the ethical integrity of such a system.

For financial markets journalist, Philip Coggan, the free-market's moral deficiencies are the price worth paying for the most efficient system. He is keen to rehabilitate the sullied reputation of financial institutions, which he thinks, "perform an immensely valuable service: imagine life without cheque books, cashpoint cards, mortgages and hire-purchase agreements."[13] Part of the problem with audience reception of *Serious Money* is precisely that the play takes for granted the desire for a world *without* "cheque books, cashpoint cards, mortgages and hire-purchase agreements." Some sympathy with this anti-capitalist sensibility, or, at the very least, an opposition to an unconstrained free-market is a prerequisite to the spectator's cooperation with the play's satirical code. Clearly some stockbrokers in the audience refused the inducement of parodic self-recognition, favouring instead a complacent or, perhaps, somewhat anarchic identification with dynamic and morally unrestricted moneymaking.

Serious Money also serves to highlight the internal contradictions and incoherence of the moral codes of the enterprise culture, a culture that the Thatcher government was attempting to establish. Thatcher famously said, "there is no such thing as society. There are individual men and women and there are families."[14] Religious Studies scholars, Paul Heelas and Paul Morris claim that in attempting to diminish communities and abolish the idea of society, the Thatcher government needed more urgently to impose specific cultural values that would facilitate an enterprise culture, "'individuals,' *themselves*, must acquire the values associated with the culture," values such as "generosity, responsibility, discipline, hard work" and a sense of duty "if selfish, indeed anarchical, forces are not to be unleashed when people are given the opportunity to take greater control over their lives."[15] Lord Young of Graffham, one of the chief architects of

---

[13] Philip Coggan, *The Money Machine: How the City Works*, 2nd ed. (London: Penguin, 1989; first published 1986), 3.

[14] Margaret Thatcher, Interview by Douglas Keay, *Woman's Own* (31 October 1987): 8-10.

[15] Paul Heelas and Paul Morris, "Enterprise Culture: its Values and Value," in *The Values of the Enterprise Culture: The Moral Debate*, eds. Heelas and Morris, (London: Routledge, 1992), 1-25, 2-3.

the enterprise discourse, claims that in order for the market to function effectively "trust between individuals is needed," trust that will result from "a just set of rules," ensuring that "competition is fair," for "the market of the enterprise culture is not to be equated with the nineteenth-century laissez-faire economy," since "it is not a jungle without rules."[16] The incompatibility between trust and competition, justice and the market, fairness and the enterprise culture is played out to its full potential in *Serious Money*. In the same way, the tension between a ceaseless drive for profit and adherence to moral codes of conduct contributes towards the ironic mode of the play.

Indeed, in contrast to Young's perception, *Serious Money* depicts the City as a jungle with few rules, and the small numbers of rules in place are frequently broken. The inclusion of a scene from Thomas Shadwell's 1693 play, *The Volunteers, Or, The Stock-jobbers*, works in three ways. Firstly, it challenges the notion that the enterprise culture is new; secondly, it places *Serious Money* within a tradition of city comedy; and thirdly, it identifies the historical location of capitalism's birth. Fabian historian, R. H. Tawney dates "the rise of modern economic relations ... from the latter half of the seventeenth century." By the eighteenth-century society had "assumed something of the appearance of a great joint-stock company, in which political power and the receipt of dividends were justly assigned to those who held the most numerous shares."[17] Historian, Harold Perkin claims the enterprise culture reached "maturity in the Victorian age to boost the self-image of the self-made man." He traces its revival in the 1980s as an attempt "to boost the self-image of the corporate business man," and points to,

> the great advantage for its protagonists of implying that its opponents are lazy and supine dependants on the 'nanny state' and that other cultures and earlier ages were anything but enterprising.[18]

The inclusion of this short vignette from Shadwell's play in *Serious Money*, a vignette dramatising the beginnings of capitalist economy, works then to denude the free-market of its seemingly innate and trans-

---

[16] Lord Young of Graffham, "The Enterprise Regained," in *The Values of the Enterprise Culture*, eds. Heelas and Morris, 29-35, 30.

[17] R. H. Tawney, *The Acquisitive Society* (London: G. Bell and Sons, 1952), 10; 14-15.

[18] Harold Perkin, "The Enterprise Culture in Historical Perspective: Birth, Life, Death–and Resurrection?," in *The Values of the Enterprise Culture*, eds. Heelas and Morris, 36-60, 36.

historical claim as *the* natural state. Additionally, Shadwell was an oppositional figure, an anti-Royalist, and an early Whig, whose plays displayed, according to Helen Pellegrin, "a robust anticlericalism," as well as the "notion that freedom must be wrested from the grip that a harsh, dissembling older generation retains on the young." Shadwell's wife was Margaret Cavendish, "an early and vocal feminist," a partner who is clearly a counterpart to, and perhaps informs Shadwell's independent "forceful and unconventional heroines."[19]

The End of History?

Fukuyama's famous 1989 article in the North American journal, *National Interest*, is a cogently argued right–Hegelian critique (influenced by Alexandre Kojève) and development of such claims as Daniel Bell's notion of the end of ideology and the postmodernist philosopher Richard Rorty's declaration that the grand narratives of human emancipation are now defunct.[20] Fukuyama argues,

> the century that began full of self-confidence in the ultimate triumph of Western liberal democracy seems at its close to be returning full circle to where it started: not to an 'end of ideology' or a convergence between capitalism and socialism, as earlier predicted, but to an unabashed victory of economic and political liberalism.[21]

Fukuyama's thesis posits that history arises out of the conflict of ideologies, that liberalism has achieved a supreme and lasting victory, and hence, that this enduring victory equates with the end of history. As well as referring to the decline of global communism, Fukuyama points to the demise of class struggle as an index of the collapse of liberal democracy and free-market capitalism's major competitor.[22] Five years after the article, Fukuyama reasserted his central thesis that "liberalism does not have many serious competitors," and that "there is only 'one language,'

---

[19] Helen Pellegrin, Introduction to *Thomas Shadwell's The Libertine: A Critical Edition* (London: Garland Publishing, 1987), xii-xcix, xxxv; xcv.
[20] See Daniel Bell, *The End of Ideology* (Illinois: Free Press of Glencoe, 1960); Richard Rorty, *Contingency, Irony, and Solidarity* (Cambridge: Cambridge UP, 1989).
[21] Francis Fukuyama, "The End of History," *The National Interest* 16 (Summer 1989): 3-18, 3.
[22] Although Fukuyama's article preceded the Eastern European revolutions, the demise of communism swiftly followed its publication and served to give the article further impact.

that of liberal democracy."[23] Although dependent itself upon an engagement with a Hegelian, idealist, grand narrative, Fukuyama's argument can be placed in dialogue with postmodernist claims made earlier in the decade. The most high profile of these was Jean Baudrillard's (cynical) appropriation of Frankfurt School thinking concerning culture, politics, and ideology, leading to his declaration that struggles against oppression are now lost in mass consumerist society, a society that is dominated by simulacra and the hyper-real.[24]

Predictably, Fukuyama's end-of-history argument caught the imagination of the establishment in the United States. In his searing critique of Fukuyama's arguments in *Spectres of Marx*, Jacques Derrida notes the important contribution of the end-of-history thesis to an attempt to establish "an unprecedented form of hegemony," part of this attempt consisting in "a great 'conjuration' against Marxism."[25] But as well as fuelling new attempts by the right to neutralise socialist discourses, the end-of-history thesis also increased the general malaise of the Left in Britain and elsewhere. The "post-isms" and "end-isms" were accommodated to a significant degree by the academic Left, *New Left Review*, and *Marxism Today*. Although Eric Hobsbawm recognised the emptiness of Fukuyama's predictions ("few prophesies look like being more short-lived than that one"), he nevertheless inadvertently buttressed some of Fukuyama's main tenets when he viewed the 1989 revolutions as the permanent closure of the revolutionary narrative initiated in 1917, "for over 70 years all Western governments and ruling classes were haunted by the spectre of social revolution and communism." For Hobsbawm, then, the Eastern European revolutions were "the end of the era in which world history was about the October Revolution."[26] However, as Jürgen Habermas rightly argues,

> the presence of large masses gathering in squares and mobilising on the streets managed, astoundingly, to disempower a regime that was armed to the teeth. It was, in other words, precisely the sort of spontaneous mass

---

[23] Fukuyama, "Reflections on *End of History*, Five Years Later," in *After History? Francis Fukuyama and His Critics,* ed. Timothy Burns (London: Rowman, 1994), 239–58, 257.

[24] See Jean Baudrillard, *Simulations* (New York: Semiotext, 1983); Jean Baudrillard, *The Consumer Society: Myths and Structures* (London: Sage, 1998).

[25] Jacques Derrida, *Spectres of Marx: The State of the Debt, the Work of Mourning, and the New International*, trans. Peggy Kamuf (New York: Routledge, 1994), 50.

[26] Eric Hobsbawm, "Goodbye To All That," *Marxism Today* (October 1990): 18–23, 23; 18.

action that once provided so many revolutionary theorists with a model, but which had recently been presumed to be dead. [27]

That said, Vladimir Tismaneanu is, of course, persuasive in his assertion that "Ceauşescu's more than two decades of rule succeeded in compromising the very name of Marxist political and social doctrine."[28] Yet, during the Romanian revolution, large numbers of young people, students, and workers participated in revolutionary activities, some forming committees, temporarily taking control of key civic sites, such as government buildings and radio and television stations, or engaging in armed conflict against a belligerently resistant political establishment. The ghosts of Marx and the spectre of the 1917 revolution (to borrow again from Derrida) are undoubtedly present in the 1989 revolutions, and particularly in the Romanian instance.

Mad Forest certainly does not dramatise a tangible alternative to free-market capitalism. However, neither does the narrative of the play treat the characteristics of Western political economy as a panacea for healing the ills of the Ceauşescu regime. In fact, specific and unmistakable signifiers of the United States (*the* emblematic capitalist power) are presented only to expose them as undesirable, if not objectionable. The first of two weddings is between Lucia and the American, Wayne. Wayne's presence is limited to the wedding scene, and he has no lines, but he is significant as the encroaching presence of values represented by the centre of neoliberal power, a power gleefully awaiting the destruction of the Eastern European regimes. It is because of Wayne that the Vladu family benefits from extra produce, such as eggs and American cigarettes. It is also because of Wayne's money that Lucia is able to bribe the doctor to abort illegally what we find out later is her Hungarian lover, Ianoş's, baby. But most insidiously, the marriage between Lucia and Wayne has aroused the suspicion and disapproval of the authorities. Bogdan is questioned by Securitate over his loyalty, demoted from the position of foreman, and warned that life will be made more difficult for his family; and indeed, Irina is also affected: she is moved to a workplace much further away from home. Association with this emblematic American figure, a figure that the

---

[27] Jürgen Habermas, "What Does Socialism Mean Today? The Rectifying Revolution and the Need for New Thinking on the Left," *New Left Review* 183, (September/October 1990): 3-21, 7.
[28] Vladimir Tismăneanu, "From Arrogance to Irrelevance: Avatars of Marxism in Romania," in *The Road to Disillusion: From Critical Marxism to Postcommunism in Eastern Europe*, ed. Raymond Taras (London: M. E. Sharpe, 1992), 135-50, 135.

audience never hears speak but whose impact is considerable, increases the level of repression for the family. This is clearly a further indictment of the Ceauşescu regime. However, American "assistance" is also subtly menacing: private American money is offered as the solution to an unwanted pregnancy and to the shortage of family resources; impinging neo-imperialism is an alternative reading of this assistance.

Notably, the marriage between Lucia and Wayne fails, as she prefers Ianoş. But she also ends up rejecting America; "I don't like America" (152) she replies to Ianoş, who says he would like to go there. Lucia's fickle and self-centred disposition is suggested at several times–particularly in her insensitive response to Toma, a Romanian orphan whom Ianoş's family adopts–but also in her first words on returning from America after the revolution: "in America everyone's thrilled" (144). However, her description of American consumerism is laden with anxiety,

> there are walls of fruit in America, five different kinds of apples, and oranges, grapes, pears, bananas, melons, different kinds of melon, and things I don't know the name–and the vegetables, the aubergines are a purple they look as if they've been varnished, red yellow green peppers, white onions red onions, bright orange carrots somebody has shone every carrot, and the greens, cabbage spinach broad beans courgettes, I still stare every time I go shopping. And the garbage, everyone throws away great bags full of food and paper and tins, every day, huge bags, huge dustbins, people live out of them. (144)

The celebratory discourse of consumerism, with its seductive promise of fulfilment, is shown to be an illusion, an illusion signified by the futility of having access to "five different kinds of apples" and the doubtful nutritional value of eating the chemically vivid "bright orange carrots." The last lines of Lucia's speech reveal her shock at the disparity between the needs and desires of middle-class Americans, who discard bagfuls of food each week, and the privation of those who take the remains because they cannot afford to satisfy basic needs.[29] Lucia's rejection of Wayne and America is also, in an important sense, the play's articulation of antipathy towards the free market.

While *Mad Forest* intimates the undesirability of capitalist restoration, *Serious Money* contains no suggestion of competition or threat to its

---

[29] Churchill's notes taken during the Bucharest production of *Mad Forest*, read, "long late-night talk about free market in which I mention the homeless in New York and London. 'But only because they want. Yes, I read about a doctor who slept outside for two months in California.'" Quoted in Philip Roberts, *About Churchill: The Playwright and the* Work (London: Faber, 2008), 239.

enclosed world of the City. However, if this is the pinnacle of human achievement–the end of history–the play indicates that it is an achievement comprising an anachronistic economic mode, one that restricts human agency to economic activity confined within a matrix of super-exploitation. In the first scene from Shadwell's seventeenth-century play, Hackwell says to his wife during the discussion over the utility of certain products, "it's no matter whether it turns to use or not; the main end verily is to turn the penny in the way of stock jobbing, that's all" (196). As well as historicising stocks and shares dealing, an activity constituting the very "heart of capitalism," according to Coggan, this scene also connects with a literary tradition of city comedies that dramatise a sullied and debased world of greedy cheats and swindlers.[30] Indeed, one of the most famous seventeenth-century city comedies, Ben Jonson's *Volpone* (1606), compares favourably in moral terms with *Serious Money*, since at least Volpone cons an Advocate, a Gentleman, and a Merchant, all of whom are arguably fair game.[31] In *Serious Money* there is an unapologetic fleecing of workers, developing countries, and the poor.

The sense of political and economic anachronism created by the play's employment of an old genre and its use of verse is offset by its keen allusion to the contemporary moment. Churchill comments,

> as usual the group opened the subject up in a way one person couldn't possibly have done in the time or in many times the time, and gave me a sense of that appalling and exciting world that carried me through weeks of reading and researching alone during Big Bang, the Guinness scandal, Boesky, all of which, with extraordinary timing, happened between the workshop and the beginning of rehearsal.[32]

In Act 1, Greville mentions the "Big Bang" (97), a reference to the deregulation of stock markets in October 1986, less than six months before the play's first performance in March 1987. There are mischievous mentions of the Guinness scandal (213; 236) and offensive allusions to AIDS (Scilla exclaims, "at work they ask for tea in an Aids cup, they mean a disposable" [218]). There is more than one mention of the Boesky affair (233), a reference to space invaders (244), Bob Geldof (261), the US-backed Contras in Nicaragua (272), filofaxes (302), and the Channel Tunnel (307). In addition to these topical cultural allusions, the play is full

---

[30] Coggan, *The Money Machine*, 95.
[31] Ben Jonson, *Volpone*, ed. Philip Brockbank (London: A & C Black Publishers, 1968; first published in 1607).
[32] Churchill, Introduction to *Caryl Churchill Plays: 2*, ix-x, x.

of City jargon both old and new, "Paris intervention rate" (202), "treasury bond dealer" (203), "insider dealing" (221), "arbitrage" (233), and "hedging" (244).

Hence, the play communicates through a fine balance of contemporary idiom and an old style, structure, and genre. The glossiness that complements the sense of immediacy resulting from the topical references is, however, threatened by old-style Hobbesian tropes that make up the dramatic imagery. This is not the endpoint of human history but an old world of backstabbing, dog eat dog, and haggling at the market place. The banker, Merrison, proclaims, "man is a gambling animal" (208); we hear from Zac, "the new guys are hungrier and hornier," and that it is "like Darwin says, survival of the fit" (211). Scilla says, "trading options and futures looks tricky if you don't understand it. But if you're good at market timing you can make out like a bandit" (243), and Joanne likens the floor of the London International Financial Futures Exchange to "animals in a zoo" (244). Animal metaphors are part of the discourse of trading, as illustrated in Nigel's assertion, "I assure you that the stag is not my role" (266).[33] The predatory masculinist connotations of this are not subtle and the resonance of the animal motifs of *Volpone* is clearly visible.

In contrast to Young's earlier defence of the culture of enterprise as not akin to the nineteenth-century laissez-faire economy, and not "a jungle without rules," *Serious Money* depicts the values of the City to be precisely reflective of these attributes. The play also represents the City "community" as defined entirely by community members' financial activities; when Dave, Martin, Brian, Terry, and Vince are out socialising, the subjects of Martin's sexist joke are "two eurobond dealers" (303). Jake says, "I never dream. (I never sleep)" (231); trading becomes the very essence of life, with dreaming, the imagination, and even sleep, unimportant. On a rare occasion when Jake employs his imagination and expresses desire, it is desire for "owning the spring" and "a big cube of sea, right down to the bottom, all the fish, the weeds, the lot" (231). Scilla plays the game, Pass the Pig with Grimes since "it's a good way to unwind because when trading stops you don't know what to do with your mind" (277). Zac and Jacinta's highly comical "romantic" exchange is perhaps the most poignant example of this,

---

[33] The stag is an investor who seeks to profit from new issues. Bears are investors who believe that share or bond prices are likely to fall. Bulls are investors who believe that share or bond prices are likely to rise. See Coggan, Glossary to *The Money Machine*, 194-202, 194; 195.

JACINTA: I love the way you are so obsessed when you're thinking about your bids.
ZAC: I love that terrible hospital scam and the drug addicted kids.
JACINTA: I love the way you never stop work, I hate a man who's lazy.
ZAC: The way you unloaded your copper mines drove me completely crazy. (300)

A Fukuyama-informed vision of a mature civilisation produced by the optimum social and economic system is replaced, instead, in *Serious Money* by a financial world populated by caricatures that reflect a severe reduction of the human subject and the erasure of human community.

Beyond the sparkle and shininess that signifies the new, lays the rot so recognisable in seventeenth-century city comedies; backstabbing, acts of revenge, murder, exploitation, dishonesty and the cheapening of human life are the main activities of this world. The play responds to the Fukuyama end-of-history moment by firstly portraying the City utopia as in part an effect of a perceived victory of free-market capitalism, and secondly by satirising that world and performing its absence of humanity to chilling effect. The future prospects for this world are challenged in *Serious Money*, not through the presence of a tangible threat within the play, but rather through the City's dependence on the unbridgeable contradictions between freedom and the free-market, trust and competition, and fairness and contest. In this sense, *Serious Money* relies on the spectator to recognise the play's deconstructive nature and to perceive the unstable basis upon which the jubilatory discourse of the City rests.

The political narrative of *Mad Forest* cautiously guards against the recuperation of the play as part of this jubilant, neoliberal discourse, a discourse that is both "very novel and so ancient" as well as "both powerful and, as always, worried, fragile, anxious."[34] Derrida's assertion, "never in history, has the horizon of the thing whose survival is being celebrated (namely, all the old models of the capitalist and liberal world) been as dark, threatening, and threatened,"[35] provides a useful illumination of the political coordinates within which *Mad Forest* locates itself. Indeed, the signifiers of the old models of capitalism in the play are represented as fragile and stale, as well as threatening and undesirable. In addition to imbuing the Ceauşescu regime with a heavily outmoded significance, the play also indicates that the NSF's (capitalist) competitors are equally burdened with historical anachronism. The main parties to choose from in

---

[34] Derrida, *Spectres of Marx*, 50.
[35] Derrida, *Spectres of Marx*, 52.

the election were the NSF, the Hungarian Democratic Union of Romania, the National Liberal Party, and the National Peasants Party. The latter two were the NSF's main rivals and were led by veterans of the pre-communist period; thus, significantly, there was nothing new to reflect the revolutionary spirit of the moment, only old-communist versus pre-communist parties, and a choice between gradual, or rapid, return to free-market capitalism. In part three, scene five, at Lucia's grandparents, the family discuss the murder of a man who put up posters for the National Peasants Party,

> GRANDFATHER: A lot of people didn't like him because he used to be a big landowner. The Peasants Party would give him back his land.
> FLORINA: So was he killed because / the rest of the
> LUCIA: I thought the Peasants Party was for peasants.
> IANOŞ: No, they're millionaires the leaders of it.
> FlORINA: village didn't want him to get all the land?
> LUCIA: He should get it / if it's his.
> FlORINA: No after all this time working on it / everyone (155)

The old pre-communist parties promoted the rapid restoration of a free-market economy with no rejuvenated thinking to reflect the newfound political agency that the revolution had inspired. Furthermore, the overlaps between the old parties including the communists abounded, as illustrated in the grandfather's assertion, "he was a party member. He was very big round here. He was a big Securitate man," to which Lucia responds, "so whose side was he on?"(155).

Rather than conceding the ideological supremacy of a neoliberal agenda, *Mad Forest* represents the revolution as an expression of a myriad of social and political impulses, none of which, however, is conterminous with Fukuyama's triumphant end-of-history discourse. As with the revolutionary hopes in Churchill's 1976 play *Light Shining*, a dominant social class quickly appropriates the space for self-realisation. But the anti-communist expressions of many of the characters are shown not to be equivalent to a desire for the restoration of a capitalist economy; Flavia says, "black market prices have shot up," to which Irina responds," it's not black market, it's free market" (168). Bogdan worries about privatisation, "private schools, private hospitals. I've seen what happens to old people. I want to buy my father a decent death" (174). The play points towards the consciousness, activities, and relationships among ordinary people as the location of historical development, and these become fluid and dynamic, opening up sites of discussion usually closed or at least muted in communist and capitalist systems alike.

Ideological, Political and Moral (un)certainties

Klaus Peter Müller emphasises *Serious Money's* exposure of the City's permeation of society as a whole.[36] The last scene, "Everybody," consists of characters reporting to the audience what happens to them after the main action of the play.[37] Corman, the corporate raider, who was persuaded by the Tory minister to halt the takeover in order to prevent any scandal from affecting the party's election chances, has been made a Lord and is also Chairman of the Board of the National Theatre. The white knight, Biddulph, is "big in ITV" (307) as well as running Albion. The American arbitrageur, Marylou Baines runs for the United States Presidency in 1996 and the banker Merrison has been "ambassador to London, Paris, Rome" (307). The presence of the City in politics, high culture, the media and international diplomacy reveals the extent of its influence in all sections of public life.

The play's insistence on emphasising the pervasive presence of City speculators in public life seems not to support a reading of the play that suggests only a certain section of the financial community are deserving of condemnation. As discussed in Chapter 2, Churchill removes the option of morally differentiating between old and new money. She also rejects the idea that social and economic reform by a Labour government would make a significant difference. As part of Zac's concluding narration he says,

> And the Conservatives romped home with a landslide victory for five more
> glorious years.
> (Which was handy though not essential because it would take far more
> than Labour to stop us.) (306)

The arguments on the Centre Left for reforming the stock market–such as those made by Fabians, David Goodhart and Charles Grant ("there is probably no better means–the October 1987 crash and crazy lurches in the market notwithstanding"[38])–are clearly not entertained in *Serious Money*.

---

[36] Klaus Peter Müller, "A Serious City Comedy: Fe/Male History and Value Judgements in Caryl Churchill's *Serious Money*," *Modern Drama* 33. 3 (September 1990): 347-62, 356.

[37] This, ironically, recalls the last scene, "After," of *Light Shining*. The political radicals in the 1976 play face defeat, poverty, and censorship, whereas the stockbrokers in *Serious Money* are rewarded with titles and top public positions.

[38] David Goodhart and Charles Grant, "Making the City work," *Fabian Tract* 528 (July 1988), 3.

The reach of international capital exceeds national boundaries, and, according to American journalist, Doug Henwood, is organised around,

> a set of institutions designed to maximise the wealth and power of the most privileged group of people in the world, the creditor-rentier class of the First World and their junior partners in the Third.[39]

Henwood's analysis is an appropriate description of the politico-economic perspective of the play.

Unlike other Churchill plays, raced and gendered identities are less of a preoccupation in *Serious Money*. This is partly due to the economic power that the characters hold, a power that partially raises them above the effects of the divisions and oppressions constituted by global capitalism. Linda Kintz states,

> while gender, race, and class seem to disappear, as each subject indistinguishably competes with every other Neo-individual, the ostensible disappearance of divisions–for instance between men and women, metropolitan and third-world traders–at the very top levels of speculative finance is achieved only by their exacerbation at every level below.[40]

Jacinta has no empathy with her fellow Peruvians, who suffer under economic imperialism: "Peru leads the way resisting the IMF, refusing to pay the interest, but I don't want to make things difficult for the banks, I prefer to support them, why should my money stay in Peru and suffer?" (255). Parasitically, she thrives on adversity, as does Nigel Abjibala, who, in concurrence with Zac ("The IMF is not a charity. It has to insist on absolute austerity" [260]), replies,

> Absolutely. It can't be namby pamby.
> These countries must accept restricted diets.
> The governments must explain, if there are food riots,
> That paying the western banks is the priority. (261)

The immunity of Nigel and Jacinta from discrimination, however, is subject to their cooperation with white, male, Western capitalist codes of individualism, codes that constitute the subject positions within the financial community.

---

[39] Doug Henwood, *Wall Street: How it Works and for Whom* (London: Verso, 1997), 7.
[40] Linda Kintz, "Performing Capital in Caryl Churchill's *Serious Money*," *Theatre Journal* 50. 3 (October 1999): 251-65, 259.

The unifying point of connection in this ruthless world of greedy backstabbers is the belief in the market. Part of the discourse of this world is informed by theories of the classic political economists, Thomas Malthus, Friedrick Hayek and Milton Friedman, who view liberty and equality as mutually exclusive.[41] Marxist philosopher, Sean Sayers comments, "to its defenders, the market is the very system of liberty in economic life; and one that leads to freedom in the wider social and political sphere as well."[42] Indeed in this view, inequality necessarily exists as a result of individual freedoms but is also a condition considered to be both essential and sought-after in order to guarantee competition and the production of wealth. *Serious Money* berates this thinking through its exposure of the "efficiency" of the market as a fallacy and its identification of individual liberty as the sole preserve of those making "serious money." Even then, the liberty enjoyed seems rather limited, taking the form of gambling, decadent consumption of food and alcohol, drug taking, hunting, and participating in brief, sexual encounters. Most of all what the play sneers at is the idea that the free-market leads to a better, more progressive world for all. Zac's speech exposes the ludicrous nature of this claim,

> the so-called third world doesn't want our charity or aid.
> All they need is the chance to sit down in front of some green screens and trade.
> (They don't have the money, sure, but just so long as they have freedom from communism so they can do it when they do have the money.)
> Pictures of starving babies are misleading and patronising.
> Because there's plenty of rich people in those countries, it's just the masses that's poor … (255)

The unequivocal contempt for the City and its "community" is spelled out in much of the dialogue, with the characters revealing an alarming disregard for anything other than the accumulation of profit.

While the world of *Serious Money* is defined clearly as ideologically abhorrent, and contains no political ambivalence, the social and political landscape dramatised in *Mad Forest* is full of ambiguity and uncertainty.

---

[41] See T. R. Malthus, *The Principles of Political Economy* (London: International Economic Circle: London School of Economics and Political Science, 1936; first published in 1836); Friedrich A. von Hayek, *Economic Freedom* (Oxford: Basil Blackwell, 1991); Milton Friedman, *Capitalism and Economics* (London: University of Chicago Press, 1962).
[42] Sean Sayers, "The Human Impact of the Market," in *The Values of the Enterprise Culture*, eds. Heelas and Morris, 120-38, 121.

The ideological hesitation of the play's perspective is reiterated in many aspects of the drama. A prime example of this is in the first act, which is characterised by several long silences (*"Bogdan and Irina Vladu sit in silence"* [107]; *"Mihai thinking and making notes, Flavia correcting exercise books, Radu drawing. They sit in silence for some time"* [108]; and *"Flavia and Mihai sitting silently over their work"* [118]). The silences are certainly reflective of the stifling context of the Ceauşescu regime but they also mark the absence of narrative in the play, a narrative providing a coherent account of the plot but also a political narrative *explaining* the revolutionary period. The lack of a clear sense of political direction in the play is both a purposeful depiction of the dearth of political options in revolutionary Romania as well as a reflection of the lack of clarity and weakening of confidence on the part of the British Left in relation to its response to the demise of the Eastern bloc. However, there is, too, an attempt not to appropriate the revolution–not to speak *for* Romanians but allow instead a cultural difference to remain, a difference articulated in part in the play's refusal to be fully understood.

The characters develop sophisticated modes of negotiating and subverting the state's system of repression, and in the process, they repudiate their passive, complicit subject positions. This reaches a high point when Gabriel moves beyond covert and defensive modes of resistance towards more open forms of non-cooperation. In scene ten, he arrives at his parents' house and excitedly starts to inform his family–without turning the radio on–of his dealings with the Securitate. Irina's response–"wait, stop, there's no power"–and the stage directions which designate that she *"puts her hand over her ears"* (117) indicate the perceived danger of doing this. However, his newfound courage provides Gabriel with the confidence to transgress what seem like immutable boundaries, and this activates a similar impulse in the others with Florina saying, "no, what if they do hear, they know what he did"; the stage directions read, *"after a while"* Irina *"starts to listen again"* (117). Bogdan too, expresses endorsement ("you're a good boy" [118]), although appreciation of Gabriel's defiance is not unanimous; Lucia asks, "what if I don't get my passport?" (118).

Gabriel cleverly manipulates the statutory code so that he can escape the Securitate's request that he inform on his colleagues,

> and I said, 'Of course I'd like to help you,' and then I actually remembered, listen to this, 'As Comrade Ceauşescu says, "For each and every citizen work is an honorary fundamental duty. Each of us should demonstrate high professional probity, competence, creativity, devotion and passion in our work." And because I'm a patriot I work so hard that I

can't think about anything else, I wouldn't be able to listen to what my
colleagues talk about because I have to concentrate. (117)

Gabriel's skilful process of deconstruction reveals weaknesses in the
coherence of the state's disciplinary codes; how can you dedicate yourself
to your work and at the same time focus on the conversations and actions
of others? Additionally, he openly divulges this information to his family
in contravention of perceived surveillance. Furthermore, and perhaps most
importantly, Gabriel's action is one of refusing to betray his fellow
workers, and is, therefore, a thoroughly social and comradely action. His
refusal recalls a politics that depends upon a sense of collectivism,
solidarity, and unity. Gabriel gains a sense of agency and autonomy: "and
I'm so happy because I've put myself on the other side, I hardly knew
there was one" (117). The other side, however, is fluid, embryonic, and in
want of political and theoretical development, which is why the revolution
is so swiftly expropriated.

The reports that make up the revolutionary narrative in part two form a
dynamic mesh, a mesh that contains contradictory strands jostling in a
state of flux. The painter's statement ("I had an empty soul. I didn't know
who I was" [127]) gestures as much towards the potential for change,
towards transformed identities and a new sense of self-awareness, as it
does towards the fear and terror prompted by violent confrontation. We
hear from a student that "some workers from the People's Palace came
with construction material to make barricades" (125); he says a little later,
"we tried to make a barricade in Rosetti Place. We set fire to a truck"
(126). The following day, the housepainter sees "thousands of workers
from the Industrial Platforms … more and more, two three kilometres"
(129). The translator says, "I've noticed in films people scatter away from
gunfire but here people came out saying, 'What's that?' People were
shouting, 'Come with us,' so we went in the courtyard and shouted too'"
(129). A student describes the fear of seeing the "police in front of the
Intercontinental Hotel" but adds "in a crowd you disappear and feel
stronger" (130). The translator, who says, "everyone was hugging and
kissing each other, you were kissing a chap you'd never seen before"
(130), reinforces this sense of solidarity and comradeship. But this
renewed feeling of commonality and shared sense of militancy sits
alongside residual divisions; "we hadn't gone far when we saw a crowd of
people with banners with Jos Ceauşescu, shouting, 'Come and join us.'
They were low class men so we didn't know if we could trust them" (130),
reports one of the students.

The most visible divisions in the play are those arising from racism,
xenophobia, and ethnic hatred. The fascism of the Iron Guard that

resurfaces in post-revolutionary Romania appears in scene nine, where the angel tells the priest "the Iron Guard used to be rather charming and called themselves the League of the Archangel Michael and carried my picture about" (116). Rady describes Iron Guard ideology as owing "much to the peasant populist movement of the nineteenth century, but with the rational element burnt out leaving only a malignant emotionalism."[43] The priest's challenge to the angel over his flirtation with fascism places other instances in the play of racism and xenophobia in the context of an established history of fascism in Romania, a history formed out of complicity of the Orthodox Church with the Iron Guard and the pre-war pro-Nazi governments. Notably, the mode of representation of these fascist impulses is anti-realist. In the New York premiere, the angel appeared "in resplendent Byzantine artifice under brilliant illumination and to the accompaniment of stirring ecclesiastical music."[44] Una Chaudhuri interprets the angel's fantastical presence first, as a joke; second, as a manifestation of the priest's conscience; and third, after both of these have been rejected, as intentionally inexplicable: "it is recognition of the actual enigma of the supposedly familiar."[45] Yet the angel is undoubtedly spectral in nature, and its importance can be attributed to its capacity to haunt. Like the radical currents of the October 1917 revolution, a predilection for fascism lingers, threatening to resurface at any moment. In this way, the experience of contemporary events played out in the intensely realist nature of many of the scenes is supplemented by an alternative, anti-realist discourse that facilitates the representation of past and future histories.

Most racist incidents occur after the revolution. Pre-revolution, the characters operate in stifling conditions, speaking in code, and repressing thoughts and desires. The gap of anticipation created by revolution provides them with the opportunity to express their means of making sense of past and present, including voicing beliefs steeped in bigotry and reactionary frameworks for thinking. Lucia, whose lover is Hungarian, seeks to reposition Hungarians in the ethno-political matrix: "Hungarians were fighting beside us they said on TV. And Ianoș wasn't hurt, that's good. I think Americans like Hungarians" (145). In response to Gabriel's xenophobia ("the poor Hungarians have a bad time because they're not treated better than everyone else" [145]), Lucia replies, "this is what we

---

[43] Rady, *Romania in Turmoil*, 24.
[44] Stanton B. Garner Jr., Review of *Mad Forest*, *Theatre Review* (1992): 399-401, 399.
[45] Una Chaudhuri, *Staging Place: The Geography of Modern Drama* (Ann Arbor: University of Michigan Press, 1998), 152.

used to say before. Don't we say something different?" (145) But her desire to move away from anti-Hungarian sloganeering seems selfishly motivated and does not extend to a more enlightened anti-racism:

> in America they even like the idea of gypsies, they think how quaint. But I said to them you don't like blacks here, you don't like hispanics, we're talking about lazy greedy crazy people who drink too much and get rich on the black market. That shut them up. (146)

Fukuyama's model of liberal democracy, America, is once again undermined, as Lucia appeals to American racism to justify discriminating against Romanian gypsies.

Mad Forest is often approached as a postmodern play that, in Tony Mitchell's description, "eschews the 'master narratives' of totalising social-realist paradigms on the one hand and epic pageantry on the other for an open-ended, quasi-cinematic series of cryptic vignettes portraying everyday life in Romania."[46] Donna Soto-Morettini describes the play as "reinforcing neither a 'meta-narrative' of progress, nor the ideals of reason";[47] and Chaudhuri claims, "in the extreme, *Mad Forest* presents place itself as a function of change, and change, in turn, as an effect of language, especially spoken language."[48] While the uncertainty expressed in the drama can be characterised as fractured and mosaic, the play is, nonetheless, more than a postmodern articulation of what Soto-Morettini describes as a "post-Enlightenment sphere," where the examination of "political cynicism" takes place.[49] Although the play does not offer a coherent clarification of the revolutionary narrative or provide tangible political solutions, *Mad Forest* nevertheless communicates a faith in emancipatory goals. Notwithstanding the play's ideological hesitation and its construction of a certain cultural untranslatability, there remains a strong commitment to the potential of both individual and collective resistance and a faith in the characters' desire for self-empowerment and self-realisation. Unlike other British Left plays on the break-up of the Eastern bloc, such as David Edgar's *The Shape of the Table* (on the subject of political negotiations in Czechoslovakia) and Howard Brenton and

---

[46] Tony Mitchell, "Caryl Churchill's *Mad Forest*: Polyphonic Representations of Southeastern Europe," *Modern Drama* 36.2 (1993): 499-511, 500.
[47] Donna Soto-Morettini, "Revolution and the Fatally Clever Smile: Caryl Churchill's *Mad Forest*," *Journal of Dramatic Theory and Criticism* 9. 1 (Fall 1994): 105-18, 114.
[48] Chaudhuri, *Staging Place,* 148.
[49] Soto-Morettini, "Revolution and the Fatally Clever Smile," 114; 115.

Tariq Ali's *Moscow Gold* (concerning power struggles between Gorbachev and Yeltsin with three cleaners representing the mass of ordinary people), Churchill populates the stage with ordinary people.[50] Through the play's emphasis on and sympathy with figures, families, and communities that lack official political agency, it intimates its interest and faith in cooperative and popular resistance. The political silences in *Mad Forest*, then, can be read partly as an objectification of the challenges confronting British Left engagement with the Eastern European revolutions; partly an attempt to construct and contribute towards a certain Romanian self-determination; and partly as an interrogation of the process of history making, but the effect of these silences is not an insistence on privileging a representation of the world that–in Terry Eagleton's description of postmodernism–is "contingent, ungrounded, diverse, unstable, indeterminate."[51]

The Triumph of Capitalism?

The demise of the Stalinist regimes in Eastern Europe and the acceleration and expansion of the global free market no doubt strengthened the hegemony of capitalist discourses. The Left too, conceded some ground to this thinking. Alex Callinicos holds that *New Left Review* perceived the Eastern European regimes as a "distorted expression of revolutionary impulses" and "thus, while supporting anti-bureaucratic movements in the Soviet bloc," it "gave its critical support to the East against the West in what it regarded as the 'Great Contest' between capitalism and communism." This led to the conclusion that the Eastern European revolutions were "a historical setback for the left."[52] Because much of the British Left had not prioritised opposition to the Stalinist regimes, the perception that socialism was synonymous with Stalinism was not adequately challenged. Edward Thompson proposed "the third way" as a path out of the "two-camps [capitalism/communism] thinking" along the lines of "the peace and human-rights movements of the 1980s, and their associated or supportive 'new social movements.'"[53] Thompson's "third way" was an attempt to exist within the framework of capitalist

---

[50] David Edgar, *The Shape of the Table* (London: Nick Hern, 1990); Tariq Ali and Howard Brenton, *Moscow Gold* (London: Nick Hern, 1990).

[51] Terry Eagleton, Preface to *The Illusions of Postmodernism* (Oxford: Blackwell, 1996), vii-x, vii.

[52] Callinicos, *The Revenge of History*, 14.

[53] Edward Thompson, "The Ends of the Cold War," *New Left Review* 182 (July/August 1990): 139-46, 144.

economics, but with a reforming agenda, an agenda that gave a greater voice to constituencies historically less empowered, radically decreased military expenditure, and spent much more on welfare and the environment.[54] However, as Halliday states, "much of what masquerades as 'third' was in reality one or other of the first two in disguise."[55] Significantly, the "third way" no longer engaged with the notion of socialism as a separate, autonomous system in itself, a socio-economic structure extraneous to and incompatible with capitalism. Charlie Leadbeater's comment in *New Times*–"the Left has to acknowledge the obvious; the market, competition, can be useful economic tools to deliver consumer choice"–is an unequivocal index of the move rightwards of influential sections of the British Left.[56]

The fall of communism was coterminous with capitalist indulgence in unfettered profit making, and this juncture connects *Mad Forest* and *Serious Money*. Hobsbawm argues that Western anxiety over the possible subversive effects of Soviet communism on Western workers was so great that Western governments attempted to ward this danger off by prioritising full employment, relatively decent wages, and a strong welfare state. However, with the fall of Eastern Europe, Hobsbawm asked, "why should the rich, especially in countries such as ours, where they now glory in injustice and inequality, bother about anyone except themselves?"[57] With the communist threat defused and the Labour movement weakened, the necessity for capitalists to curtail exploitation in order to appease workers, according to Hobswawm, no longer had a basis.

---

[54] Thompson's "third way" shows some continuity with non-Stalinist communism, in contrast to the New Labour third way, which is significantly more pro-capitalist. One of the chief architects of this latter third way is Anthony Giddens. See *Beyond Left and Right: The Future of Radical Politics* (Cambridge: Polity Press, 1994); *The Third Way: The Renewal of Social Democracy* (Cambridge: Polity Press, 1998).

[55] Halliday, "A Reply to Edward Thompson," *New Left Review* 182 (July/August 1990): 150.

[56] Charlie Leadbeater, "Power to the Person," in *New Times: The Changing Face of Politics in the 1990s*, eds. Stuart Hall and Martin Jacques (London: Lawrence & Wishart in association with Marxism Today, 1989), 137-49, 146.

[57] Hobsbawm, "Goodbye to All That," 23.

Serious Money dramatises this renewed sense of freedom.[58] The play sparkles with the delight of financiers who experience an unencumbered liberty to accumulate, to freely trade products, and as Scilla says, to "buy and sell money" [244]). The emancipation of the market produces an anti-civic sensibility, a sensibility that is reinforced by the lack of cultural texture characterising this world. The play is denuded of the traditional signifiers of cultural cohesion such as familial bonds, community ties, and municipal networks.

Many characters in the play are contemptuous of the customary high brow values of the appreciation of education and art. Jake "didn't go to university and learn to think twice" (205); trading does not require the skills of academic appraisal, as evidenced by Grimes, a gilts trader who has "a CSE in metalwork" (207). Durkfield, a trader and co-chief executive of Klein Merrick, is associated with the new "hungrier and hornier" (210) guys; "screw the Picassos," he says to his partner Merrison, the banker: "traders make two dollars profit for this company for every dollar made by you bankers" (209). High art is consumed by Gleason, the cabinet minister, who discusses the City with Corman in the interval of *King Lear* at the National Theatre. "Enjoying the show?" Gleason asks, to which Corman responds, "I'm not watching it" (296; 297). The exchange between Gleason and Corman is a sardonic reinvention of a speech by King Lear, which in turn is an anticipation of "third way" welfare statism.[59] Gleason misidentifies Cordelia as Ophelia, and with topical humour, Regan as Reagan. Gleason and Corman miss or misidentify the moral and political meanings in Shakespeare's play, which in turn, ironically, connects with the City spectators' misinterpretation of *Serious Money*, discussed in Chapter 2.

There is clearly a cultural class difference in the financial world; Scilla says, "if we've a Porsche in the garage and champagne in the glass we

---

[58] Although *Serious Money* was written and performed before the collapse of the USSR, the beginnings of the deterioration of Stalinism can be located earlier in the decade. In 1985 Gorbachev was in dialogue with Western leaders; he initiated key changes in political reform, Glasnost (openness), and in economic reform, Perestroika (reconstruction).

[59] "Poor naked wretches, whereso'er you are, / That bide the pelting of this pitiless storm, / How shall your houseless heads and unfed sides, / Your loop'ed and window'd raggedness, defend you / From seasons such as these? O! I have ta'en / Too little care of this. Take physic, Pomp; / Expose thyself to feel what wretches feel, / That thou mayst shake the superflux to them, / And show the Heavens more just." (3.4.28-36) William Shakespeare, *King Lear*, edited by R. A. Foakes (London: The Arden Shakespeare, 1997; first published in 1608).

don't notice there's a lot of power still held by men of daddy's class" (205). The Dickensian name, Grimes, is further reinforced by his headmaster's representation of him as a "hooligan" (4). The "frightful yobs" (213), as Greville describes Dave, Martin, Brian, Terry, Vince, Joanne, and Kathy, who work with Scilla on the floor of LIFFE, are the upwardly mobile ex-working-class, the "Romford scholar(s) in Eurodollars" (253) and the "barrow boys" (215), as Frosby calls them. While the Essex boys and girls are superciliously dismissed by the upper-class section of the financial community, this latter group are in turn portrayed as sadistic parasites:

> His mouth's rather hard and he is very strong,
> Don't fight him, he'll pull out your arms by the socket.
> There's not a horse faster,
> So don't step on hounds and don't override master. (212)

They are figured as vulgar vestiges left over from a past, more barbaric, age as they repeat the same refrain at the meet of a foxhunt.

Serious Money depicts the financial world–the centre of capitalist systems–as irreformable. Both old and new money are portrayed as equally odious and united in their commitment to nothing except the liberty to accrue limitless hoards of financial products, stocks, shares and money. The free market could not be made to submit to a third way, particularly since the influence of the City can be located in every sector of society. In this analysis, the play is fundamentally anti-capitalist. However, in privileging this small, but powerful world of financial operators as the object of dramatic enquiry, the play omits the presence of competing communities or alternative ideologies. Yet, its political potential is drawn from the more progressive context of the play's performance; it is assumed the audience's value systems will reject this appalling vision of humanity, a vision that masquerades as the pinnacle of human achievement.

In *Mad Forest* Churchill presents the characters' far from simple and at times contradictory engagement with the Ceauşescus, communism, revolution, Western capitalism, and elections; nevertheless, the diverse engagements are always contextualised. Radu's vehement anti-communism, for example, continues in his attitude towards the NSF, and his middle-class identification with the opposition is made clear: "Iliescu's going to get in because the workers and peasants are stupid" (153). This class arrogance causes problems in his relationship with Florina, who feels "in a panic," after the revolution, since before she could "keep everything out" (153). Radu says to her, "but you didn't have me then," to which she replies, "no but I thought you were perfect"; "I am perfect," he answers (153). Their relationship becomes more fraught when Radu joins the occupation of University Square; "so what have you done today? Sat in the square and talked?" (165) says Florina. As their argument intensifies, Radu retorts, "let's forget we know each other" and brands her "communist," to which Florina replies, "you don't know me" (165).

Radu's father, Mihai, a middle-class architect, is the character who identifies most clearly as communist. Mihai continues the discourse of the old regime:

> MIHAI: Radu, I don't know what to do with you. Nothing is on a realistic basis.
> RADU: Please don't say that.
> MIHAI: What's the matter now?
> RADU: Don't say 'realistic basis.'
> FLAVIA: It's true, Mihai, you do talk in terrible jargon from before, it's no longer correct. (159)

Of course, what is now correct is still in the making, as is the revolutionary narrative itself. Mihai supports the NSF, claiming "the revolution is in safe hands" (175), whereas his wife, Flavia, once reinforcing the cult of personality of Ceauşescu in her school lessons, now votes Liberal (as does Florina) although "Mihai doesn't know" (171). Flavia hides how she votes from her husband, while at the same time encouraging him to openly acknowledge his allegiances: "you never dared speak out against Ceauşescu, Mihai, and you don't dare speak out now. Say it, I'm a communist and so what" (176).

Bogdan expresses frustration with the occupation of University Square ("we can't have a traffic jam forever" [170]) because of the persistent claim of the protesters that the revolution was hijacked by a coup; "'was it a revolution?' of course it was. My son was shot for it," he says (170). His old peasant aunt shouting ritual chants at Florina ("little bride, little bride, you're laughing, we've cried" [169]), provides a thematic connection with Bogdan's declaration, "I support the Peasants Party because my father's a peasant. ... They should have their land because their feet are in the earth and they know things nobody else knows" (175). But he retreats into what he thinks he knows best; his roots in the peasantry, growing up in the countryside, folklore, the earth, and nature provide a sense of security amidst the confusion: "CIA, KGB, we're all in the hands of foreign agents. That's one point where I'm right behind Ceauşescu" (175).

Racist comments, violent incidents, and misunderstandings compete with moments of kindness, understanding, and unity. The exchanges at the wedding of Florina and Radu in part three over land ownership, the revolution, the occupation in University Square, the nature of the NSF and the other parties, the relationship between Romania and Hungary, and the related Transylvanian question end up deteriorating into a drunken brawl. But the play does not end here, as the stage directions read, "*they pick themselves up, see if they are all right. ... They begin to enjoy themselves*" (178). Although initially disruptive, the fight also appears to be cathartic as they resume the wedding rituals, seemingly, or at least temporarily, reconciled.[60] In the final moments of the play, the characters "*start to talk while they dance, sometimes to their partner and sometimes to one of the others, at first a sentence or two and finally all talking at once*" (178). They switch from speaking English to speaking Romanian, which prevents English-speaking audiences from fully comprehending the conclusion to the play. Producing a certain indecipherability for audiences (readers are provided with translations) is a reminder, too, that, as the subtitle of the play indicates, *Mad Forest* is to be seen as "a play from Romania," and, as such, seeks to construct a sense of cultural specificity for the Romanian revolution.[61] It is, of course, a play from Britain as well, and the intercultural discourse that takes place seems to oscillate between different geopolitical as well as macro- and micro-political perspectives.

The political vision in *Mad Forest* seems to be dispersed obliquely through a commitment to the potential and desire of ordinary people for self-emancipation. Furthermore, the play refuses to perceive the revolutionary events of 1989 as heralding the end of socialist paradigms. Of course, confidence in a clearly identifiable socialist solution is absent in the play, just as it is in much of British Left debate of the moment. At the same time, rather than welcoming the free market, or viewing postmodern relativity as a political impasse, the play seems to indicate the continuing importance of discussion and debate, as well as individual and collective resistance. The drama was created out of "the company's intense involvement" with "Romanian students and other people," when "emotions in Bucharest were still raw."[62] This also informs the play's political position; it reflects the continuing dynamic of political fluctuation and emotional engagement of Romanian participants. The play dramatises

---

[60] I saw the Birmingham School of Speech and Drama production of *Mad Forest* on 1 March 2003 at the Crescent Studio, Birmingham, UK, which closed with a strong sense of unity and celebration. Many audience members joined in with the dancing by invitation of cast members.

[61] This is the subtitle of the stand-alone version: (London: Nick Hern, 1990).

[62] Churchill, Introduction to *Caryl Churchill Plays: 3* (London: Nick Hern, 1998), vii-viii, vii.

the revolution as a utopian moment of possibility but also as a vulnerable space, a space of disputation, a space that is ultimately lost to forces of tradition and anachronism, most potently symbolised by the vampire who smells blood and comes to feed. *Mad Forest* implicitly acknowledges that the likelihood of a democratic socialist movement's emerging in Romania in the near future is slight, but the buoyant, self-realisation of huge numbers of people dramatised in the play clearly demonstrates the potential for future collective resistance and upheaval. Rather than endorsing what Michael Evenden describes as "an apocalypse of stasis" brought about by the end of history, *Mad Forest* suggests that political impulses extraneous to capitalist democracy continue to remain significant in their threatened destabilising of a fragile hegemony.[63] *Mad Forest* tells us that history has not ended; history's radical unpredictability, if anything, is its defining characteristic.

---

[63] Michael Evenden, "'No Future without Marx': Dramaturgies of 'The End of History' in Churchill, Brenton and Barker," *Theatre* 29.3 (1999): 100-13, 100.

CHAPTER SIX

STILL A SOCIALIST?
THE SKRIKER AND *FAR AWAY*

Have you noticed the large number of meteorological phenomena lately? Earthquakes. Volcanoes. Drought. Apocalyptic meteorological phenomena. The increase of sickness. It was always possible to think whatever your personal problem, there's always nature. Spring will return even if it's without me. Nobody loves me but at least it's a sunny day. This has been a comfort to people as long as they've existed. But it's not available any more. Sorry. Nobody loves me and the sun's going to kill me.
(*Skriker*, 282-83)

Of course. I'm not surprised you can't sleep, what an upsetting thing to see. But now you understand, it's not so bad. You're part of a big movement now to make things better. You can be proud of that. You can look at the stars and think here we are in our little bit of space, and I'm on the side of the people who are putting things right, and your soul will expand right into the sky.
(*FA*, 14-15)

Introduction

I argued in the previous chapter that Churchill's dramatic response in *Serious Money* and *Mad Forest* to a newfound neoliberalist confidence, a confidence based upon increased liberation of the market, the collapse of the USSR, and the accompanying declaration of the end of history, is one that is far *less* complicit with the political relativism of postmodern discourses than many commentators have claimed. The polemical revulsion expressed at the horrors of the financial markets in *Serious Money* and the faith articulated in the collective potential of ordinary people in *Mad Forest* demonstrate a continuing commitment to the political possibilities of grassroots resistance and oppositional activities. This does not seem to continue, however, as a coherently articulated political force in Churchill's later plays. This final chapter will explore two innovative, yet disturbing, oblique and difficult to interpret plays, written and performed at the end of the millennium, *The Skriker* (1994) and *Far Away* (2000). Here the focus is Churchill's treatment of these plays' thematic concerns of environmental destruction, alienation, brutality, and war together with an exploration of the ways in which a continuing commitment to socialist politics still forms an appropriate framework within which to make sense of these works.[1]

Environmental Destruction

The situation is complicated by the theoretical issues raised by environmental politics. The birth of ecocriticism and the rise of the Radical Environmental Movement in the 1990s reflect an acute perception in Liberal Left thinking and in socialist and anarchist circles of imminent environmental destruction.[2] Simon C. Estok talks of "an age of environmental crisis," Steven Rosendale of the "human-caused environmental catastrophe," the French philosopher Michel Serres says that what is "at stake is the Earth in its totality, and humanity, collectively," and Alan Bleakley tells us that "ecological crisis is an established part of the postmodern condition," before going on to declare that "it is a crisis so huge that it has led to an apocalyptic numbing, an anaesthetic."[3] An apocalyptic idiom through which environmental damage is expressed is indeed the dominant register of political discourse in both *The Skriker* and *Far Away*.

While class oppression, gender inequality, racism, imperialism, and nuclear proliferation are the foci of Left campaigns during the 1970s and 1980s, environmental devastation, the exploitation of animals, globalisation, and the politics of space characterise the targets of oppositional struggle in

---

[1] For a shorter version of this discussion, see Siân Adiseshiah, "Still a Socialist? Political Commitment in Caryl Churchill's *The Skriker* and *Far Away*," in *Drama and/after Postmodernism*, eds. Christoph Henke and Martin Middeke (Trier: WVT Wissenschaftlicher Verlag, 2007), 277-91.

[2] The emergence of a coherent ecocritical body of work is reflected in *The Ecocriticism Reader: Landmarks in Literary Ecology*, eds. Cheryl Glotfelty and Harold Fromm (London: University of Georgia Press, 1996).

[3] Simon C. Estok, "A Report Card on Ecocriticism," *AUMLA: The Journal of the Australasian Universities Language and Literature Association* 96 (November 2001): 220-38, 221; Steven Rosendale, Introduction to *The Greening of Literary Scholarship* (Rosendale Iowa City: University of Iowa Press, 2002), xv-xxix, xvi; Rosendale, "In Search of Left Ecology's Usable Past," *The Greening of Literary Scholarship*, 59-76, 61; Michel Serres, *The Natural Contract* (Ann Arbor: University of Michigan Press, 1995), 4; Alan Bleakley, *The Animalising Imagination* (London: Macmillan, 2000), 51.

the 1990s. These differing political inflections, of course, remain a presence in each decade and there are crossovers between them, but because of the disintegration of the counter-cultural movement and the fragmentation of the Left, environmental concerns begin to eclipse others and come to be recuperated as a way of sustaining Left political activity in a context that increasingly brands a certain idiom, an idiom that talks of "class," "socialism," "feminism," "anti-racism," and even "equality" as outdated. This is not to underestimate the fact that many Ecocritics do, in fact, *prioritise* an environmental focus over and above these other political campaigns; Cheryll Glotfelty's introduction to *The Ecocriticism Reader* identifies "the most pressing contemporary issue of all" to be "the global environmental crisis."[4] However, a number of ecocritical readings address the specific dynamics of gender, race,[5] and class[6] in connection with environmental concerns. Moreover, within the field of ecocriticism and environmentalism, unfashionable political agencies (those based around class, race, and gender) seem to have partially re-emerged in more culturally digestible forms, forms that have not yet been fully absorbed by discourses of consumption or deemed to be no longer relevant to the contemporary moment.

Ecocriticism's growing presence in scholarship in the 1990s is associated more with the United States, coming a little later to Britain and constituting a smaller body of work. The Radical Environmental Movement in contrast is active and vibrant in Britain throughout this decade, although seems to have been much less visible in the 2000s. The movement's political diversity makes it difficult to characterise, but some distinguishing features include the negotiation of a variety of different kinds of activism that draw on several political traditions; anarchism is the most visible but (post-)Marxism is also an uneasy co-presence. Engagement with theorists such as Gilles Deleuze, Henri Lefebvre and ideas drawn from French Situationism reflect the negotiation of anarchist

---

[4] Glotfelty, Introduction to *The Ecocriticism Reader*, xv-xxxvii, xv.
[5] For gender and race, see Karla Armbruster and Kathleen Wallace, eds., *Beyond Nature Writing: Expanding the Boundaries of Ecocriticsm* (London: University Press of Virginia, 2001). There is also a growing body of ecofeminism. See Maria Mies and Vandana Shiva, eds., *Ecofeminism* (London: Zed, 1993); Ariel Salleh, *Ecofeminism as Politics: Nature, Marx and the Postmodern* (London: Zed, 1997); Beate Littig, *Feminist Perspectives on Environment and Society* (Upper Saddle River, NJ: Prentice Hall, 2001); Barbara Cook, ed., *Women Writing Nature: A Feminist View* (Lanham, MD: Lexington Books, 2007).
[6] See Rosendale, ed., *The Greening of Literary Scholarship*.

and Marxist thinking; the neglect of trade unionism and a weak critique of class-privilege demonstrate a middle-class, liberal preponderance.

An accompanying dynamic is the conflicted relationship of ecocriticism and postmodernism. Derek Wall discusses the environmental group Earth First!, which displays concern at postmodern suspicions over cause and effect, and postmodern reservations over a knowable, extra-discursive reality. Wall says,

> EF! (UK) activists would argue that global environmental issues, such as potential nuclear war and the greenhouse effect have 'real' implications for human beings and the non-human environment. How can green politics fight for the earth if practical conclusions about the effectiveness of environmental action are impossible to judge?[7]

A discussion of environmental causes and effects that correspond to a knowable, extra-textual reality (as opposed to existing only as social construction) and the necessity of recognising the essential utility of political activism are key political imperatives for committed environmentalists, who, somewhat ironically, are often identified as postmodern activists in cultural discourse.

Of course, there are many different political positions both between and within environmentalism, ecocriticism, and the Radical Environmental Movement, which range from a liberal concern for animal welfare and the natural environment, to a revolutionary challenge to green issues, globalisation, and the political economy. A strong tendency within academic ecocriticism has been to critique the traditional binary opposition between nature and culture, or to view, as Kathleen Wallace and Karla Armbruster do, "nature and culture as interwoven rather than as separate sides of a dualistic construct."[8] This is taken up particularly in a form that critiques the pervasive anthropocentrism of our culture, an anthropocentrism that is part of the Enlightenment narrative of human rationality and mastery of nature. Deconstructing the dualisms of human/animal and culture/nature in dialogue with poststructuralist preoccupations with representation has allowed discussion to emphasise the constructed nature of these traditional separations and has prompted enquiry into the relationship between discursive representations and particular historical moments. However, privileging language and text–although with very

---

[7] Derek Wall, *Earth First! And the Anti-Roads Movement: Radical Environmentalism and Comparative Social Movements* (London: Routledge, 1999), 12.

[8] Wallace and Armbruster, Introduction to *Beyond Nature Writing*, 1-25.

different emphases–is a common project in both Enlightenment and poststructuralist thinking; the Enlightenment identification of the supposedly uniquely human realm of language and culture as justification for human mastery of nature is oddly comparable to Jacques Derrida's "il n'ya pas de hors-texte."[9] If nature is only accessible through textual representation, its independent presence, its extra-discursive reality remains remote and voiceless. Textual appropriation of nature thus restricts efforts to perceive the autonomy of nature–the ultimate voiceless Other. Deconstructing the nature/culture or human/animal opposition has included Alan Bleakley's hope for what he thinks of as,

> animal life revived–living, present, hailed and celebrated as the born-again god–not so that we can hack and slice it to death in the same breath, but so that we can appreciate (and learn from) its beauty, its self-display, its aesthetic presence and worth.[10]

This in turn involves acknowledgment that experience is necessarily mediated through discourse and that this recognition undermines our ability to appreciate the subjectivity of the non-human world.

The degradation of the non-human world–the marauding of it as a resource for humanity–is justified by humanist discourses, which have deemed the best of human nature to be furthest away from the bestial. However, The Jungian analyst, Russell Lockhart, reported in 1987 that patients were experiencing,

> a simultaneous and increasing appearance of animals, animals coming, animals watching, animals speaking, animals wanting to lead us, animals undergoing all manner of transformation.[11]

The non-human world, so long repressed in the human consciousness returns in apocalyptic dreaming. Of course, the idea of the avenging animal has been claimed on a number of occasions and from a variety of political locations. The bacteria salmonella, the parasitic amoeba E. coli, BSE and most recently avian and swine flues have all been related to environmental reprisal. Serres opens his *The Natural Contract* with a

---

[9] Jacques Derrida, *Of Grammatology*, trans. Gayatri Chakravorty Spivak (Baltimore: John Hopkins University Press, 1976), 158.
[10] Bleakley, *The Animalising Imagination*, 14.
[11] Russell A. Lockhart, *Psyche Speaks: A Jungian Approach to Self and World* (Wilmette: Chiron Publications, 1987), 84.

description of Goya's painting of two men duelling "knee-deep in the mud." Serres states,

> quicksand is swallowing the duellists; the river is threatening the fighter; earth, waters, and climate, the mute world, the voiceless things once placed as a décor surrounding the usual spectacles, all those things that never interested anyone, from now on thrust themselves brutally and without warning into our schemes and manoeuvres. They burst in on our culture, which had never formed anything but a local, vague, and cosmetic idea of them: nature. What was once local–this river, that swamp–is now global: Planet Earth.[12]

The destructive consequences of pollution, the devastating effects of climate change, and the ominous impact of global warming are the non-human natural world's reply to humanity's parasitic behaviour, which, according to Serres has precipitated the apocalyptic tenor of nature's retribution.

War

Added to the threat of environmental degradation is the impact of Britain's participation in several military interventions in the 1990s. The first Gulf War in 1991, although represented as a "clean" precision bombing campaign resulted in what became known as Gulf War Syndrome. Several thousand veterans claimed to be experiencing the effects of the by products of depleted uranium munitions. Estimates of Iraqi civilian deaths, uncounted by the US military, range from a few thousand to 200,000. 1991 additionally saw the conflict in Sierra Leone, swiftly followed by the Bosnian war (1993-1995), the Chechen war (1994-1996), and the Kosovan intervention in 1999. These are interspersed with repeated coalition bombings of Baghdad. This Orwellian dystopia of permanent warfare, was famously predicted by Frederick Engels, who, according to Rosa Luxemburg, claimed, "capitalist society faces a dilemma, either an advance to socialism or a reversion to barbarism."[13] Serres's alternative prophecy, this time with an environmental focus, is, "this is history's bifurcation: either death or symbiosis."[14]

---

[12] Serres, *The Natural Contract*, 3.
[13] Frederick Engels, quoted in *The Junius Pamphlet*, by Rosa Luxemburg (London: Merlin Press, 1915), 16.
[14] Serres, *The Natural Contract*, 34.

Western initiation, intervention in, and exacerbation of war around the world dominate the political context of the 1990s. Growing cynicism, political evasion, and numbness form part of the public discourse that in turn becomes a target for the shock-inducing dramaturgy of the "in-yer-face" playwrights, such as Sarah Kane, Mark Ravenhill, and Anthony Neilson.[15] In contrast to the 1982 Falklands War, the self-declared altruistic motives of Western intervention in the 1990s are treated in public discourse with mounting suspicion, as financial interests, oil, and NATO's hegemony are increasingly recognised as motivations for war. The 1999 Kosovan war is met in *New Left Review* with various analyses of the American imperialist project. Edward Said writes, "punishment is its own goal, bombing as a display of NATO authority its own satisfaction, especially when there is little chance of retaliation from the enemy."[16] Tariq Ali talks of NATO's new mission statement as converting "a defensive alliance into a mobile, global police force which can hit a target state anywhere in the world to defend the interests of the United States, defined, of course, as 'human rights' and the 'free market.'"[17] And Slavoj Žižek correctly predicts,

> the NATO bombing of Yugoslavia will change the global geopolitical co-ordinates. The unwritten pact of peaceful coexistence–the respect of each state's full sovereignty, that is, non-interference in internal affairs, even in the case of the grave violation of human rights–is over.[18]

Robin Blackburn's contribution is equally chilling, "those who sow the wind, reap the whirlwind. The West does not tackle rogue states so much as imitate and produce them breeding a future fascism."[19] As is Peter Gowan's, "NATO electorates thought their states were trying to help in Yugoslavia, even if they were not 'doing enough.' In reality, Western

---

[15] Good examples of "in-yer-face" plays include: Sarah Kane, *Blasted* (London: Methuen, 2001; first published in 1996); Mark Ravenhill, *Shopping and F***ing* (London: Methuen, 1996); Anthony Neilson, *The Censor* (London: Methuen, 1997).

[16] Edward Said, "Protecting the Kosovars?" *New Left Review* 234 (March/April 1999): 73-75, 74.

[17] Tariq Ali, "Springtime for NATO," *New Left Review* 234 (March/April 1999): 62-72, 62.

[18] Slavoj Žižek, "Against the Double Blackmail," *New Left Review* 234 (March/April 1999): 76-82, 81.

[19] Michael Blackburn, "Kosovo: The War of NATO Expansion," *New Left Review* 235 (May/June 1999): 107-23, 123.

policies promoted the descent into barbaric wars."[20] Indeed, "barbaric wars," the devastation of the environment, the ongoing retreat from socialist discourses and the dispersal of a coherent, progressive, political idiom provides the peculiarly hostile context within which to make sense of these two plays.

The Skriker

What *The Skriker* is about was a question that many theatre critics puzzled over with some irritation after the play's first performance. Firstly, it contains several modes of performance; acting, music, singing, dance, and mime all form significant contributions to the event of the play. Churchill's explanation of this is that "a number of stories are told but only one in words."[21] Secondly, many of the speeches–particularly the Skriker's–seem impenetrable and thus a coherent narrative is difficult to identify. Furthermore the different dramatic forms through which stories are told do not seem to form part of an integrated expression. James Christopher in *Time Out* writes,

> what doesn't work so well is Churchill's greater ambition to marry disparate forms of theatrical expression: notably the ever-present Grimm fairies who dance and wander aimlessly around Annie Smart's neutral, boxy set. Apart from the surreal swirling banquet party to welcome Josie to hell their presence is distracting, inexplicable, almost intrusive. [22]

Neil Smith in *What's On* describes the play as "bizarre," although "bewildering and bewitching in equal measures," the narrative as "pretty incomprehensible," and the total theatrical event as an experience "that quite literally defies explanation."[23] Michael Billington in *The Guardian* finds the play "strangely opaque,"[24] Clive Hirschhorn from the *Sunday Express* is not sure if there is "any discernible thread of significance"

[20] Peter Gowan, "The NATO Powers and the Balkan Tragedy," *New Left Review* 234 (March/April 1999): 83-105, 103.

[21] Churchill, Introduction to *Caryl Churchill Plays: 3*, vii-viii, viii.

[22] James Christopher, *Time Out* (2 February 1994) reprinted in *Theatre Record* (15-28 January 1994): 96.

[23] Michael Billington, *The Guardian* (29 January 1994) reprinted in *Theatre Record* (15-28 January 1994): 97.

[24] Neil Smith, *What's On* (2 February 1994) reprinted in *Theatre Record* (15-28 January 1994): 96.

informing Churchill's "weird new play,"[25] and Maureen Paton of the *Daily Express* calls it "a work of quite awesome pretentiousness," like "some dreadful exercise to help actors lose their inhibitions about movement."[26]

In contrast, academics have tended to view the play's supposed resistance to comprehension as a postmodern frustration of interpretative mastery. However, I would argue that this reading of *The Skriker* seems instead to be one of the play's targets of critique. The politics of *The Skriker* resides in a radical environmental discourse that warns of an apocalypse in contemporary capitalist development as well as proffering ironic comment on the political stasis of postmodern perspectives. The fragmented language, fractured and mutated identities, and incoherent speeches are as much a parody of the impasse produced by the logic of indeterminacy as they are reflective of the slipperiness of language and the hollowness of the contemporary moment. Indeed the dramatisation of the different discourses of speech, dance, mime, and song, a dramatisation that so many critics found incomprehensible as an entire expression, is as much a satirical comment on the ever-increasing disintegration of the collective, the social unit, and the individual subject, as it is evidence of the altogether ubiquitous, but incoherent nature of political agency.

While language, subjectivity, identity and political agency might be fluid and indeterminate within academic and cultural discourses, the non-human world is potentially determinate: it can be damaged irreparably. The avenging Skriker ("*a shapeshifter and death portent, ancient and damaged*" [243], as the stage directions describe it) is a repository of human and non-human attributes; the Skriker is a conglomeration of human myth and Pagan folklore, at the same time as signifying an altogether non-human dimension of the natural world. The Skriker's reprisal is in one sense the non-human natural world's reaction to continued repletion and pollution of the environment, and in another, a satirical response to the "post-Marxist" neglect of liberal discourses to mount a coherent challenge to the ideologies of capital. Furthermore, as French philosopher, Alain Badiou, discusses in his *Ethics* essay, orientating cultural politics around the concept of the Other, around the idea of radical alterity, tends to produce at best a politically restrictive self-reflexivity and at worst a politics of inertia and the maintenance of the

---

[25] Clive Hirschhorn, *Sunday Express* (30 January 1994) reprinted in *Theatre Record* (15-28 January 1994): 94.

[26] Maureen Paton, *Daily Express* (1 February 1994) reprinted in *Theatre Record* (15-28 January 1994): 94.

existing socio-economic terrain.[27] Indeed the Skriker's bearing of a caricature of postmodernist preoccupations is presented as part of the problem: as contributing to a political impasse.

The Skriker reflects a complex engagement with the discourses of modernism and postmodernism. As many commentators have noted, the Skriker's speeches bear a resemblance to Joycean prose, *Ulysses* in particular. The institutionalisation of modernist art in the academy has softened its radical edge; its absorption within the mainstream of culture prevents it from proffering the dissidence it once signified. Furthermore, postmodern art is often, as Frederic Jameson has said, "at one with the official culture of Western society."[28] In contrast, Ann Wilson argues that *The Skriker's* (postmodern) incoherence is its political expression; she says, "Churchill's refusal to allow the audience access to a position of interpretative 'mastery' over *The Skriker* is an act of political resistance."[29] However, refusing interpretive mastery is limited in its impact as a performative act of political resistance. An audience's incomprehension and confusion by no means leads to its politicisation. Some means of making sense of the play's political narrative is necessary if one of the most repeated political concerns in the play—environmental destruction—is to be taken up by an audience.

Indeed, *The Skriker* is not incoherent. The play offers enough moments of sense to be tantalisingly provocative. The Skriker's first long monologue contains recognisable patterns of figurative speech, most of which are cultural references. Several mentions of fairytales (Rumplestiltskin, Beauty and the Beast) are interspersed with cinematic and literary allusions ("chainsaw massacre," "bloody chamber," "whale moby" [244; 245]), some of which in turn are predicated on proverb and cliché ("loch stock and barrel" [244]). The linguistic patterns comprise metaphor, and this, in turn, foregrounds the topics of language, sense, and understanding. The slipping of one hackneyed phrase into another: the fusing together of conventionally separate units by drawing twice on the same word, in this example "do": "or pin prick cockadoodle do you feel it?" (244) is also a common feature. There are some explicit allusions to political figures from the Right and Left; Enoch Powell is imagined in "they poison me in my rivers of blood poisoning" (246), and Leon Trotsky's infamous murder

---

[27] See Alain Badiou, *Ethics: An Essay on the Understanding of Evil* (London: Verso, 2002).

[28] Frederic Jameson, "Postmodernism, or The Cultural Logic of Late Capitalism," *New Left Review* 146 (July-August 1984): 57-92, 56.

[29] Ann Wilson, "Failure and the Limits of Representation in *The Skriker*," in *Caryl Churchill: Contemporary Re-presentations*, ed. Sheila Rabillard, 174-88, 187.

resounds in "ice pick in your head long ago" (246). This medley of mostly recognisable references, references that can be categorised in identifiable ways challenges the spectator to consider the damaged ways in which the Skriker's speech speaks to contemporary concerns. Rather than refusing interpretive mastery (and in doing so bearing a postmodern challenge to the violence of representation), the Skriker's speech can be read instead as ironising postmodern non-sense, and both a symptom and critique of postmodern, political inarticulacy.

Churchill scholar, Amelia Howe Kritzer, discusses the politics of Churchill's late plays in terms of their tendency to present a "subject-less tragedy, in which individuals are never fully revealed or defined." She says "indeed, a sense of identity and coherence seems to be what these characters seek in their futile attempts to connect with others."[30] In *The Skriker*, the protagonists, Lily and Josie appear to be located outside of a wider social network. Unlike many of Churchill's earlier plays these working-class women are no longer situated in a tangibly felt social context but are rather positioned outside of a shared sense of social space. Indeed Lily and Josie's inchoate identities are produced largely through the absence of a social texture, except, of course, in the punitive form of Josie's confinement to the mental hospital where Foucauldian codes of discipline and punishment are inscribed in the representation of her hospitalisation. This scene is also a reminder of Connie's confinement to a mental hospital in Marge Piercy's socialist-feminist utopia, *Woman on the Edge of Time*, where Connie slips in and out of a utopian future; however, the utopian future that is oriented around equality, solidarity, and respect for the natural environment in Piercy's novel is replaced in *The Skriker* for a nightmarish dystopia with a toxic landscape and human regret.[31]

Another important intertext is Christina Rossetti's *Goblin Market.*[32] Lily and Josie echo Laura and Lizzie in their sisterly relationship (although *The Skriker* does not state they are sisters) and in their proneness to temptation, the theme of which is introduced in the Skriker's opening speech where it makes reference to "forbidden fruit" (245). In *Goblin Market* the sexualised danger symbolised by the fruit, which is associated with the depraved masculinity of goblin men is initially yielded to by

---

[30] Amelia Howe Kritzer, "Political Currents in Caryl Churchill's Plays at the Turn of the Millennium," in *Crucible of Cultures: Anglophone Drama at the Dawn of the New Millennium*, eds. Maufort & Bellarsi (Brussels: Peter Lang, 2002), 57-67, 58.

[31] Marge Piercy, *Woman on the Edge of Time* (London: Women's Press, 1979).

[32] Christina Rossetti, *Goblin Market* (London: Macmillan, 1971; first published in 1862).

Lizzie; however, Laura's saving of her–borne out of her unwavering commitment to their continued intimacy and sorority–results in Lizzie's redemption. This nineteenth-century feminist tale is thus reworked in what Elin Diamond calls "Churchill's ecological millennial parable" to speak to the (dystopian) contemporary moment.[33] The significant acmes in the feminist and socialist movements that coincided with the publication of *Goblin Market* and *Woman on the Edge of Time* seem long gone and *The Skriker*, instead, speaks to this loss, a loss that signifies in the absence of collective political commitment and the lack of a substantive sense of resistance. The so-called "third-wave" of feminism or "postfeminism" does not seem to figure in the play as something to celebrate.

Indeed gender politics appears to be less visible as a driving force in the narrative of *The Skriker*. The audacious attack on misogynist mythmaking in *Vinegar Tom* and the critique of bourgeois feminism in *Top Girls* do not seem to be superseded by something equally bold in relation to gendered themes here. That said, the play is concerned with mostly female characters and produces a variety of constructions of femininity. Claudia Barnett calls *The Skriker* "a revisionist fairy tale with a feminist twist" partly because of what she sees as Churchill's "regendering" of the Skriker from a male shape-shifting death portent to a feminised figure, played in the original production by Kathryn Hunter, and a figure who "is more witch than goblin and [who] embodies maternal desire."[34] Katherine Perrault reads *The Skriker* through an engagement with chaos theory, a theory that she sees as complementing a deconstruction of phallogocentrism. Perrault states, "the chaos that ensues from Churchill's systematic portrayal of matriarchal integers seeks to expose the historical oppression of women and deconstruct patriarchal ideology."[35]

Certainly *The Skriker's* manipulation of dramatic form, its staging of mostly female characters, and the fairy underworld's evocation of Julia Kristeva's concept of the chora lends the play to feminist readings.[36] However, gender oppression is not the primary object of the play's political impulse. Nor perhaps is class, although, along with gender, the politics of class equally forms part of the play's political texture. The play's protagonists clearly signify as young and working class. Their single-mother and single-mother-to-be identities, their lack of economic

---

[33] Elin Diamond, *Unmaking Mimesis* (London: Routledge, 1997), 36.
[34] Claudia Barnett, "'Reveangance is gold mine, sweet'" *Essays in Theatre* 19.1 (November 2000): 45-57, 55; 48.
[35] Katherine Perrault, "Beyond the Patriarchy: Feminism and the Chaos of Creativity," *Journal of Dramatic Theory and Criticism* 17.1 (2002): 45-67, 48.
[36] Julia Kristeva's chora is discussed in Chapter 2, page 85.

power, and Josie's confinement to a mental hospital also contribute to the reinforcement of their vulnerable location within the political economy. But while these two women, so resonant of previous Churchillian characters, seem especially defenceless in the socio-economic landscape of the play, their class and gender subjugation is symptomatic of the wider social neglect that has given rise to environmental destruction, alienation, and social discordance.

Jameson talks of postmodernism replacing Nature and the unconscious. He describes late capitalism–"this purer capitalism"–as abolishing "the enclaves of precapitalist organisation it had hitherto tolerated and exploited in a tributary way"; he speaks of a "new and historically original penetration and colonisation of Nature and the Unconscious."[37] The Skriker's underworld is, of course, symbolic of both nature's base and the human unconscious. Several critics have discussed the Jungian collective unconscious reflected in the Skriker and the underworld. István Nagy suggests that the "delicate net of cultural references" indicates the Skriker's containment of "pre-eminently the English," but also "in a wider sense, the whole of Western culture in her unconscious."[38] Indeed, the Skriker itself asks Josie, "haven't I wrapped myself up rapt rapture ruptured myself in your dreams, scoffed your chocolate creams, your Jung men and Freud eggs, your flying and fleeing?" (272).

The pollution of the natural world is also implicated in the representation of the dying underworld. The Skriker's references to "wars," "drought," "sunburn," "toxic waste," "salmonelephantiasis," and "poison in the food chain" (271) are the cause for disintegration, a disintegration symbolised dramatically in the crumbling of the feast. The reverberations of Prospero's disappearing feast are evident; however, in *The Tempest* Prospero loses control over his power momentarily, seemingly due to his remembrance of Caliban's plot of insurrection;[39] contrastingly in *The Skriker*, it is not an individual's loss of control but rather a collective retreat from environmental, social, and political responsibility that has produced this crisis in the underworld. The underworld seems to fuse the human and non-human natural worlds in its conglomeration of mythical archetypes and its close relationship with the non-human natural world, and as such the underworld is indicative, in its

---

[37] Jameson, "Postmodernism, or The Cultural Logic of Late Capitalism," *New Left Review* 146 (July-August 1984): 57-92, 78.

[38] István Nagy, "The Modern Fairy of an Urban Folktale," *The Anachrist* (1998): 233-47, 239.

[39] William Shakespeare, *The Tempest*, eds. Alden T. Vaughan and Virginia Mason Vaughan (London: The Arden Shakespeare, 1999; first published in 1623).

demise, of the noxious effects of human activity on the environment in the late twentieth century. The idea of the underworld containing within it a sense of (uneasy) fusion between the human and non-human worlds, a fusion that is progressively disaggregating, provides a sinister vision of the effects of the breakdown of this once benign relationship.

The sense of dislocation embodied in the underworld is also performed by the Skriker in its mimicking of human social organisation. The different human roles the Skriker plays include, "a dowdy woman in her fifties" (251), "a derelict woman ... shouting in the street" (252), "an American woman of about forty" (253), "a small child" (263), "a smart woman in [her] mid thirties" (275), "a man about thirty" (280), "a young woman about Lily's age" (285), "a shabby respectable man about forty" (287), and "a very ill old woman" (288). This assortment of individuals makes up a community characterised by dislodgement and alienation. The perversions of human traits in these characters are not immediately apparent; indeed, these figures often seem like ordinary, albeit lonely and eccentric, people. One of the Skriker's mutations, the "very ill old woman" ("I've enemies in here. Shh." [289]) mimics the speech of a demented, old woman confined to hospital. This old woman, along with other damaged human personas the Skriker slips in and out of so convincingly, reflects the sense of isolation and ill-health that characterises the range of subject positions available in the late-twentieth century.

Like the vampire in *Mad Forest*, the Skriker is from the past. Kritzer says, "having been damaged, the Skriker does damage. Being frightened ... she becomes frightening."[40] The re-emergence of this vengeful "death portent" (243) is in part a resistance to nature's eclipse in the postmodern moment. The avant-garde mode of dramatic expression–the form of the drama–is in tension with the content of the dramatic narrative, a narrative that contains within it much older ideas. The disintegration of the totality– and in this case the total matrix of human and non-human lived experience–is signified in the crisis of the underworld. However, more significant is the dissipation of a coherent idiom facilitating the articulation of political resistance, and in this case resistance to the destruction of the natural environment. This leads inevitably to the climactic apocalyptic moment of permanent historical closure; Lily accompanies the Skriker to what she thinks will be the underworld only to find herself one hundred years in the future where she sees her granddaughter and her great great granddaughter:

---

[40] Kritzer, "Systemic Poisons in Churchill's Recent Plays," in *Essays on Caryl Churchill*, ed. Sheila Rabillard, 159-73, 169.

> *The girl bellows wordless rage at Lilly.*
> 'Oh they couldn't helpless,' said the granddaughter,
> 'they were stupid stupedfied stewpotbellied not evil
> weevil devil take the hindmost of them anyway.'
> But the child hated the monstrous.
> *Girl bellows.*
> … So Lily bit off more than she could choose. And she
> Was dustbin. (290-91)

The "wordless rage" of Lily's great great granddaughter suggests where the current trajectory of contemporary political (non-)intervention leads. Her rage is wordless because we cannot hear: it does not signify within the dystopian perimeters of our current modes of representation. It is also wordless because of the eclipse of collective political activity by a postmodern fixation with the representational nature of language and the demise of human agency.

Far Away

Although there is a consensus amongst critics and academics that *Far Away* is political theatre, the nature of the political narrative in the play is far less certain. While each vignette in the play resonates as politically meaningful (the sinister activities involving Harper's husband and the violation of people in a lorry; the ominous threat of the corrupt hat company, which is shockingly undercut by the flamboyant hat parade of prisoners before their execution; all-out global war involving the elements, humans, and the non-human natural world) the precise nature of this meaningfulness is less clear. Kritzer reads the politics of *Far Away* as residing in "a kind of parable indicting the Left for its failures in the twentieth century."[41] She states,

> the three primary scenes of the play refer to three failures of modern European socialism. The first scene, between Harper and young Joan, represents the era of Stalinism, under which those supposedly being helped were often harmed, while its apologists defended the system through constantly shifting lies. The second scene, in which Joan and Todd create hats for a competition, points to the narrow perspective of trade unionism–the aspect of Leftist politics with which many British dramatists have been closely associated. While Joan and Todd focus on the rewards of personal achievement and the problems of their particular workplace, they are ignoring the conditions of a world in which their artistic creations serve as

---

[41] Kritzer, "Political Currents in Caryl Churchill's Plays," 64.

absurd adornments for people in chains being marched to their deaths. The
final scene suggests the factionalism that characterises the contemporary
Left, along with the chaotic proliferation of intense but indecipherable
conflicts around the globe.[42]

The sense of loss and impotence–an absence of a coherent and tangibly-
felt Left presence–certainly seems to be signified in the play's political
vision, but Kritzer's claim that the play represents the failure of the Left in
three forms of socialism is unconvincing. The tableau of each scene of *Far
Away* is multidimensional, drawing on several political allusions, and is
thus difficult to recruit to a reading that imposes a single metaphorical
meaning. The first scene, for example, alludes as much to contemporary
discourses on ethnic cleansing, asylum seekers, and Palestinian
displacement, as it does to Nazi and Stalinist regimes. Kritzer's analysis of
the second scene–a scene that offers a critique of the perversity of Joan
and Todd's preoccupation with pay and conditions at the expense of
recognition that their work contributes towards the activities of a
gruesomely ritualised death camp–is more persuasive. But the final
scene's extraordinary use of animals, the elements, and the natural world,
should be addressed on its environmental terms as well as with respect to
its metaphorical function. Furthermore, this scene's metaphorical
signification is as much an expression of bewilderment at postmodern
representations of agency as it is a satire on Left factionalism.

Kritzer rightly acknowledges that "deconstruction of social and
political categories and goals in the perspectives of postmodern theory
further complicates the situation," creating a "difficult environment" that
has "silenced many playwrights on the Left."[43] However, she does not
seem to view the demise of the Left and the rise of postmodern theory as
interdependent. While dramatising political inarticulacy as a product of the
demise of collective agencies, *Far Away* equally depends on "political
categories and goals" in its response to the social, political, and
environmental crisis at the turn of the millennium. According to Jameson,

> postmodern culture is the internal and superstructural expression of a
> whole new wave of American military and economic domination
> throughout the world: in this sense, as throughout class history, the
> underside of culture is blood, torture, death and horror.[44]

---

[42] Kritzer, "Political Currents in Caryl Churchill's Plays," 65.

[43] Kritzer, "Political Currents in Caryl Churchill's Plays," 57.

[44] Jameson, "Postmodernism, or The Cultural Logic of Late Capitalism," 57.

Indeed, *Far Away* expresses the relationship between the demise of the Left, the hegemony of postmodern discourses, permanent warfare, exploitation, and terror as constituting an inter-dependent political and cultural milieu.

The first scene of *Far Away* establishes the play's disjunction between the horror of the real world and society's nonchalant response to it. Joan visits her Aunt in what appears to be a house in the English countryside, only to discover that her uncle is active in sinister activities involving adults and children, a lorry, violence, and blood. Harper's attempts to cover up these activities soon give way to her disclosure that Joan has "found out something secret" (11). But Harper continues to shift uneasily as Joan persists in her questioning. Christine Dymkowski thinks "Joan's gradual but relentless revelations and Harper's shifting responses have so destabilised the idea of 'the truth' that it no longer exists as a valid concept for the audience."[45] However, this aspect of the scene works precisely through its orientation around Joan and the audience's desire to discover "the truth." Joan's representation of what she sees acts as a reliable report of what happens; Harper's explanation (but not a refutation) of what Joan sees, serves to reinforce the "truth" of what Joan has witnessed further; it is Harper's justification that the audience doubts: not because truth "no longer exists as a valid concept" but precisely the opposite: because Harper's dubious response acquires its dubiousness through the sense that it masks the "truth."

However, the notion of obfuscating "truth" is related to the shortage of political clarity that characterises the postmodern moment. In the absence of grand narratives that provide explanatory frameworks within which political circumstances can be read, the politics of relativity become the predominant mode of making sense of the social context. Here the audience is not able to explain or understand its suspicions of Joan's uncle's actions, which are in Harper's words, "part of a big movement now to make things better" (14) and, even if Harper is telling the truth, the audience is denied the opportunity of judging the political perspective of this "big movement." Without fixed coordinates of political principle, the ability to identify the location and nature of power recedes into ambiguity and ambivalence. The audience is disturbed by the sense of menace expressed in the drama but what disturbs more is the construction of the implied spectator as one who is unable to translate the dystopian drama of the play into a politically legible articulation. The audience knows things

---

[45] Christine Dymkowski, "Caryl Churchill: *Far Away* ...but Close to Home," *European Journal of English Studies* 7.1 (2003): 55-68, 57.

are terribly wrong but no longer has the means to express or explain this intelligibly.

The second scene begins with a familiar scenario in Churchill's plays: the activity of work. The grown-up Joan and Todd sit at a workbench making hats. They are not factory workers mass producing the same hats but skilled craftspeople undertaking their millinery with individualism and flair. Educated and imaginative, Joan and Todd seem to straddle the blue and white collar worker divide. Although their roles as artists in Marxist theory are considered as comprising non-alienated work–there is no division of labour and they invest their creative power (their "life-force") into their production–here the "proletarianisation" of Joan and Todd as workers is evidenced in the worsening of their pay and conditions and their exploitation by company management. However, it is a complex set of circumstances since hat production is usually carried out by factory workers, the hats sold as commodities with a use-value. Here, the function of the hats is purely aesthetic and transitory: the hats are produced only to be destroyed immediately along with the prisoners who wear them. Their function is symbolic; Todd says, "the hats are ephemeral. It's like a metaphor for something or other" (25).

The relationship between work, exploitation, art, and politics crystallises in an extraordinarily evocative moment. Chaudhuri describes the hats as "colossal creations of grotesque proportions, bizarre shapes, and riotous colours" that "silently scream out the horror that results when aesthetics loses all concern for the material reality from which it works."[46] Todd's likening of the hats' ephemeral nature to "a metaphor for something or other" is suggestive. Robert Brustein proposes, "it is indeed, a metaphor for something or other, and that something grows increasingly monstrous and threatening in the phantasmagoric final scene."[47] Brustein's reluctance to offer a clear reading of what the metaphor signifies echoes most commentary on *Far Away*, although there is at the same time a consensus over the magnitude of significance of this metaphor. However, Todd seems to miss the point; the hats' ephemeral, beautiful, and flamboyant nature is not a metaphor *for* something else, but rather a signifier of metaphor. In other words, the hats produce meaning through their signification of metaphor, through their display of the power to represent.

---

[46] Una Chaudhuri, "Different Hats," Review of *Far Away*, *Theatre* 33. 3 (2000): 132-34, 132.

[47] Robert Brustein, "Robert Brustein on Theater: Prescient Plays," *The New Republic* (23 December 2002): 27-28, 27.

Todd and Joan are unusual in terms of their access to the means of creating meaning. Most forms of production, including millinery work, involve the division of labour, repetition, monotony, and regimentation; production workers do not control what they produce and are denied the opportunity to invest creativity into the product. Kritzer is right to point to the resonance of a trade union idiom in the conversations between Todd and Joan ("we used to get two weeks before a parade and then they took it down to one and now they're talking about cutting a day" [17]); however, unlike Churchill's protagonists in many of her other plays, Todd and Joan do not fit easily into a working-class category; rather, middle-class identities are produced through their educated dialogue and aesthetic sensibilities. This scene does not just work, therefore, through a sinister satire on the insularity of syndicalist politics; it also makes connections between the privilege of a (middle-class) access to opportunities for generating meaning and the consequences of acting on that privilege in narcissistic and reckless ways. The hats as metaphor–the means of signification–are created solely for the pleasure of their subsequent incineration; "you make beauty and it disappears, I love that" (25) is Todd's response to the weekly death rituals.

Joan indicates her regret over the destruction of the hats, but this regret ("it seems so sad to burn them with the bodies" [25]) displays her grotesque lack of interest in the ritualised killings of the prisoners. The parade is described in the stage directions as, "*a procession of ragged, beaten, chained prisoners, each wearing a hat, on their way to execution. The finished hats are even more preposterous than in the previous scene*" [24]). The shocking effect of this works through the sharp disjunction between the vulnerability of the human body, marked with degradation through prison uniforms, and the extravagant head adornment with its flamboyant display of excess. This is undoubtedly a grim exposure of the potential of art to collude with brutality; however, the power of the hats to signify as metaphor–as the means of creating meaning–serves to implicate not just art but all creative practice (including intellectual discourse) that has a privileged access to the construction of meaning. The preoccupation with signifying practices in postmodern culture has often been exercised at the expense of confronting the material conditions of human experience, a human experience that is framed in some contexts by exploitation, oppression, torture, and execution.

The last scene is set "*several years later*" (28) in Harper's house. The bizarre tenor of the scene is quickly established; from an exchange between Todd and Harper that grows increasingly strange it becomes apparent that all animals are partisans of one faction or another in a global war: "the cats have come in on the side of the French" (29) says Harper. A familiar way of speaking about certain groups ("but some cats are still ok" [30]) is made strange through its reference to animals, and the complex politics of alliance is conveyed through an ever mutating set of identities:

> TODD: But we're not exactly on the other side from the French. It's not as if they're the Moroccans and the ants.
> HARPER: It's not as if they're the Canadians, the Venezuelans and the mosquitoes.
> TODD: It's not as if they're the engineers, the chefs, the children under five, the musicians.
> HARPER: The car salesmen.
> TODD: Portuguese car salesmen.
> HARPER: Russian swimmers.
> TODD: Thai butchers.
> HARPER: Latvian dentists. (30-31)

As Kritzer has suggested, echoes of Left factionalism in the dialogue are certainly identifiable, particularly through the use of a Left idiom to speak about different groups–"no, the Latvian dentists have been doing good work in Cuba" (31). However, as Beth Watkins' review of *Far Away* rightly argues, "clearly, Churchill has responded to a post-Bosnian world, where atrocities of unimaginable magnitude are made familiar and trivial by media saturation."[48]

The neglect in the media to explain and contextualise conflicts in the 1990s reverberates in *Far Away* as the audience is denied the ability to make sense of this war. But this confusion over the causes and make-up of coalitions also works to deride the justification for wars. Harper remarks, "but Latvia has been sending pigs to Sweden. The dentists are linked to international dentistry and that's where their loyalty lies, with dentists in Dares-Salaam" (31). The phrase "international dentistry" picks up satirically on more familiar political phrases ("international Jewry"). These phrases serve to mock the act of investing in such categorisations, categorisations that are used in turn as a means of justifying particular alliances in conflict. This Orwellian vision of permanent warfare sees side-changing taking place without reference to a comprehensible set of political principles or moral codes. Parallels abound between these tactics and the shifting alliances that typify modern politics, with particularly prominent examples in the 1990s such as the West's swiftly changing construction of Iraq from ally to enemy.

---

[48] Beth Watkins, Review of *Far Away*, *Theatre Journal* 53.3 (2001): 481-82, 482.

In addition to the evocation of the bewildering multiplicity of conflicts that characterise the end of the millennium, this scene in *Far Away* continues to probe the postmodern preoccupation with language, representation, and identity. The ever-continuing splitting of subjectivity ("Portuguese car salesmen" [30]; "Russian swimmers"; "Thai butchers"; "Latvian dentists" [31]) creates a ludicrous picture of unending difference. An identifiable paradigm of power is lost amidst the incessant mutation of the subject. The negative implications of a fetish of identity politics, informed increasingly by an interminable alterity has produced a breakdown in the social texture of human relations and created a hostile landscape where only temporary (and distrustful) alliances can be made. A proliferation of different forms of identity in this scene work to perpetuate suspicion, division, and alienation between different groups of humans and animals. The logical extreme of a politics of difference both between and within subjects has led to a global community, the members of which identify with each other mostly through their common experiences of isolation, estrangement, and enmity.

Like *The Skriker*, *Far Away* also focuses on the natural environment. As well as functioning metaphorically (as expressive of the apocalyptic nature of global conflict), the animals, landscape, and natural elements are all meaningful in terms of their own independent and autonomous agencies. No longer a passive depository of resources for humanity or an idealised backdrop for the development of human history, the non-human natural world has discovered the potential of its agency and is fighting back. Butterflies "can cover your face" (28), cats have been "killing babies" (30), mallards "commit rape" (33), and "fawns get under the feet of shoppers and send them crashing down escalators" (34). Furthermore, the "weather here's on the side of the Japanese" (37), "the Bolivians are working with gravity" (p37), and Joan does not know "whose side the river was on" (38). There is universal involvement in this war, or at least, nearly universal: "who's going to mobilise darkness and silence? that's what I wondered in the night" (38). Chaudhuri writes,

> the fraying of the social order in the domestic, professional, artistic, and political spheres leaves her characters, finally, face-to-face with an ecocidal free-for-all. All of creation has joined the fray–animals, plants, rivers, and even the weather is part of the new reality of total enmity, universal dissension.[49]

---

[49] Chaudhuri, "Different Hats," 133.

Although inter-animal conflict comprises a dimension of the war, there is a vivid sense of the natural world's (united) retribution on humanity, a humanity that ends up as "piles of bodies." Joan continues, "and if you stopped to find out there was one killed by coffee or one killed by pins, they were killed by heroin, petrol, chainsaws, hairspray, bleach" (37).

Our "self-imposed incarceration in the prison house of language," as ecocritic Lance Newman describes the situation, prevents us from exploring the "dialectical interaction between texts and ... the extra-textual material world."[50] *Far Away*, and the last scene of the play in particular, is a vision of what could happen if political critique remains an inward-looking, text-based activity. The anthropomorphic nature of the narrative of humanism is deconstructed by postmodern theory only to be replaced by an outlook that by implication is equally negligent of the non-human natural world. The identification that our self-realisation is mediated by text has served to produce a fetish of language, text, and signification in postmodern culture. In contrast, the extra-textual material world in *Far Away*, although it has no dialogue, has a tangible independence of its own. Not only does it display its agency through active participation in war but it also expresses an autonomous, albeit amorphous and inchoate, sense of presence. Joan speaks the last few lines of the play,

> but I didn't know whose side the river was on, it might help me swim or it might drown me. In the middle the current was running much faster, the water was brown, I didn't know if that meant anything. I stood on the bank a long time. But I knew it was my only way of getting here so at last I put one foot in the river. It was very cold but so far that was all. When you've just stepped in you can't tell what's going to happen. The water laps round your ankles in any case. (38)

Joan's inability to decipher the river ("I didn't know if that meant anything") along with the unknowable but nevertheless perceptible expression of the river's subjectivity reflected in the strangely opaque last phrase, "the water laps round your ankles in any case," begins a new trajectory that attempts to redefine the relationship between the human and non-human natural world.

Nevertheless, although there is a definite reverberation of Serres's *The Natural Contract*, the play's politics work through a concern with human displacement, exploitation, and the corrosion of a social network as well as

---

[50] Lance Newman, "Marxism and Ecocritism," *Interdisciplinary Studies in Literature and Environment* 9.2 (Summer 2002): 1-25, 7.

through bewilderment and repugnance at the sense of ultimate breakdown of the relationship between the human and non-human natural world. The natural environment in this way is the last frontier; it is, as the Skriker says, what is always assumed to be there, even as it suffers erosion. *Far Away's* ecocritical dystopia is framed within a wider attack on the imperialist projects that seem to define the historical moment within which the play is produced. The first scene includes many allusions to war, prisoners, and refugees. We hear that Joan's uncle "was bundling someone into a shed" (8) and that there are children with "blood on their faces" (12). This evocation of war victims, asylum seekers, and refugees contributes further to the sense of displacement that is already present in the scene. The setting, after all, is not concretely placed; the stage directions indicate only that it is "*Harper's house*" (3). The audience is encouraged to presume that it is in a rural location because Joan notes "the stars are brighter here" and Harper explains "it's because there's no street lights" (5). Harper also says "people come here specially to watch birds" and remarks "what a beautiful place it is" (6). But it seems peculiarly out of space; Harper says to Joan: "it's always odd in a new place" (4), but this place's oddness seems to be reinforced by the strange Pinteresque dialogue and the fractured sense of coherence that permeates the play's political narrative. At the end of the second scene, the frequent need for Joan and Todd to assert themselves through the repeated use of personal pronouns ("I go for a"; "I've got a"; "I stay up till"; "I'm getting a"; "I've got my" (18; 19) intimates an anxiety surrounding notions of subjectivity, articulation, and communication.

The final act of total enmity is thus contextualised through the sense of displacement and disarticulation expressed in the first and second acts. Dymkowski suggests "there is a sense of progression from what seems to have been the local conflict of the first scene, to the totalitarian oppression of the second, to this (presumably) civil war situation of the third."[51] Although *Far Away* contains a diachronic narrative, it can also be read synchronically, a reading that depends upon viewing each scene as containing parallel articulations of the same political code. Images of displacement and violence in the first scene are continued into the second, although they are played out in a different context in negotiation with ideas relating to aesthetics, labour relations, and alienation. The final scene can be viewed as yet another form in which similar political impulses are reflected. In other words, each scene constitutes and is constituted by the others. There is an inter-dependence of each facet (exploitation, alienation,

---

[51] Dymkowski, "Caryl Churchill: *Far Away* …but Close to Home," 62.

fragmentation, displacement, war), an interdependence that is reflective of similar political impulses.

Far Away's political vision can be seen as the consequence of the dissolution of the totality, the collapse of collective agency, and the displacement of political critique from a committed position towards a shifting and transient location. Some critics, such as Kritzer, look for moments of optimism in the play ("Joan, who has braved all the bizarre dangers of her conflict-ridden world to be with Todd ... demonstrates her choice to make a meaningful commitment"[52]) and see these as instances of hope for the future, or a "Brechtian 'way out' of the dystopia of a world disintegrating in chaotic conflict."[53] But although the global crisis envisioned in *Far Away* works through the shocking closeness of the political predicament to the existing socio-economic landscape, it remains a dystopia, and a dystopia serving as a warning of what might occur if preventative action (or activism) is not undertaken. There is no going back from the apocalypse of *Far Away*; however much courage and commitment Joan displays in her final speech, this is the moment of historical closure: the end of human history. There is no hope for Joan, Todd, Harper or anyone else. If there is hope, it is located in the potential of the audience to reject this prophesy, to re-ignite their sense of social and political agency, and to transform the contemporary political trajectory.

Churchill's socialist inclination is present in *Far Away*, perhaps not with the same sense of palpability that figured in many of the 1970's and 1980's plays, but nevertheless it is still discernible. A more conventional socialist narrative would have struggled to communicate, since the language of socialism had been deemed anachronistic and irrelevant in postmodern culture. In order for political articulation to be effective–to get through as it were–it has to negotiate the contemporary idiom, however de-politicised that may be. *Far Away* does exactly this: it embraces the preoccupations of postmodern culture–multiple subjectivities, fragmentation, displacement, ironic art, the primacy of signifying practices–only to implicate them in the nightmare of the play's political vision. The lack of unity, absence of a collective vision, and neglect of social responsibility are not recuperated as an invigorating jettisoning of humanist or Marxist narratives, but rather serve as a haunting of the play, reflecting the sense of disruption and disturbance that forms its psychic and social texture. *Far Away* may not be a play that foregrounds a socialist narrative, but it is certainly a play informed by socialist politics.

---

[52] Kritzer, "Political Currents in Caryl Churchill's Plays," 66.
[53] Kritzer, 'Political Currents in Caryl Churchill's Plays," 66.

CONCLUSION

Churchill's work has been rightly celebrated as innovative, rich, and diverse. She has been recognised for her pioneering approach to theatrical form, a form that consistently breaks down barriers in its discovery of new dramatic structures, and equally for her diversity of content, which gives full expression to the abundant experiences of individuals and groups of people struggling to make sense of themselves and their social contexts. An unapologetic commitment to anti-capitalist resistance and struggle is a major element of her drama. The exploration of different manifestations of this commitment helps to open up and (re)ignite the vibrant Left debates with which the plays evidently display interest. Janelle Reinelt introduces Churchill as someone who,

> came to prominence concurrently with the development of Second Wave feminism in Britain, both its activism and its academic thrust; and at the time when Marxism was being re-thought in the academy in light of Althusser and Lacan, and challenged by feminists for ignoring gender, and, later, sexuality.[1]

Gramscian theory and the Frankfurt School should also be included in this list. Indeed Marxist and socialist departures, as well as the Left as a political and intellectual body are of at least equal importance as sources of preoccupation and inspiration in much of Churchill's drama, as feminist, poststructuralist, and postmodernist discourses.

I hope to have shown that the vibrant field of utopian studies and Left appropriations of utopian theory in particular, form a stimulating apparatus within which to reinterpret Churchill's plays. The application of utopian theory to theatrical space, to social relations of theatrical production, as well as to the politics of performance–such an enormously under explored area–has proved to be a fruitful prelude to responding to Churchill's plays individually and in pairs. From the explicitly class-based revolutionary desire of *Light Shining* to the anarchic-feminist imaginative space in the

---

[1] Janelle Reinelt, "Caryl Churchill and the Politics of Style," in *The Cambridge Companion to Modern British Playwrights*, eds. Elaine Aston and Janelle Reinelt (Cambridge: Cambridge UP Press, 2000): 174-94, 174.

first Act of *Top Girls*, and the utopian transformative drive of *Mad Forest*, Churchill's drama shows a persistent alertness to the role of utopia in political struggle as well as to its capacity as an escape from, and a way of managing individual and collective despair. Churchill's commitment to the potential of human emancipation at times leads to a representation of social activity where individuals employ various forms of non-compliance, disobedience, and resistance in intransigent and repressive contexts. These representations alternate with more confident displays of solidarity, confrontation, and collective uprising. Utopian theory facilitates the exploration of the interaction between different modes of non-cooperation with, and challenge to, oppressive networks of power.

One of the most prolific areas of socialist and Marxist intervention in research has been in the discipline of historical studies. Churchill's contribution to the reinstatement of the 1640s English revolutionary narrative displays an unequivocal commitment to defend, reinforce, and refresh a body of (socialist) knowledge, knowledge that forms an intellectual bedrock in socialist thinking. *Light Shining* holds in the balance the celebration of the courage and foresight of grass-roots militants and an appraisal of why the revolution stopped short of full emancipation. The play is steeped in the vibrant discussions engendered by socialist, communist, and History Workshop historiography, and utilises Brechtian form to maximise the audience's critical engagement. The explicit dialogue between *Light Shining* and Left historiography is mirrored, once more, in *Vinegar Tom*. This time, a more conscious Marxist-*feminist* challenge to the gender bias in Marxist, as well as liberal, historiography, *Vinegar Tom* reflects the move by socialist-feminist historians in History Workshop to do the same, resulting in the *History Workshop Journal* adopting the subtitle *A Journal of Feminist and Socialist History* in 1982.[2] The intense reciprocity of these two plays (both dramatically and politically) has been made helpfully visible by exploring them together in the contexts of Left academic discussion and political activity.

Similarly, *Top Girls* is once more symptomatic of the tensions between Marxism and feminism, class and gender. This time liberal feminism is shown to be highly inadequate in its response to the needs and desires of most women. An intensely complex play, *Top Girls* has been prone to such unfortunate (mis-)readings as, "the conflicting claims of motherhood versus female equality," or worse, a play about "different life-style

---

[2] Note too publications such as Judith L. Newton, Mary P. Ryan and Judith R. Walkowitz, eds., *Sex and Class in Women's History* (London: Routledge & Kegan Paul, 1983).

choices" in its movement "between the domestic Joyce and the business-world Marlene."[3] To analyse *Top Girls* with reference to an exploration of the dynamics of the relationship between class and gender helps to release the political potential of the play. The play's Marxist-feminist critique of liberal feminism is expressed through its incisive rejection of Thatcherite economics, and a deepening sense of dismay at the fracture of the oppositional Left, which seems impotent to respond to Angie's "frightening" (141) context. Working-class women are, once more, the central protagonists in *Fen*, but this time they are women neglected by both feminists and the British Left. Their isolation from trade unionism, the Labour Movement, women's groups and municipal politics is echoed in the closed community that nurtures superstition, folklore, and repression. The politics of *Fen*, like *Light Shining* and *Vinegar Tom*, resides partly in the play's recording of the lives of rural, working-class women, whose stories would otherwise remain marginal, if not silenced. The play also traces the ways in which these women from a remote countryside village negotiate lives dominated by hard labour, the ideologies of motherhood, and patriarchal relationships. In this sense, the play confronts the topic of working-class women's oppression obliquely–through the stories of Fen women, women who rarely emerge as protagonists in any historical narrative. In doing so, the play attempts to reshape socialist and feminist discourses by prioritising this usually neglected constituency of women, as well as expressing opposition to the capitalist context within which these women struggle to survive.

Despite the problems with its reception and its focus on a self-contained world, bereft of ordinary people, *Serious Money* remains a socialist satire on the financial centre of capitalism. *Serious Money's* brazen pastiche of the economic organisation of capitalism should not be recuperated as a morality play that critiques acquisitiveness but rather appreciated for the full force of its aggressive assault on the sordid spectacle of capitalist self-congratulation. *Serious Money* is careful not to emphasise *sections* of the financial world as targets of attack; instead, the whole system is represented as inveterately exploitative. In this way, the play is implicitly revolutionary in its exclusion of a get-out clause for capitalist economics. Capitalist self-congratulation, articulated so seminally by Francis Fukuyama, is also an important context for *Mad Forest*. The play is so often approached as a postmodern work that at best expresses a political ambivalence too indistinct to decipher and at worst is

---

[3] Christopher Innes, *Modern British Drama 1890-1990* (Cambridge: Cambridge UP, 1992), 460; Michelene Wandor, *Look Back in Gender* (London: Methuen, 1987), 125.

an irrational space where the playfulness of language and multiple subjectivities eclipse the play's enunciation of revolutionary practices. Examining *Mad Forest* as an intervention into the associated political events of the demise of the USSR, the deregulation of the stock market, and the resulting claims of the end of history and the triumph of capitalism reinvigorates its political impact and provides it with a dynamism that does much more than its commonly perceived attributes of innovating dramatic form and articulating political uncertainties.

Again, so often discussed in postmodern terms, Churchill's more recent plays also benefit from being placed within a socialist framework. Although written in a politically hostile climate, *The Skriker* and *Far Away* still signify an anti-capitalist politics. *The Skriker* offers a complex dreamscape, where confusion produced by the endless mutation of subjectivity and a postmodern fetish of the irrational results in political inarticulacy and environmental travesty. *Far Away* follows similar themes, but this time the breakdown in social connection produces an apocalyptic world of all out war. The outcome of repeated wars and environmental abuse is a complete destruction of society and the total breakdown of the relationship between humanity and the non-human natural world. Both of these plays express bewilderment in response to this breakdown. They also articulate a critique of the postmodern discourses that seem to celebrate our supposedly post-ideological world, discourses that within the plays are considered to both reflect and reinforce this breakdown. Socialist commitment certainly survives in these plays but it seems to reside and take refuge in an ecocritical politics, a politics more attuned to the contemporary oppositional idiom.

There is no doubt that revolutionary socialist commitment–be it in traditional political forms, in the academy, or in the arts–has receded over the last two to three decades. Leninist party structures seem anachronistic and inappropriate to contemporary anti-capitalist activity, activity that demands a looser, less-disciplined, more democratic organisational structure. The "decentralised, nonauthoritarian, communist, non-sexist ... society" for which Churchill expressed desire in the early 1980s has been articulated in an idiom that has departed increasingly from the language of the Marxist tradition.[4] However, Churchill's plays have continually reflected an investment in the critique as well as the optimism embodied by socialist and Marxist thinking. From explicit intervention into communist historiography in *Light Shining*; the critical dialogue (from a socialist-feminist perspective) with Marxist and liberal engagements with

---

[4] Churchill, Interview by Judith Thurman, 54.

the seventeenth century witch hunts in *Vinegar Tom*; the socialist challenge to the liberal feminist neglect of class oppression in *Top Girls*; the critique of the delimitations of both feminist and socialist discourses in their disregard of agricultural, working-class women in *Fen*; and a fierce satirical assault on the financial centre of capitalism in *Serious Money*, Churchill's plays from the 1970s and 1980s contain a strong and explicit socialist inflection.

Lastly, although a confident socialist discourse is more difficult to trace in the later plays, it is undoubtedly present. *Mad Forest* is antipathetic to capitalist solutions for post-Ceauşescu confusion, undermines neoliberal jubilation, and celebrates individual and collective forms of resistance and struggle. *The Skriker* critiques an increasingly illegible society, where disparate forms of communication fail to connect with one another, and where the poisoning of the nonhuman, natural world continues in a relentless fashion. *Far Away* continues this dissension from a postmodern world that seems more embracing of multiple subjectivities and political inarticulacy than it is oppositional to the breakdown of human society and the collapse of the relationship between the human and nonhuman natural worlds. Socialist commitment is expressed in these last two plays through parody of postmodern self-reflexivity, and by means of an ecocritical attempt to reignite political agency in an audience living through social and environmental breakdown, a breakdown strengthened by collective apathy, confusion, and bewilderment.

AFTERWORD

In an article in *The Guardian* in 2002 on the legacy of John McGrath, Roland Muldoon is quoted as stating,

> the anti-globalisation movement, and the fact that people are again beginning to understand the nature of capitalism, will give birth to these cultural phenomena [campaigning theatre]. At the height of 7:84, they really did go out there and reflect people's lives, have a good time and organise politically. The question is: how can a theatre movement become vital again? Well, it will. Well, it should. I think we should make it happen.[1]

Muldoon's optimism seems to have been justified. There has been a re-emergence of explicitly political drama, particularly in the rise of Verbatim Theatre, which has included such high profile plays as Richard Norton-Taylor's *The Colour of Justice* (1999), *Justifying War* (2003), *Bloody Sunday* (2005), and *Called to Account* (2007); Victoria Brittain and Gillian Slovo's *Guantanamo* (2004); Alan Rickman and Katherine Viner's *My Name is Rachel Corrie* (2005); Gregory Burke's *Black Watch* (2006); and Robin Soans's *Talking to Terrorists* (2005).[2]

As *The Guardian's* Michael Billington observes, "the disastrous Iraq invasion has galvanised political theatre," and Kate Kellaway correctly detects in *The Observer* that "9/11, the Iraq War and the Bush administration [have] energised playwrights."[3] However, this flurry of

---

[1] Roland Muldoon, quoted in Brian Logan, "What did you do in the class war, Daddy?" *The Guardian* (15 May 2002): 16-17, 17.

[2] Richard Norton-Taylor, *The Colour of Justice* (London: Oberon, 1999); *Justifying War: Scenes from the Hutton Inquiry* (London: Oberon, 2003); *Bloody Sunday: Scenes from the Saville Inquiry* (London: Oberon, 2005); *Called to Account* (London: Oberon, 2007); Victoria Brittain and Gillian Slovo, *Guantanamo* (London: Oberon, 2004); Alan Rickman and Katherine Viner, *My Name is Rachel Corrie* (London: Nick Hern, 2005); Gregory Burke, *Black Watch* (London: Faber, 2006); Robin Soans, *Talking to Terrorists* (London: Oberon, 2005).

[3] Michael Billington, Theatre Blog, *The Guardian* (03 May 2007); Kate Kellaway, "Theatre of War," *The Observer* (29 August 2004).

politics on stage is tempered by a resistance, a resistance reflected in Harold Pinter's comments, "this remains a conservative country in many ways with a deeply held tradition of mockery and dismissal," and Richard Eyre's claim that "this country does not like artists to be politically engaged."[4] Notwithstanding this, The National Theatre staged David Hare's 2003 play, *The Permanent Way* (about the disastrous and deadly consequences of the privatisation of the railways) and his 2004 play about the Iraq war, *Stuff Happens*, as well as Roy Williams's 2000 play *Sing yer Heart out for the Lads* (about English nationalism and racism).[5] In 2003, The National Theatre hosted a series called "Collateral Damage," where artists including Judi Dench, Tony Harrison, and Patrick Marber, came together to articulate their responses to the Iraq war, and in 2004 the theatre put on a "National Headlines Series," comprising five monologues from playwrights including Mark Ravenhill and Tanika Gupta focusing on such "headline" topics as asylum seekers, foot and mouth disease, and hospitals.

Churchill, too, has returned to a more overtly political theatre in recent times. *Drunk Enough to Say I Love You*,[6] first performed in 2006, was an expression of, in Benedict Nightingale's words, "quiet fury"[7] at Britain's seduction by, and complicity in, American-led, imperialist adventurism, neoliberal agenda setting, and the Americanisation of culture and the arts.[8] Dramatised through the metaphor of a sexual relationship between two men, Jack and Sam, the play's politics is expressed through the contemporary idiom of sexuality and personal relationships. At the same time the play implicates the spectator in Jack's obsequious feelings for Sam and, by extension, everyone's acquiescence to US belligerence and global exploitation. Whilst Billington praised the play's "brilliant conceit" and appreciated that it "nails American double-think and manipulation of

---

[4] Both quoted in Kellaway, "Theatre of War."
[5] David Hare, *The Permanent Way* (London: Faber, 2003); *Stuff Happens* (London: Faber, 2004); Roy Williams, *Sing yer Heart out for the Lads* (London: Methuen, 2002).
[6] Churchill, *Drunk Enough to Say I Love You* (London: Nick Hern, 2006).
[7] Benedict Nightingale, *The Times* (23 November 2006).
[8] Although Churchill did not intend the character, Jack, to represent Britain specifically; she imagined him as "just a person." She missed the association of Jack with union jack. She says, "what I wanted to write was about the way most people (in Britain, or other Western countries, or anywhere, almost) are a bit in love with America, whether it's movies, ice-cream or ideals, and are then implicated in all this stuff it does." Churchill, quoted in Philip Roberts, *About Churchil:The Playwright and the* Work (London: Faber, 2009), 269.

language," *The Observer's* Susannah Clapp dismissed it as "polemic," complaining, "it doesn't discuss; it states. It doesn't surprise; it confirms."[9] It seems that Eyre's reference to the continuing lack of appreciation in public discourse of politically engaged art remains a strong presence. Indeed, it is interesting to note Ben Brantley's review in *The New York Times* of a revival of the play, which likens it to a "political poison-pen letter," but also claims that the "rabid venting takes the form of a brave, canny exploration of theatrical language," concluding that Churchill's "natural talent can't help asserting itself."[10]

Perhaps the most significant political play on stage in Britain in the 2000s was Churchill's *Seven Jewish Children: A Play for Gaza*,[11] a play that responded to the Israeli siege of Gaza in January 2009, which resulted in the widely reported deaths of 13 Israelis compared with over 1300 Palestinians. A short ten-minute play, it stages seven characters discussing Israeli and Jewish history, particularly focusing on how violent events are explained to children. Churchill writes in a letter to *The Independent*, "in the early scenes, it is violence against Jewish people; by the end, it is the violence in Gaza."[12] On the Royal Court Theatre website Mark Brown quotes Churchill as saying that the play was a result

> of feeling strongly about what's happening in Gaza–it's a way of helping the people there. Everyone knows about Gaza, everyone is upset about it, and this play is something they could come to. It's a political event, not just a theatre event.[13]

The play was famously free to attend, spectators instead asked to make a donation to the charity, Medical Aid to Palestine (MAP). Churchill made the script available free to download, inviting anyone to perform it on condition that it should be free to attend and donations to MAP should be collected from the audience.

---

[9] Billington, "*Drunk Enough to Say I Love You?*" *The Guardian* (24 November 2006); Susannah Clapp, "Divided by a Common Language," *The Observer* (26 November 2006).

[10] Ben Brantley, "They Don't Call it a Special Relationship for Nothing," *The New York Times* (17 March 2008).

[11] See Chapter 1, note 87.

[12] Churchill, Letter, *The Independent* (21 February 2009).

[13] Mark Brown, "Royal Court Acts Fast with Gaza Crisis Play," http://www.royalcourttheatre.com/whatson_article_detail.asp?ArticleID=21&play=548

This convergence of theatre and politics–the fact that *Seven Jewish Children* is a political as well as a theatrical event, as Churchill sees it–is also a rehabilitation of a Left cultural tradition. Many performances across Britain and the US scheduled discussions after the play, this rejuvenation of the after-show discussion, an activity resonant of socialist theatre practices in the 1970s. Of course, the play was accused by some of being anti-semitic, an accusation seemingly difficult to avoid for those campaigning against Israeli occupation and expressing Palestinian solidarity.[14] Nevertheless, the furore that the play incited in the media ensured that this slight but powerful play made a global impact and revived debate on the Israel/Palestine conflict as well as contributing financially to the relief of Palestinian suffering. These events seem to reflect the re-emergence of theatre as a vital political form, a form that can intervene in contemporary events with rapidity, and question, challenge, and provide alternatives to dominant political representations.

Churchill, it seems, is likely to continue to be at the forefront of political playwrighting and continue to reflect socialist themes and concerns, although–as several other Churchill scholars have successfully demonstrated–she has always written interestingly and provocatively on a whole range of issues including philosophical, psychological, and emotional aspects of human experience. Churchill's advantage as a playwright, an advantage that has provided her with an admiring global audience, has always been her immense talent for producing remarkable theatre. This talent and wide coverage of diverse issues and themes have meant that whilst much scholarly engagement has neglected the socialist dimensions of Churchill's work and theatre critics have at times displayed an embarrassment at her more explicit political representations, the extraordinarily high quality of her work has, simultaneously, guaranteed the plays a global hearing and serious critical attention.

---

[14] The most vociferous attack on the play from Britain came from Melanie Phillips, who described it as "a direct attack on the Jews" and accused it of being "a ten-minute blood-libel." "The Royal Court's Mystery Play," *The Spectator* (8 February 2009).

BIBLIOGRAPHY

Abelove, Henry, Betsy Blackmar, Peter Dimock and Jonathan Schneer, eds. *Visions of History*. Manchester: Manchester UP, 1976.

Abott, Pamela and Roger Sapsford. *Women and Social Class*. London: Tavistock Publications, 1987.

Acker, Joan. "Women and Social Stratification: A Case of Intellectual Sexism." *American Journal of Sociology* 78 (1973): 936-45.

Adiseshiah, Siân. "Revolution and the End of History: Caryl Churchill's *Mad Forest*." *Modern Drama* 52.3 (Fall 2009): 283-99.

—. "Still a Socialist? Political Commitment in Caryl Churchill's *The Skriker* and *Far Away*." In *Drama and/after Postmodernism*. Edited by Christoph Henke and Martin Middeke, 277-91. Trier: Wissenschaftlicher, 2007.

—. "Utopian Space in Caryl Churchill's History Plays: *Light Shining in Buckinghamshire* and *Vinegar Tom*." *Utopian Studies* 16.1 (Spring 2005): 3-26.

Adorno, Theodor. "Commitment." In *Aesthetics and Politics*. Edited by Frederic Jameson, 177-95. London: Verso, 1977.

Ali, Tariq. "Springtime for NATO." *New Left Review* 234 (March/April 1999): 62-72.

Ali, Tariq and Quintin Hoare. "Socialists and the Crisis of Labourism." *New Left Review* 132 (March-April 1982): 59-81.

Ali, Tariq and Howard Brenton. *Christie in Love*. London: Methuen, 1970.

—. *Moscow Gold*. London: Nick Hern, 1990.

Althusser, Louis. "Contradiction and Overdetermination." In *The New Left Reader*. Edited by Carl Oglesby, 57-83. New York: Grove Press, 1969.

Anderson, Perry. *Arguments Within English Marxism*. London: Verso, 1980.

Anonymous. "The Appeal from the Sorbonne." In *The New Left Reader*. Edited by Carl Oglesby, 267-73. New York: Grove Press, 1969.

Armbruster, Karla and Kathleen Wallace, eds. *Beyond Nature Writing: Expanding the Boundaries of Ecocriticsm*. London: University Press of Virginia, 2001.

Artaud, Antonin. "Mise en scène and Metaphysics." In *The Routledge Reader in Politics and Performance*. Edited by Lizbeth Goodman and Jane de Gay, 98-101. London: Routledge, 2000.

Ascherson, Neal. "Eastern Europe On the Move." In *New Times: The Changing Face of Politics in the 1990s*. Edited by Stuart Hall and Martin Jacques, 222-44. London: Lawrence and Wishart in association with *Marxism Today*, 1989.

Asquith, Ros. *City Limits* (2 April 1987) reprinted in *London Theatre Record* (26 March-22 April 1987): 369.

Aston, Elaine. *Caryl Churchill*. Plymouth: Northcote House, 1997.

—. *An Introduction to Feminism and Theatre*. London: Routledge, 1995.

Aylmer, G. E. *The Levellers in the English Revolution*. London: Thames and Hudson, 1975.

—. *Rebellion or Revolution: England 1640-1660*. Oxford: Oxford UP, 1987.

Badiou, Alain. *Ethics: An Essay on the Understanding of Evil*. London: Verso, 2002.

Baker-White, Robert. "Caryl Churchill's Natural Visions." In *Caryl Churchill: Contemporary Re-presentations*. Edited by Sheila Rabillard, 142-58. Winnipeg: Blizzard Press, 1997.

Barnes, Harry, Jr. Introduction. In *Romania After Tyranny*. Edited by Daniel N. Nelson, 1-7. Oxford: Westview Press, 1992.

Barnett, Anthony. "Raymond Williams and Marxism: A Rejoinder to Terry Eagleton." *New Left Review* 99 (September-October 1976): 47-64.

—. "A Revolutionary Student Movement." *New Left Review* 53 (January-February 1969): 43-53.

Barnett, Claudia. "'Reveangance is gold mine, sweet.'" *Essays in Theatre* 19.1 (November 2000): 45-57.

Barrett, Michèle. *Women's Oppression Today: Problems in Marxist Feminist Analysis*. London: Verso, 1980.

Barrett, Michèle and Mary McIntosh. "Christine Delphy: Towards a Materialist Feminism?" *Feminist Review* 1 (1979): 95-106.

Barstow, Anne Llewellyn. *Witchcraze: A New History of the European Witch Hunts*. London: Pandora, 1994.

Bartkowski, Frances. *Feminist Utopias*. London: University of Nebraska Press, 1989.

Baudrillard, Jean. *The Consumer Society: Myths and Structures*. London: Sage, 1998.

—. *Simulations*. New York: Semiotext, 1983.

Bell, Daniel. *The End of Ideology*. Illinois: Free Press of Glencoe, 1960.

Bellamy, Edward. *Looking Backward*. Harmondsworth: Penguin, 1982 (first published in 1888).

Belsey, Catherine. *Desire: Love Stories in Western Culture.* Oxford: Blackwell, 1994.

Benjamin, Walter. *The Arcades Project.* London: Belknap Press of Harvard University Press, 1999.

—. "Theses on the Philosophy of History." In *Illuminations.* Translated by Harry Zohn, 245-55. London: Fontana Press, 1992.

Bennett, Susan. "Growing Up on *Cloud Nine*: Gender, Sexuality, and Farce." In *Caryl Churchill: Contemporary Re-presentations.* Edited by Sheila Rabillard, 29-40. Winnipeg: Blizzard Press, 1997.

Betsko, Kathleen and Rachel Koenig, eds. *Interviews with Contemporary Women Playwrights.* New York: Beech Tree Books, 1987.

Billington, Michael. *The Guardian* (29 January 1994) reprinted in *Theatre Record* (15-28 January 1994): 97.

—. *The Guardian* (25 September 1997) reprinted in *Theatre Record* (10-23 September 1997): 1193.

—. "*Far Away*: Surreal Shocks from Caryl Churchill." *The Guardian* (2 December 2000).

Blackburn, Michael. "Kosovo: The War of NATO Expansion." *New Left Review* 235 (May/June 1999): 107-23.

Bleakley, Alan. *The Animalising Imagination.* London: Macmillan, 2000.

Bloch, Ernst. *The Principle of Hope.* Volume One. Translated and edited by Neville Plaice, Stephen Plaice and Paul Knight. Oxford: Blackwell, 1986.

Bond, Edward. *Restoration.* London: Methuen, 1992.

Bradbury, Malcolm and David Palmer, eds. *Contemporary British Drama.* Stratford-upon-Avon Studies 19. London: Edward Arnold, 1981.

Brailsford, H. N. *The Levellers and the English Revolution.* Edited by Christopher Hill. London: Cressett Press, 1961.

Brecht, Bertolt. *Brecht on Theatre.* Translated and edited by John Willett. New York: Hill and Wang, 1957.

Brenton, Howard. *Magnificence.* London: Methuen, 1973.

Brighton, Pam. "Theatre in Thatcher's Britain: Organising the Opposition." *New Theatre Quarterly* 5.18 (May 1989): 113-23.

Brittain, Victoria and Gillian Slovo. *Guantanamo.* London: Oberon, 2004.

Brook, Peter. *The Empty Space.* London: MacGibbon & Kee, 1968.

Bronner, Stephen Eric. "Between Art and Utopia: Reconsidering the Aesthetic Theory of Herbert Marcuse." In *Marcuse: Critical Theory and the Promise of Utopia.* Edited by Robert Pippin, Andrew Feenberg and Charles P. Webel, 107-40. London: Macmillan, 1988.

Brown, Janet. "Caryl Churchill's *Top Girls* Catches the Next Wave." In
  Caryl Churchill: A Casebook. Edited by Phyllis R. Randall, 117-30.
  London: Garland Publishing, 1988.
Brown, Mark Thacker. "'Constantly Coming Back': Eastern Thought and
  the Plays of Caryl Churchill." In *Caryl Churchill: A Casebook*. Edited
  by Phyllis R. Randall, 25-47. London: Garland, 1988.
Brustein, Robert. "Robert Brustein on Theater: Prescient Plays." *The New
  Republic* (23 December 2002): 27-28.
Burchill, Julie. "A Woman's Work is Never Done." In *The Guardian
  Weekend* (16 February 2002).
Burke, Gregory. *Black Watch*. London: Faber, 2006.
Burstyn, Varda. "Masculine Dominance and the State." *The Socialist
  Register* (1983): 45-89.
Burwell, Jennifer. *Notes on Nowhere: Feminism, Utopian Logic, and
  Social Transformation*. London: University of Minnesota Press, 1997.
Butler, Judith. *Bodies that Matter: On the Discursive Limits of Sex*.
  London: Routledge, 1993.
Callaghan, John. *The Far Left in British Politics*. Oxford: Blackwell, 1987.
Callinicos, Alex. *Against Postmodernism: A Marxist Critique*. Oxford:
  Blackwell, 1989.
—. *The Revenge of History: Marxism and the East European Revolutions*.
  Oxford: Polity Press, 1991.
Campbell, Donald. "Traditional Movement." *Plays and Players*
  (November 1976): 20-21.
Carver, Terrell. "Engels' Feminism." *History of Political Thought* 4.3
  (Winter 1985): 479-89.
Case, Sue-Ellen. "The Power of Sex: English Plays by Women, 1958-
  1988." *New Theatre Quarterly* 7.27 (August 1991): 238-45.
Castleden, Rodney, ed. *British History: A Chronological Dictionary of
  Dates*. London: Parragon, 1994.
Chamberlain, Mary. *Fenwomen: A Portrait of Women in an English
  Village*. London: Routledge & Kegan Paul, 1983.
Chaudhuri, Una. "Different Hats." *Theatre* 33.3 (2000): 132-34.
—. "Hell in the Heartland: Mapping Post-Abu Ghraib America in Sam
  Shepherd's *The God of Hell*." In *Mapping Uncertain Territories:
  Space and Place in Contemporary Theatre and Drama*. Edited by
  Thomas Rommel and Mark Schreiber, 49-60. Trier: Wissenschaftlicher,
  2006.
—. *Staging Place: The Geography of Modern Drama*. Ann Arbor:
  University of Michigan Press, 1995.

Chesters, Graeme. "Resist to Exist? Radical Environmentalism at the End of the Millennium." *ECOS* 20.2 (1999): 19-25.

Chodorow, Nancy. "Mothering, Male Dominance, and Capitalism." In *Capitalist Patriarchy and the Case for Socialist Feminism*. Edited by Zillah R. Eisenstein, 83-106. London: Monthly Review Press, 1979.

Christopher, James. *Time Out* (2 February 1994) reprinted in *Theatre Record* (15-28 January 1994): 96.

Churchill, Caryl. *Blue Heart*. London: Nick Hern, 1997.

—. "Caryl Churchill." In *Interviews with Contemporary Women Playwrights*. Edited by Kathleen Betsko and Rachel Koenig, 75-84. New York: Beech Tree Books, 1987.

—. "Caryl Churchill." In *Joint Stock: The Making of a Theatre Collective*. Edited by Rob Ritchie, 118-21. London: Methuen, 1987.

—. *Caryl Churchill: Plays: 3*. London: Nick Hern, 1998.

—. *Cloud Nine*. London: Nick Hern, 1989 (first published in 1979).

—. "The Common Imagination and Individual Voice." Interview by Geraldine Cousin. *New Theatre Quarterly* 4.13 (February 1988): 3-16.

—. *Drunk Enough to Say I Love You*. London: Nick Hern, 2006.

—. *Far Away*. London: Nick Hern, 2000.

—. *Fen*. In *Caryl Churchill Plays: 2*, 143-90. London: Methuen, 1990.

—. *Icecream*. In *Caryl Churchill Plays: 3*, 55-102. London: Nick Hern, 1998.

—. *Icecream* with *Hot Fudge*. London: French, 1990.

—. Interview by Judith Thurman. *Ms* (May 1982): 54.

—. Interview by Laurie Stone. In "Making Room at the Top." *The Village Voice* XXVIII.9 (1 March 1983): 80-81.

—. Interview by Lizbeth Goodman. In *Approaching Top Girls Video*. Produced by the Open University BBC. London: Routledge, 1996.

—. Introduction. *Caryl Churchill Plays: 2*, ix-x. London: Methuen, 1990.

—. Introduction. *Caryl Churchill Plays: 3*, vii-viii. London: Nick Hern, 1998.

—. Introduction. *Fen*. In *Caryl Churchill: Plays 2*, 146. London: Methuen, 1990.

—. Introduction. *Light Shining in Buckinghamshire*. In *Caryl Churchill: Plays: 1*, 183. London: Methuen, 1985.

—. Introduction. *Vinegar Tom*. In *Caryl Churchill Plays: 1*, 129-31. London: Methuen, 1985.

—. *The Legion Hall Bombing*. Transmitted 22 August 1978 BBC1.

—. Letter to the Chairman of the English Stage Company (3 November 1989). Reprinted in *About Churchill: The Playwright and the Work* by Philip Roberts, 115-17. London: Faber, 2008.

—. Letter to Dear Weekend. *The Guardian Weekend*. (23 February 2002)

—. Letter to the Editor. *The Guardian* (10 April 1999)

—. Letter to the Editor. *The Guardian* (8 January 2009)

—. *Light Shining in Buckinghamshire*. In *Caryl Churchill Plays: 1*, 181-241. London: Methuen, 1985.

—. *Mad Forest*. London: Nick Hern, 1990.

—. *Mad Forest*. In *Caryl Churchill Plays: 3*, 103-81. London: Nick Hern, 1998.

—. A Note on the Production. *Light Shining in Buckinghamshire*. In *Caryl Churchill Plays: 1*, 184-85. London: Methuen, 1985.

—. *A Number*. London: Nick Hern, 2002.

—. *Owners*. In *Caryl Churchill: Plays 1*, 1-67. London: Methuen, 1985.

—. Production Note to *Fen*. In *Caryl Churchill: Plays 2*, 145. London: Methuen, 1990.

—. *Serious Money*. In *Caryl Churchill Plays: 2*, 193-309. London: Methuen, 1990.

—. *Seven Jewish Children: A Play for Gaza*. London: Nick Hern, 2009.

—. *The Skriker*. In *Caryl Churchill Plays: 3*, 239-91. London: Nick Hern, 1998.

—. *Top Girls*. In *Caryl Churchill Plays: 2*. 51-141. London: Methuen, 1990.

—. *Top Girls*. BBC/Open University Video Production, directed by Max Stafford-Clark, 1991.

—. *Vinegar Tom*. In Caryl *Churchill Plays: 1*, 129-79. London: Methuen, 1985.

—. "A Woman's Point of View." Interview by Maggie Rose. *Sipario* (November-December 1987): 99-100.

Cixous, Hélène. "The Laugh of the Medusa." Translated by Keith Cohen and Paula Cohen. *Signs* 1 (1976): 875-93.

Claeys, Gregory. Introduction. *Utopias of the British Enlightenment*, vii-xxviii. Cambridge: Cambridge UP, 1994.

Clapp, Susannah. "A Son for Every Occasion." *The Observer Review* (29 September 2002).

Clum, John M. Review of *The Plays of Caryl Churchill* by Amelia Howe Kritzer. *Modern Drama* 38.1 (Spring 1995): 131-32.

—. "'The Work of Culture': *Cloud Nine* and Sex/Gender Theory." In *Caryl Churchill: A Casebook*. Edited by Phyllis R. Randall, 91-116. London: Garland, 1988.

Coates, David. "Labourism and the Transition to Socialism." *New Left Review* 129 (September-October 1981): 3-22.

Cody, Garbrielle. *"Icecream*: Caryl Churchill's Invisible Meltdown." *Theater* 3.9 (Fall 1990): 58-67.

Coggan, Philip. *The Money Machine: How the City Works*. 2nd ed. London: Penguin, 1989 (first published in 1986).

Cohn, Ruby. "Modest Proposals of Modern Socialists." *Modern Drama* 25 (1982): 457-68.

—. *Retreats from Realism in Recent English Drama*. Cambridge: Cambridge UP, 1991.

Cook, Barbara, ed. *Women Writing Nature: A Feminist View*. Lanham, MD: Lexington Books, 2007.

Coontz, Stephanie and Peta Henderson, eds. *Women's Work, Men's Property: The Origins of Gender and Class*. London: Verso, 1986.

Cornish, Roger and Violet Ketels. *Landmarks of Modern British Drama: The Plays of the Seventies*. London: Methuen, 1986.

Cousin, Geraldine. *Churchill: The Playwright*. London: Methuen, 1989.

—. "Owning the Disowned: *The Skriker* in the Context of Earlier Plays by Caryl Churchill." In *Caryl Churchill: Contemporary Re-presentations*. Edited by Sheila Rabillard, 189-205. Winnipeg: Blizzard Press, 1997.

—. *Women in Dramatic Place and Time: Contemporary Female Characters on Stage*. London: Routledge, 1996.

Coveney, Michael. *Daily Mail* (24 September 1997) reprinted in *Theatre Record* (10-23 September 1997): 1193.

—. *Financial Times* (17 February 1983) reprinted in *London Theatre Record* 3.4 (12-25 February 1983): 112-13.

Coward, Rosalind. "Sexual Liberation and the Family." *m/f* 1 (1978): 7-24.

Craig, Sandy, ed. *Dreams and Deconstructions: Alternative Theatre in Britain*. Ambergate: Amber Lane Press, 1980.

Crosland, Anthony. *The Future of Socialism*. London: Cape, 1956.

Cushman, Robert. *The Observer* (5 September 1982).

Daly, Mary. *Gyn/Ecology: The Metaethics of Radical Feminism*. London: The Women's Press, 1979.

Davies, A. *Other Theatres: The Development of Alternative and Experimental Theatre in Britain*. London: Macmillan, 1987.

Davis, J. C. *Fear, Myth and History: The Ranters and the Historians*. Cambridge: Cambridge UP, 1986.

de Beauvoir, Simone. *The Second Sex*. London: Vintage, 1997 (first published in 1949).

de Certeau, Michel. *The Practice of Everyday Life*. Translated by Steven Randall. London: University of California Press, 1984.

de Gay, Jane. "Colour Me Beautiful? Clothes Consciousness in the Open University/BBC video production of *Top Girls*." In *Caryl Churchill:*

Contemporary Re-presentations. Edited by Sheila Rabbillard, 102-13. Winnipeg: Blizzard Press, 1997.

Delphy, Christine. *Close to Home: A Materialist Analysis of Women's Oppression.* London: Hutchinson, 1984.

——. "Women in Stratification Studies." In *Close to Home,* 28-39. London: Hutchinson, 1984.

Derrida, Jacques. *Of Grammatology.* Translated by Gayatri Chakravorty Spivak. Baltimore: John Hopkins University Press, 1976.

——. *Specters of Marx: The State of the Debt, the Work of Mourning, and the New International.* Translated by Peggy Kamuf. Routledge: New York, 1994.

Diamond, Elin. "Closing No Gaps: Aphra Behn, Caryl Churchill, and Empire." In *Caryl Churchill: A Casebook.* Edited by Phyllis R. Randall, 161-74. London: Garland, 1988.

——. "(In)Visible bodies in Churchill's Theater." In *Making a Spectacle: Feminist Essays on Contemporary Women's Theatre.* Edited by Lynda Hart, 259-81. Ann Abor: University of Michigan Press, 1989.

——. *Unmaking Mimesis.* London: Routledge, 1997.

Dolan, Jill. *Utopia in Performance: Finding Hope at the Theater.* Ann Arbor: University of Michigan Press, 2005.

Dow, F. D. *Radicalism in the English Revolution 1640-1660.* Oxford: Blackwell, 1985.

Dunn, Nell. *Poor Cow.* London: Virago, 1988.

Dymkowski, Christine. "Caryl Churchill: *Far Away* ...but Close to Home." *European Journal of English Studies* 7.1 (2003): 55-68.

Eagleton, Terry. "Criticism and Politics: The Work of Raymond Williams." *New Left Review* 95 (January-February 1976): 3-23.

——. Preface. *The Illusions of Postmodernism,* vii-x. Oxford: Blackwell, 1996.

——. "In the Gaudy Supermarket." Review of *A Critique of Post-Colonial Reason: Towards a History of the Vanishing Present,* by Gayatri Chakravorty Spivak. *London Review of Books* (13 May 1999): 3-6.

——. *Literary Theory: An Introduction.* Oxford: Blackwell, 1983.

——. *Marx and Freedom.* London: Phoenix, 1997.

Edgar, David. *Maydays.* London: Methuen, 1983.

——. *The Second Time as Farce: Reflections on the Drama of Mean Times.* London: Lawrence and Wishart, 1988.

——. *The Shape of the Table.* London: Nick Hern, 1990.

Ehrenreich, Barbara and Deirdre English. *Witches, Midwives and Nurses: A History of Women Healers.* London: Writers and Readers Publishing Cooperative, 1976.

Eisenstein, Zillah, ed. *Capitalist Patriarchy and the Case for Socialist Feminism*. London: Monthly Review Press, 1979.

—. "Capitalist Patriarchy and Female Work." In *Capitalist Patriarchy and the Case for Socialist Feminism*, 169-172. London: Monthly Review Press, 1979.

—. "Developing a Theory of Capitalist Patriarchy and Socialist Feminism." In *Capitalist Patriarchy and the Case for Socialist Feminism*, 5-40. London: Monthly Review Press, 1979.

Engels, Frederick. Letter to Joseph Bloch (21-22 September 1890). In *Marxist Literary Theory*. Edited by Terry Eagleton and Drew Milne, 39. Oxford: Blackwell, 1996.

—. Preface to the First Edition. In *The Origin of the Family, Private Property and the State*, 8. Moscow: Foreign Languages Publishing House, 1954 (first published in 1884).

—. *The Origin of the Family, Private Property and the State*. Moscow: Foreign Languages Publishing House, 1954 (first published in 1884).

—. *Socialism: Utopian and Scientific*. Peking: Foreign Languages Press, 1975 (first published in 1880).

Estok, Simon C. "A Report Card on Ecocriticism." *AUMLA: The Journal of the Australasian Universities Language and Literature Association* 96 (November 2001): 220-38.

Evenden, Michael. "'No Future without Marx': Dramaturgies of 'The End of History' in Churchill, Brenton and Barker." *Theatre* 29.3 (1999): 100-13, 100.

Firestone, Shulamith. *The Dialectic of Sex: The Case for Feminist Revolution*. London: Jonathan Cape, 1970.

Fitzsimmons, Linda. *File on Churchill*. London: Methuen, 1989.

—. "'I won't turn back for you or anyone': Caryl Churchill's Socialist-Feminist Theatre." *Essays in Theatre* 6.1 (November 1987): 19-29.

Fortier, Mark. *Theory/Theatre: An Introduction*. London: Routledge, 1997.

Foucault, Michel. "Of Other Spaces." *Diacritics* 16.1 (Spring 1986): 22-27.

Fox-Genovese, Elizabeth. "Placing Women's History in History." *New Left Review* 133 (May-June 1982): 5-29.

Friedman, Milton. *Capitalism and Economics*. London: University of Chicago Press 1962.

Fukuyama, Francis. "The End of History." *The National Interest* 16 (Summer 1989): 3-18.

—. "Reflections on *End of History*: Five Years Later." In *After History?: Francis Fukuyama and His Critics*. Edited by Timothy Burns, 239-58. London: Rowman & Littlefield, 1994.

Galbraith, J. K. *The Affluent Society*. London: Hamish Hamilton, 1958.

Galloway, George and Bob Wylie. *Downfall: The Ceausescus and the Romanian Revolution*. London: Futura, 1991.

Garner Jr., Stanton B. Review of *Mad Forest*. *Theatre Review* (1992): 399-401.

Garton Ash, Timothy. *We the People: The Revolution of '89 Witnessed in Warsaw, Budapest, Berlin and Prague*. Cambridge: Granta in association with Penguin, 1990

Gearhart, Sally Miller. *The Wanderground: Stories of the Hill Women*. London: Women's Press, 1988

Gems, Pam. *Queen Christina*. London: Methuen, 1986.

Geoghegan, Vincent. *Utopianism and Marxism*. London: Methuen, 1987.

Giddens, Anthony. *Beyond Left and Right: The Future of Radical Politics*. Cambridge: Polity Press, 1994.

—. *The Third Way: The Renewal of Social Democracy*. Cambridge: Polity Press, 1998.

Gilman, Charlotte Perkins. *Herland*. London: Women's Press, 1979.

Gilmour, Ian. *Dancing with Dogma: Britain Under Thatcherism*. London: Simon and Schuster, 1992.

Glotfelty, Cheryl and Harold Fromm, eds. *The Ecocriticism Reader: Landmarks in Literary Ecology*. London: University of Georgia Press, 1996.

Goldthorpe, John. "Women and Class Analysis: In Defence of the Conventional View." *Sociology* 17 (1983): 465-88.

Gooch, Steve. *Will Wat, If Not, Wat Will?* London: Pluto Press, 1975.

Goodhart, David and Charles Grant. "Making the City work." *Fabian Tract* 528 (July 1988).

Goodman, Lizbeth. "Overlapping Dialogue in Overlapping Media: Behind the Scenes of *Top Girls*." In *Essays on Caryl Churchill: Contemporary Re-presentations*. Edited by Sheila Rabillard, 69-101. Winnipeg: Blizzard Publishing, 1998.

Goodwin, Barbara and Keith Taylor. *The Politics of Utopia: A Study in Theory and Practice*. London: Hutchinson, 1982.

Gordon, Linda. "Interview with Carol Lasser." In *Visions of History*. Edited by Henry Abelove et. al., 73-96. Manchester: Manchester UP, 1976.

Gorz, André. *Farewell to the Working Class: An Essay on Post-Industrial Socialism*. London: Pluto Press, 1982.

—. "From *Strategy For Labour.*" In *The New Left Reader*. Edited by Carl Oglesby, 41-42. New York: Grove Press, 1969.

Gowan, Peter. "The NATO Powers and the Balkan Tragedy." *New Left Review* 234 (March/April 1999): 83-105.

Gramsci, A. *Selections from the Prison Notebooks*. London: Lawrence and Wishart, 1976.

Graves, Robert. *The Greek Myths*. London: Penguin, 1992.

Gray, Frances. "Mirrors of Utopia: Caryl Churchill and Joint Stock." In *British and Irish Drama since 1960*. Edited by James Acheson, 47-59. London: Macmillan, 1993.

Griffiths, Trevor. Interview. *Socialist Review* 185 (April 1995): 22-23.

—. *Occupations*. London: Faber, 1980.

Gross, Robert. "Making Relations: *Icecream's* Dramaturgy of Scepticism." In *Caryl Churchill: Contemporary Re-presentations*. Edited by Sheila Rabillard, 114-28. Winnipeg: Blizzard Press, 1997.

Grunmann, Reiner. "The Ecological Challenge to Marxism." *New Left Review* 187 (May/June 1991): 103-20.

Habermas, Jürgen. "What Does Socialism Mean Today? The Rectifying Revolution and the Need for New Thinking on the Left." *New Left Review* 183 (September/October 1990): 3-21.

Hall, Stuart. *The Hard Road to Renewal: Thatcherism and the Crisis of the Left*. London: Verso, 1988.

—. "The Meaning of New Times." In *New Times: The Changing Face of Politics in the 1990s*. Edited by Stuart Hall and Martin Jacques, 116-34. London: Lawrence and Wishart in association with *Marxism Today*, 1989.

Hall, Stuart and Martin Jacques. Introduction. In *New Times: The Changing Face of Politics in the 1990s*. Edited by Stuart Hall and Martin Jacques, 11-20. London: Lawrence and Wishart in association with *Marxism Today*, 1989.

Hall, Stuart, Raymond Williams and Edward Thompson. "From *The May Day Manifesto*." In *The New Left Reader*. Edited by Carl Oglesby, 111-43. New York: Grove Press, 1969.

Halliday, Fred. "The Ends of Cold War." *New Left Review* 180 (March/April 1990): 5-23.

Hanna, Gillian. "Feminism and Theatre." *Theatre Papers* 8. 2nd Series (1978): 9-10.

Hardy, Thomas. *Jude the Obscure*. London: Penguin, 1996 (first published in 1895).

Hare, David. *Fanshen*. London: Faber, 1986.

—. *The Permanent Way*. London: Faber, 2003.

—. *Plenty*. London: Faber, 1978.

—. *Stuff Happens*. London: Faber, 2004.

Harman, Chris. "Why they Can't Deliver." *Socialist Worker Review* 133 (July/August 1990): 10-13.

Hartman, Heidi. "Capitalism, Patriarchy, and Job Segregation by Sex." In *Capitalist Patriarchy and the Case for Socialist Feminism*. Edited by Zillah Eisenstein, 206-47. London: Monthly Review Press, 1979.

Harvey, David. *Spaces of Hope*. Edinburgh: Edinburgh UP, 2000.

Haslett, Moyra. *Marxist Literary and Cultural Theories*. London: Macmillan, 2000.

Haug, Frigga. "Daydreams." *New Left Review* 162 (March/April 1987): 51-66.

Hayek, Friedrich A von. *Economic Freedom*. Oxford: Basil Blackwell, 1991.

Hebdige, Dick. "After the Masses." In *New Times: The Changing Face of Politics in the 1990s*. Edited by Stuart Hall and Martin Jacques, 94-102. London: Lawrence and Wishart in association with *Marxism Today*, 1989.

Heelas, Paul and Paul Morris, eds. *The Values of the Enterprise Culture: The Moral Debate*. London: Routledge, 1992.

—. "Enterprise Culture: its Values and Value." In *The Values of the Enterprise Culture: The Moral Debate*, 1-25. London: Routledge, 1992.

Hemming, Sarah. "Caught in the Crossfire." *Independent* (8 January 1992).

Henwood, Doug. *Wall Street: How it Works and for Whom*. London: Verso, 1997.

Hetherington, Kevin. *Expressions of Identity: Space, Performance, Politics*. London: Sage, 1998.

Hill, Christopher. *The World Turned Upside Down: Radical Ideas during the English Revolution*. London: Penguin, 1972.

Hirschhorn, Clive. *Daily Express* (29 March 1987) reprinted in *London Theatre Record* (26 March-22 April 1987): 371.

—. *Sunday Express* (30 January 1994) reprinted in *Theatre Record* (15-28 January 1994): 94.

Hobsbawm, Eric. *Age of Extremes: The Short Twentieth Century 1914-1991*. London: Michael Joseph, 1994.

—. "Goodbye to All That." *Marxism Today* (October 1990): 18-23.

Hollis, Andy ed. *Beyond Boundaries: Textual Representations of European Identity*. Amsterdam: Rodopi, 2000.

Howard, Roger. *Siege*. Colchester: Theatre Action Press, 1981.

Hutcheon, Linda. *Narcissistic Narrative: The Metafictional Paradox.* London: Methuen, 1984.

Huxley, Aldous. *Brave New World.* London: Flamingo, 1994 (first published in 1932).

Inglis, Fred. "The Figures of Dissent." *New Left Review* 215 (January/February 1996): 83-92.

Innes, Christopher. *Modern British Drama 1890-1990.* Cambridge: Cambridge UP, 1992.

Itzen, Catherine. *Stages in the Revolution: Political Theatre in Britain Since 1968.* London: Eyre Methuen, 1980.

Jaggar, Alison M. *Feminist Politics and Human Nature.* Sussex: Harvester Press, 1983.

Jaggi, Maya. "Stuart Hall, Prophet at the margins." *The Guardian* (8 July 2000).

Jameson, Frederic, ed. *Aesthetics and Politics: The Key Texts of the Classic Debate Within German Marxism.* London: Verso, 1980.

—. *The Cultural Turn: Selected Writings on the Postmodern 1983-1998.* London: Verso, 1998.

—. "Postmodernism, or The Cultural Logic of Late Capitalism." *New Left Review* 146 (July/August 1984): 53-92.

Jenkins, Anthony. "Social Relations: An Overview." In *Caryl Churchill: Contemporary Re-presentations.* Edited by Sheila Rabillard, 14-28. Winnipeg: Blizzard Press, 1997.

Jonson, Ben. *Volpone.* Edited by Philip Brockbank. London: A & C Black Publishers, 1968 (first published in 1607).

Kaldor, Mary. "After the Cold War." *New Left Review* 180 (March/April 1990): 25-37.

Kane, Sarah. *Blasted.* London: Methuen , 2001 (first published in 1996).

Kershaw, Baz. "Peformance, Community, Culture." In *The Routledge Reader in Politics and Performance.* Edited by Lizbeth Goodman and Jane de Gay, 136-42. London: Routledge, 2000.

—. *The Radical in Performance: Between Brecht and Baudrillard.* London: Routledge, 1999.

Keyssar, Helene. "Doing Dangerous History: Caryl Churchill and *A Mouthful of Birds.*" In *Caryl Churchill: A Casebook.* Edited by Phyllis R. Randall, 131-49. London: Garland, 1988.

King, Kimball. "*Serious Money*: A Market Correction?" In *Caryl Churchill: A Casebook.* Edited by Phyllis Randall, 151-60. London: Garland, 1988.

Kintz, Linda. "Performing Capital in Caryl Churchill's *Serious Money.*" *Theatre Journal* 50.3 (October 1999): 251-65.

Klaić, Dragan. *The Plot of the Future: Utopia and Dystopia in Modern Drama*. Michigan: The University of Michigan Press, 1991.

Knight, Diana. *Barthes and Utopia: Space, Travel, Writing*. Oxford: Clarendon Press, 1997.

Kolakowski, Leszek. "The Concept of the Left." In *The New Left Reader*. Edited by Carl Oglesby, 144-58. New York: Grove Press, 1969.

—. "The Death of Utopia Reconsidered." *The Tanner Lectures on Human Values* IV (1983): 229-47.

Kostova, Ludmilla. "Inventing Post-Wall Europe: Visions of the 'Old' Continent in Contemporary British Fiction and Drama." In *Beyond Boundaries: Textual Representations of European Identity*. Edited by Andy Hollis, 83-84. Amsterdam: Rodopi, 2000.

Kramer, Heinrich and James Sprenger. *The Malleus Maleficarum: The Hammer of the Witches*. Edited by Montague Summers. New York: Dover, 1971 (first published in 1487).

Kristeva, Julia. *Revolution in Poetic Language*. Translated by Margaret Waller. New York: Columbia UP, 1984.

Kritzer, Amelia Howe. *The Plays of Caryl Churchill: Theatre of Empowerment*. London: Macmillan, 1991.

—. "Political Currents in Caryl Churchill's Plays at the Turn of the Millennium." In *Crucible of Cultures: Anglophone Drama at the Dawn of the New Millennium*. Edited by Marc Maufort and Franca Bellarsi, 57-67. Brussels: Peter Lang, 2002.

—. "Systemic Poisons in Churchill's Plays." In *Caryl Churchill: Contemporary Re-presentations*. Edited by Sheila Rabillard, 159-73. Winnipeg: Blizzard Press, 1997.

Kumar, Krishan. *Utopia and Anti-Utopia in Modern Times*. Oxford: Basil Blackwell, 1987.

Landry, Donna and Gerald Maclean. *Materialist Feminisms*. Oxford: Blackwell, 1993.

Lane, Harry. "Secrets as Strategies for Protection and Oppression in *Top Girls*." In *Caryl Churchill: Contemporary Re-presentations*. Edited by Sheila Rabillard, 60-68. Winnipeg: Blizzard Press, 1997.

Laslett, Peter. *The World We Have Lost: Further Explored*. London: Methuen, 1983.

Leadbeater, Charlie. "Power to the Person." In *New Times: The Changing Face of Politics in the 1990s*. Edited by Stuart Hall and Martin Jacques, 137-49. London: Lawrence & Wishart in association with Marxism Today, 1989.

Le Guin, Ursula. *The Dispossessed: An Ambiguous Utopia*. London: Harper Collins, 1996 (first published in 1974).

Lenin, V. I. "Party Organisation and Party Literature." In *Lenin: Selected Works*. Moscow: Progress Publishers, 1968 (first published in 1905).

—. *What is to be done?: Burning Questions of Our Movement*. Beijing: Foreign Languages Press, 1978 (first published in 1902).

Levitas, Ruth. *The Concept of Utopia*. Hemel Hempstead: Philip Allan, 1990.

Lindenberger, Herbert. *Historical Drama: The Relation of Literature and Reality*. Chicago: University of Chicago Press, 1975.

Littig, Beate. *Feminist Perspectives on Environment and Society*. Upper Saddle River, NJ: Prentice Hall, 2001.

Lockhart, Russell A. *Psyche Speaks: A Jungian Approach to Self and World*. Wilmette: Chiron Publications, 1987.

Logan, Brian. "What Did You Do in the Class War, Daddy?" *The Guardian* (15 May 2002).

Luxemburg, Rosa. *The Junius Pamphlet*. London: Merlin Press, 1915.

Lyddon, Dave. "Demythologising the downturn." *International Socialism* 25 (Autumn 1984): 91-107.

Lynd, Staughton. Interview by Len Calabrese. In *Visions of History*. Edited by Henry Abelove et. al., 149-65. Manchester: Manchester UP, 1976.

Macfarlane, Alan. *Witchcraft in Tudor and Stuart England: A Regional and Comparative Study*. London: Routledge & Kegan Paul, 1970.

Mailer, Norman. *Armies of the Night: History as a Novel, the Novel as History*. Harmondsworth: Penguin, 1970.

Malthus, T. R. *The Principles of Political Economy*. London: International Economic Circle: London School of Economics and Political Science, 1936 (first published in 1836).

Mannheim, Karl. *Ideology and Utopia: An Introduction to the Sociology of Knowledge*. London: Routledge & Kegan Paul, 1936.

Manning, Brian. *1649: The Crisis of the English Revolution*. London: Bookmarks, 1992.

Manuel, Frank E. and Fritzie P. Manuel. *Utopian Thought in the Western World*. Cambridge, Massachusetts: Harvard UP, 1979.

Marcuse, Herbert. *Eros and Civilisation: A Philosophical Inquiry into Freud*. Boston: Beacon Press, 1966.

—. *One Dimensional Man*. London: Sphere Books, 1970.

Marin, Louis. *Utopics: Spatial Play*. London: Macmillan, 1984.

Marohl, Joseph. "De-realised Women: Performance and Identity in *Top Girls*." *Modern Drama* 30.3 (September 1987): 376-88.

Marshall, Peter. *Demanding the Impossible: A History of Anarchism*. London: Fontana Press, 1993.

Marwick, Arthur. *British Society Since 1945*. London: Penguin, 1982.

Marx, Karl. "The Eighteenth Brumaire of Louis Bonaparte." In *Karl Marx Selected Writings*. Edited by David McLellan, 300-25. Oxford: Oxford UP, 1977 (first published in 1852).

Marx, Karl and Frederick Engels. *The Communist Manifesto*. Introduced and notes by A. J. P. Taylor. London: Penguin, 1967 (first published in 1848).

McLennan, Gregor. *Marxism and the Methodologies of History*. London: Verso, 1981.

McGrath, John. *The Bone Won't Break*. London: Methuen, 1990.

—. *The Cheviot, The Stag and The Black, Black Oil*. London: Methuen, 1981.

Melucci, Alberto. *Challenging Codes: Collective Action in the Information Age*. Cambridge: Cambridge UP, 1996.

Middleton, Chris. "Patriarchal Exploitation and the Rise of English Capitalism." In *Gender, Class and Work*. Edited by Eva Gamarnikow et. al., 11-27. London: Heinemann, 1983.

Mies, Maria and Vandana Shiva, eds. *Ecofeminism*. London: Zed, 1993.

Miliband, Ralph. "The Future of Socialism in England." *Socialist Register* (1977): 38-50.

Miller, Arthur. *The Crucible*. London: Penguin, 2000 (first published in 1953).

Millett, Kate. *Sexual Politics*. London: Rupert Hart-Davis, 1971.

Mitchell, Juliet. *Woman's Estate*. Harmondsworth: Penguin, 1971.

—. "Women: The Longest Revolution." *New Left Review* 40 (November/December 1966): 11-37.

Mitchell, Tony. "Caryl Churchill's *Mad Forest*: Polyphonic Representations of Southeastern Europe." *Modern Drama* 36.2 (1993): 499-511.

Molyneux, Maxine. "Beyond the Domestic Labour Debate." *New Left Review* 116 (July-August 1979): 3-27.

More, Thomas. *Utopia*. Oxford: Basil Blackwell, 1923 (first published in 1516).

Morley, David and Kuan-Hsing Chen, eds. *Stuart Hall: Critical Dialogues in Cultural Studies*. London: Routledge, 1992.

Morris, William. *News from Nowhere: Or an Epoch of Rest: Being Some Chapters From a Utopian Romance by William Morris*. Cambridge: Cambridge UP, 1995 (first published in 1890).

Morton, A. L. *The World of the Ranters: Religious Radicalism in the English Revolution*. London: Lawrence & Wishart, 1970.

Moylan, Tom. *Demand the Impossible: Science Fiction and the Utopian Imagination.* London: Methuen, 1986.

Muldoon, Roland. "Cast Revival." *Plays and Players* 24.4.279 (January 1977): 40-41.

—. Interview. In *Fringe First: Pioneers of Fringe Theatre on Record.* By Roland Rees, 68-76. London: Oberon Books, 1992.

Müller, Klaus Peter. "A Serious City Comedy: Fe-/Male History and Value Judgements in Caryl Churchill's *Serious Money.*" *Modern Drama* 33.3 (September 1990): 347-62.

Myrdal, Gunnar. *Beyond the Welfare State.* New Haven, Conn: Yale University Press, 1960

Nagy, István. "The Modern Fairy of an Urban Folktale." *The Anachrist* (1998): 233-47.

Naismith, Bill, ed. Commentary. In *Top Girls.* By Caryl Churchill, xxi-liii. London: Methuen, 1991.

Neilson, Anthony. *The Censor.* London: Methuen, 1997.

Newman, Lance. "Marxism and Ecocritism." *Interdisciplinary Studies in Literature and Environment* 9.2 (Summer 2002): 1-25.

Newton, Huey. A Prison Interview. In *The New Left Reader.* Edited by Carl Oglesby, 223-40. New York: Grove Press, 1969.

Newton, Judith L., Mary P. Ryan and Judith R. Walkowitz, eds., *Sex and Class in Women's History.* History Workshop Series. London: Routledge & Kegan Paul, 1983.

Norton-Taylor, Richard. *Bloody Sunday: Scenes from the Saville Inquiry.* London: Oberon, 2005.

—. *Called to Account.* London: Oberon, 2007.

—. *The Colour of Justice.* London: Oberon, 1999.

—. *Justifying War: Scenes from the Hutton Inquiry.* London: Oberon, 2003.

Oglesby, Carl, ed. *The New Left Reader.* New York: Grove Press, 1969.

Orwell, George. "Inside the Whale." *Inside the Whale and Other Essays,* 9-50. London: Penguin Books, 1962.

—. *Nineteen Eighty-Four.* London: Penguin, 1990 (first published in 1949).

Osborne, John. *Look Back in Anger.* London: Faber, 1996 (first published in 1957).

Palmer, Richard H. *The Contemporary British History Play.* London: Greenwood Press, 1998.

Paton, Maureen. *Daily Express* (1 February 1994) reprinted in *Theatre Record* (15-28 January 1994): 94.

Peacock, D. Keith. *Radical Stages: Alternative History in Modern British Drama*. London: Greenwood Press, 1991.

—. *Thatcher's Theatre: British Theatre and Drama in the Eighties*. London: Greenwood, 1999.

Pellegrin, Helen. Introduction. *Thomas Shadwell's The Libertine: A Critical Edition*, xii-xcix. London: Garland Publishing, 1987.

Perkin, Harold. "The Enterprise Culture in Historical Perspective: Birth, Life, Death–and Resurrection?" In *The Values of the Enterprise Culture: The Moral Debate*. Edited by Paul Heelas and Paul Morris, 36-60. London: Routledge, 1992.

Perrault, Katherine. "Beyond the Patriarchy: Feminism and the Chaos of Creativity." *Journal of Dramatic Theory and Criticism* 17.1 (2002): 45-67.

Phillips, Melanie. "The Royal Court's Mystery Play." *The Spectator* (8 February 2009).

Piercy, Marge. *Woman on the Edge of Time*. London: Women's Press, 1979.

Plaice, Neville, Stephen Plaice and Paul Knight. Introduction. *The Principle of Hope*, Volume One. By Ernst Bloch, xvix-xxxiii. Oxford: Basil Blackwell, 1986.

Plant, Sadie. *The Most Radical Gesture: The Situationist International in a Postmodern Age*. London: Routledge, 1992.

Plato, *The Republic*. Translated and introduced by Desmond Lee. London: Penguin, 1987.

Ponnuswami, Meenakshi. "Fanshen in the English Revolution: Caryl Churchill's *Light Shining in Buckinghamshire*." In *Essays on Caryl Churchill: Contemporary Representations*. Edited by Sheila Rabillard, 41-59. Winnipeg: Blizzard Publishing, 1998.

Purdy, David. "British Capitalism since the War: Part 2." *Marxism Today* (October 1976): 316.

Rabillard, Sheila, ed. *Caryl Churchill: Contemporary Re-presentations*. Winnipeg: Blizzard Press, 1997.

—. Introduction. *Caryl Churchill: Contemporary Re-presentations*, 7-13. Winnipeg: Blizzard Press, 1997.

Radin, Victoria. *New Statesman* (3 April 1987) reprinted in *London Theatre Record* (26 March-22 April 1987): 369.

Rady, Martyn. *Romania in Turmoil: A Contemporary History*. London: IB Tauris, 1992.

Randall, Phyllis R., ed. *Caryl Churchill: A Casebook*. London: Garland, 1988.

—. "Beginnings: Churchill's Early Radio and Stage Plays." In *Caryl Churchill: A Casebook*. Edited by Phyllis R. Randall, 3-23. London: Garland, 1988.

Ravenhill, Mark. *Shopping and F***ing*. London: Methuen, 1996.

Rawlence, Chris. "Political Theatre and the Working Class." In *Media, Politics and Culture*. Edited by Carl Gardner, 61-70. London: Macmillan, 1979.

Rayner, Alice. "All her Children: Caryl Churchill's Furious Ghosts." In *Caryl Churchill: Contemporary Re-presentations*. Edited by Sheila Rabillard, 206-24. Winnipeg: Blizzard Press, 1997.

Rees, Roland. *Fringe First: Pioneers of Fringe Theatre on Record*. London: Oberon Books, 1992

Reinelt, Janelle. *After Brecht: British Epic Theater*. Ann Arbor: University of Michigan Press, 1994.

—. "Beyond Brecht: Britain's New Feminist Drama." In *Feminist Theatre and Theory*. Edited by Helene Keyssar, 35-48. London: Macmillan, 1996.

—. "Caryl Churchill and the Politics of Style." In *The Cambridge Companion to Modern British Playwrights*. Edited by Elaine Aston and Janelle Reinelt, 174-94. Cambridge: Cambridge UP Press, 2000.

—. "Caryl Churchill: Socialist Feminism and Brechtian Dramaturgy." In *After Brecht: British Epic Theater*, 81-107. Ann Arbor: University of Michigan Press, 1994.

—. "Feminist Theory and the Problem of Performance." *Modern Drama* 32.1 (March 1989): 44-57.

Reiter, Rayna R., ed. *Toward an Anthropology of Women*. London: Monthly Review Press, 1975.

Richards, Barry. "Enterprise, Omnipotence and Dependency: A Psychoanalytical Approach to Political Culture." In *The Values of the Enterprise Culture*. Edited by Paul Heelas and Paul Morris, 194-213. London: Routledge, 1992.

Rickman, Alan and Katherine Viner. *My Name is Rachel Corrie*. London: Nick Hern, 2005.

Ritchie, Rob, ed. *The Joint Stock Book: The Making of a Theatre Collective*. London: Methuen, 1987.

Roberts, Philip. *About Churchill: The Playwright and the Work*. London: Faber, 2008.

Rorty, Richard. *Contingency, Irony, and Solidarity*. Cambridge: Cambridge UP, 1989.

Rosendale, Steven. Introduction. *The Greening of Literary Scholarship*, xv-xxix. Rosendale Iowa City: University of Iowa Press, 2002.

—. "In Search of Left Ecology's Usable Past." In *The Greening of Literary Scholarship*, 59-76. Rosendale, Iowa City: University of Iowa Press, 2002.

Rossetti, Christina. *Goblin Market*. London: Macmillan, 1971 (first published in 1862).

Rowbotham, Sheila. "Hope, Dreams amd Dirty Nappies." *Marxism Today* 28.12 (December 1984): 8-12.

—. Interview by Dina Copelman. In *Visions of History*. Edited by Henry Abelove et. al., 49-69. Manchester: Manchester UP, 1976.

—. "The Women's Movement and Organising for Socialism." In *Beyond the Fragments: Feminism and the Making of Socialism*. Edited by Sheila Rowbotham, Lynne Segal and Hilary Wainwright, 21-155. London: Merlin Press, 1979.

Rowbotham, Sheila, Lynne Segal and Hilary Wainwright, eds. *Beyond the Fragments: Feminism and the Making of Socialism*. London: Merlin Press, 1979.

Russ, Joanna. *The Female Man*. London: Women's Press, 1985 (first published in 1975).

Russell, Conrad, ed. *The Origins of the English Civil War*. Basingstoke: Palgrave Macmillan, 1973.

Rustin, Michael. "The New Left and the Present Crisis." *New Left Review* 121 (May-June 1980): 63-89.

—. "The Trouble with 'New Times.'" In *New Times: The Changing Face of Politics in the 1990s*. Edited by Stuart Hall and Martin Jacques, 303-20. London: Lawrence and Wishart in association with *Marxism Today*, 1989.

Sabine, G. H ed., *The Works of Gerrard Winstanley*. Ithaca: Cornell University Press, 1941.

Said, Edward. "Protecting the Kosovars?" *New Left Review* 234 (March/April 1999): 73-75.

Salleh, Ariel. *Ecofeminism as Politics: Nature, Marx and the Postmodern*. London: Zed, 1997.

Samuel, Raphael. Foreword. *People's History and Socialist Theory*, xi-xiii. London: Routledge & Kegan Paul, 1981.

Sandford, Jeremy. *Cathy Come Home*. London: Marion Boyars, 1976 (first published in 1967).

Sargent, Lydia, ed. *The Unhappy Marriage of Marxism and Feminism: A Debate of Class and Patriarchy*. London: Pluto Press, 1981.

Sargent, Lyman Tower. "Is There Only One Utopian Tradition?" *Journal of the History of Ideas* 43. 4 (1982): 681-89.

Sayers, Sean. "The Human Impact of the Market." In *The Values of the Enterprise Culture: The Moral Debate*. Edited by Paul Heelas and Paul Morris, 120-38. London: Routledge, 1992.

Secombe, Wally. "The Housewife and Her Labour under Capitalism." *New Left Review* 83 (January-February 1974): 3-24.

Serres, Michel. *The Natural Contract*. Ann Arbor: University of Michigan Press, 1995.

Shadwell, Thomas. *The Volunteers, Or, The Stock-jobbers*. London: James Knapton, 1693.

Shakespeare, William. *King Lear*. Edited by R. A. Foakes. London: The Arden Shakespeare, 1997 (first published in 1608).

—. *The Tempest*. Edited by Alden T. Vaughan and Virginia Mason Vaughan. London: The Arden Shakespeare, 1999 (first published in 1623).

Sharpe, James. *Instruments of Darkness: Witchcraft in England 1550-1750*. London: Penguin, 1996.

Shields, Rob. *Lefebvre, Love and Struggle: Spatial Dialectics*. London: Routledge, 1998.

Shipley, Peter. *Revolutionaries in Modern Britain*. London: The Bodley Head, 1976.

Shklar, Judith. "The Political Theory of Utopia: From Melancholy to Nostalgia." *Daedalus* 94.2 (Spring 1965): 367-81.

Showalter, Elaine. *A Literature of Their Own: British Women Novelists from Brontë to Lessing*. London: Princeton University Press, 1977.

Smith, Neil. *What's On* (2 February 1994) reprinted in *Theatre Record* (15-28 January 1994): 96

Soans, Robin. *Talking to Terrorists*. London: Oberon, 2005.

Soper, Kate. "Postmodernism, Subjectivity, Value." *New Left Review* 186 (March/April 1991): 120-28.

Soto-Morettini, Donna. "Revolution and the Fatally Clever Smile: Caryl Churchill's *Mad Forest*." *Journal of Dramatic Theory and Criticism* 9.1 (Fall 1994): 105-18.

Taras, Raymond, ed. *The Road to Disillusion: From Critical Marxism to Postcommunism in Eastern Europe*. London: M.E. Sharpe, 1992.

Tawney, R. H. *The Acquisitive Society*. London: G. Bell and Sons, 1952.

Taylor, Paul. *Independent* (25 September 1997) reprinted in *Theatre Record* (10-23 September 1997): 1192.

Thatcher, Margaret. "Aids, Education and the Year 2000! Interview with Margaret Thatcher." By Douglas Keay, *Woman's Own* (31 October 1987): 8-10.

Therborn, Goran. "The Frankfurt School." *New Left Review* 63 (September-October 1970): 63-96.

Thomas, Jane. "The Plays of Caryl Churchill: Essays in Refusal." In *The Death of the Playwright?: Modern British Drama and Literary Theory*. Edited by Adrian Page, 160-85. London: Macmillan, 1992.

Thomas, Keith. *Religion and the Decline of Magic*. London: Penguin, 1971.

—. "Women and the Civil War Sects." *Past and Present* 13 (April 1958): 42-62.

Thompson, Edward. "The Ends of Cold War." *New Left Review* 182 (July/August 1990): 139-46.

—. Foreword to the Revised Edition. In *William Morris: Romantic to Revolutionary*, ix-xi. London: Merlin Press, 1977.

—. *The Making of the English Working Class*. London: Gollancz, 1963.

—. "Outside the Whale." In *The Poverty of Theory and Other Essays*, 1-33. London: Merlin Press, 1978.

—. "The Peculiarities of the English." In *The Poverty of Theory and Other Essays*, 35-91. London: Merlin Press, 1978.

—. "The Poverty of Theory." In *The Poverty of Theory and Other Essays*, 193-397. London: Merlin Press, 1978.

—. "Romanticism, Moralism and Utopianism: the Case of William Morris." *New Left Review* 99 (September-October 1976): 83-111.

—. *William Morris: Romantic to Revolutionary*. London: Lawrence & Wishart, 1955.

Thomsen, Christian W. "Three Socialist Playwrights: John McGrath, Caryl Churchill, Trevor Griffiths." In *Contemporary British Drama*. Edited by Malcolm Bradbury and David Palmer, 156-75. Stratford-upon-Avon Studies 19. London: Edward Arnold, 1981.

Tismaneanu, Vladimir. "From Arrogance to Irrelevance: Avatars of Marxism in Romania." In *The Road to Disillusion: From Critical Marxism to Postcommunism in Eastern Europe*. Edited by Raymond Taras, 135-50. London: M.E. Sharpe, 1992.

Tosh, John. *The Pursuit of History: Aims, Methods and New Directions in the Study of Modern History*. 2nd ed. London: Longman, 1991 (first published 1984).

Trevor-Roper, Hugh. *Catholics, Anglicans and Puritans: Seventeenth Century Essays*. London: Secker & Warburg, 1987.

Urry, John. "The End of Organised Capitalism." In *New Times: The Changing Face of Politics in the 1990s*. Edited by Stuart Hall and Martin Jacques, 94-102. London: Lawrence and Wishart in association with *Marxism Today*, 1989.

Vogel, Lise. *Marxism and the Oppression of Women: Toward a Unitary Theory*. New Jersey: Rutgers University Press, 1983.

Walker, Alice. *In Search of Our Mother's Gardens: Womanist Prose*. London: Women's Press, 1984.

Wall, Derek. *Earth First! And the Anti-Roads Movement: Radical Environmentalism and Comparative Social Movement*. London: Routledge, 1999.

Wandor, Michelene. *Look Back in Gender: Sexuality and the Family in Post-War British Drama*. London: Methuen, 1987.

Wardle, Irving. *The Times* (28 September 1976) reprinted in *File on Churchill*, by Linda Fitzsimmons, 30. London: Methuen, 1989.

Watkins, Beth. Review of *Far Away*. *Theatre Journal* 53.3 (2001): 481-82.

Waugh, Patricia. *Metafiction: The Theory and Practice of Self-conscious Fiction*. London: Methuen, 1984.

Weber, Max. *The Protestant Ethic and the Spirit of Capitalism*. London: Unwin University Books, 1971 (first published in 1930).

Weinbaum, Batya. *The Curious Courtship of Women's Liberation and Socialism*. Boston: South End Press, 1978.

Weir, Angela and Elizabeth Wilson. "The British Women's Movement." *New Left Review* 148 (November/December 1984): 74-103.

Wells, H. G. *A Modern Utopia*. London: Penguin 2005 (first published in 1905).

Wertenbaker, Timberlake. *The Grace of Mary Traverse*. London: Faber, 1989.

Williams, Gwynn A. "Gramsci's Concept of *Egemonia*." *Journal of the History of Ideas* XXI.4 (October-December 1960): 589-99.

Williams, Raymond. *Culture and Society*. London: Hogarth, 1958.

—. *Keywords*. London: Fontana Press, 1988.

—. *Marxism and Literature*. Oxford: Oxford UP, 1977

—. "Notes on Marxism in Britain since 1945." *New Left Review* 100 (November 1976-January 1977): 81-94.

—. *Politics and Letters: Interviews With New Left Review*. London: Verso, 1981.

—. "Problems of the Coming Period." *New Left Review* 140 (July-August 1983): 7-18.

—. *Problems in Materialism and Culture*. London: Verso, 1980.

Williams, Roy. *Sing yer Heart out for the Lads*. London: Methuen, 2002.

Wilson, Ann. "Failure and the Limits of Representation in *The Skriker*." In *Caryl Churchill: Contemporary Re-presentations*. Edited by Sheila Rabillard, 174-88. Winnipeg: Blizzard Press, 1997.

—. "Hauntings: Ghosts and the Limits of Realism in *Cloud Nine* and *Fen* by Caryl Churchill." In *Drama on Drama: Dimensions of Theatricality on the Contemporary British Stage*. Edited by Nicole Boireau, 152-67. London: Macmillan, 1997.

Wing, Joylynn. "*Mad Forest* and the Interplay of Languages." In *Caryl Churchill: Contemporary Re-presentations*. Edited by Sheila Rabillard, 129-41. Winnipeg: Blizzard Press, 1997.

Woods, Alan. "Romania: A Difficult Road to Restoration." *Militant International Review* 44 (Summer 1990): 32-40.

Wright, Erik Olin. "Women in the Class Structure." *Politics & Society* 17.1 (1989): 35-66.

Wright Mills, C. "The Politics of Responsibility." In *The New Left Reader*. Edited by Carl Oglesby, 23-31. New York: Grove Press, 1969.

X, Malcolm. "I Don't Mean Bananas." In *The New Left Reader*. Edited by Carl Oglesby, 207-22. New York: Grove Press, 1969.

Young, Lord of Graffham. "The Enterprise Regained." In *The Values of the Enterprise Culture: The Moral Debate*. Edited by Paul Heelas and Paul Morris, 29-35. London: Routledge, 1992.

Zamytin E. I. *We*. Bristol: Bristol Classical Press, 1994 (first published in 1921).

Žižek, Slavoj. "Against the Double Blackmail." *New Left Review* 234 (March/April 1999): 76-82.

INDEX